Library of Congress Cataloging-in-Publication Data
Stinson, Kandi M.
Women and dieting culture : inside a commercial weight loss group /
Kandi M. Stinson.
    p.   cm.
Includes bibliographical references and index.
ISBN 0-8135-2948-4 (cloth : alk. paper) — ISBN 0-8135-2949-2 (pbk. : alk.
paper)
1. Weight loss—Social aspects.   2. Overweight women.   3. Body image
in women.   I. Title.

RM222.2 S842   2001
613.7′045—dc21   00-068347

British Cataloging-in-Publication data for this book is available from the
British Library
Permission t/k

In memory of my grandmother
Gladys Squires Boedeker
who filled my childhood with wonderful
food and, by example, taught me that the
size of your heart is far more important
than the size of your hips

Contents

Acknowledgments

I received practical and psychological support from many people during the five years of researching and writing this book. I would like to thank David Myers at Rutgers University Press for his advice, encouragement, and patience. I'm sure it's not easy working with a deadline-challenged author. The two reviewers' comments were extremely helpful, and I am grateful to them as well.

Many people at Xavier University have supported me in my work. April Farah provided excellent secretarial assistance. Her calm, never-failing good humor kept me from going over the edge on more than one occasion. Neil Heighberger has encouraged me in everything I've done since I arrived at Xavier thirteen years ago. I couldn't ask for anything more from a dean. My colleagues in the department of political science and sociology, Jim McCann, Jon Moulton, John Ray, Mike Weissbuch, and Tim White, make my job as chair of the department easy, freeing much time for research and writing. Over the past several years there have also been many students, too numerous to name, who have listened to me talk about my research, asked insightful, pointed questions, and shared their own struggles with weight issues. I greatly appreciate their interest and their honesty.

I am very lucky to be surrounded at Xavier by a group of women who are wonderful colleagues and steadfast friends, including Cindy Crown, Chris Dacey, and Janice Walker. I have had the privilege of coteaching and writing with Carol Winkelmann several times, and it has been sheer pleasure. She has spent countless hours talking with me about my research and reading drafts of many chapters. She is an inspiring teacher, a relentless crusader for women on campus, and a loyal friend. Marie Giblin and Trudelle Thomas have also read parts of the manuscript and I greatly appreciate their comments and suggestions. Kathy Hart has been an endless source of humor, encouragement, and a shoulder to cry on.

Above all, my husband, Rick, and children, Allison and Zachary, deserve much credit. It is not easy living with a researcher, and it is most definitely not easy living with someone who is struggling with weight issues. Putting the two together is surely a disaster waiting to happen. Not only did they survive, but through the whole ordeal they gave me all the support, freedom, and love I needed. They make it all worthwhile.

Women and
Dieting Culture

1 | Eating, Dieting, and Being Female

On July 5, 1994, I called the local office of a commercial weight loss program and asked how to go about joining. After finding out where I lived, a friendly and sympathetic receptionist informed me that the closest location was in a nearby shopping center, directly across the breezeway from an ice cream parlor. I remember wondering how many people set out for a meeting, only to end up getting ice cream instead. I asked how much it would cost to join and was told it was thirty dollars initially and then ten dollars for each subsequent week. The receptionist suggested it would be cheaper to join the following week, since a special rate would go into effect then—"if you want to save a little money. But of course, if you want to, we encourage you to jump right in. We find that, you know, when you make the call you're pretty motivated." Feeling like I had just called Alcoholics Anonymous, I thanked her for the information. She responded, "Good luck! And take care now." She sounded sincere, and I admit I was touched by her apparent concern and support.

That evening I attended my first meeting, thus embarking simultaneously on a personal weight loss project and a research agenda that would last over two years. As an experienced researcher and a feminist scholar specializing in issues concerning women's bodies, I was prepared for the academic component. What I wasn't entirely prepared for was the personal side of the project. This was my first foray into a commercial weight loss program and I had little notion of what to expect. This was not, however, my first attempt to lose weight.

(Rodin 1992). Dieters can choose from thousands of diet books, plans, programs, and centers, all promising weight loss for a price (Hesse-Biber 1996). Although it appears that more recently fewer people are joining commercial diet programs (Fraser 1997), perhaps in part because of notoriously high failure rates (Hesse-Biber 1996), there is no shortage of commercial plans for those willing to spend the money. Dieters are further supported in their efforts by a highly profitable and expanding diet food industry, which itself is buttressed by recent public health concerns over dietary fat (Austin 1999; Hesse-Biber 1996).

Dieting in the United States is not a gender-neutral activity. It is the rare woman who has not dieted at some point in her life. In a recent national survey, 84 percent of the women and 58 percent of the men had dieted to lose weight (Garner 1997). Research consistently finds that women are more likely to diet than men, and are more likely to use even more drastic measures to lose weight, including diet pills, laxatives, and surgery (Berg 1995; Garner 1997; Wolf 1991). Women are also more likely than men to exercise specifically to lose weight (Garner 1997). Gender differences in dieting are reflected in and reinforced by differences in the content of popular women's and men's magazines, with diet-related articles appearing much more frequently in those targeted at women (Andersen and DiDomenico 1992). At the extreme, women are more likely than men to develop eating disorders, although rates may be increasing among men, especially among subgroups that are subject to strong weight or physical appearance norms, including some athletes, such as wrestlers, and possibly gay men (Hesse-Biber 1996).

Dieting is not a new phenomenon, and women in the United States today are certainly not the first women to restrict their food intake, sometimes severely (Bell 1985; Brumberg 1988; Bynum 1987). At the same time, the meaning of dieting varies historically and cross-culturally (Counihan 1998a, b). Strong antifat attitudes and pervasive prejudice and discrimination against those who are overweight contribute to high rates of dieting in the United States, and these attitudes differentially affect women and men.

Living Fat in the United States

It is not easy to live as an overweight person in the United States. Unhealthy, ugly, unkempt, lazy, sexually unattractive, and lacking in willpower are just a few of the negative traits attributed to overweight individuals (Joanisse and Synnott 1999; Lewis et al. 1997; Millman 1980). In her classic study, Millman (1980) dramatically documents the extreme denigration and disgust directed at obese people. Negative attitudes are related to negative behavior, which can profoundly restrict the life chances of those who are overweight. In a review of the literature, Cash and Roy (1999) find substantial evidence that overweight people encounter frequent discrimination in education, the labor force, housing, and treatment by others. To be fat in the United States is to be clearly and unequivocally stigmatized. A strong belief that body weight is largely, if not entirely, subject to individual control fuels the prejudice and discrimination. On top of everything else, individuals are held responsible and blamed for their obesity. Substantial research evidence suggests that antifat attitudes are learned at a young age (Caskey and Felker 1971; Flannery-Schroeder and Chrisler 1996; Lerner and Gellert 1969). At a time when many are becoming increasingly sensitized to prejudice and discrimination based on race and sex, there is little evidence that antifat biases are abating.

One does not have to be obese to encounter denigration. Relatively rigid expectations of what is regarded as ideal weight mean that even slight deviations from the norm are stigmatized. During the early 1940s in the United States, the Metropolitan Life Insurance Company issued the first of its ideal weight charts, which now set the standard for normative body weight (McKinley 1999). Medical and public health discourses reinforce the presumed association between ideal weight and health. Individuals falling within the ideal weight ranges are assumed to be living a healthy lifestyle, consuming appropriate quantities of nutritious food, and exercising sufficiently. Not only does the notion of ideal weight affect individuals' perceptions of and attitudes toward their own bodies, but the Metropolitan standards are used to calculate official rates of overweight and obesity in the United States. Because the ranges have been raised and lowered several times since their inception, reports of increasing rates of overweight and obesity in recent years (Hesse-Biber 1996) should be interpreted cautiously. Fluctuations in the rates may have as much to do with changes in the ideal ranges as actual changes in body weight (McKinley 1999).

Antifat attitudes affect women and men differently. There is substantial evidence that women are more dissatisfied with their bodies than are men (Cash and Henry 1995; Cash, Winstead, and Janda 1986; Freedman 1986; Garner 1997; Muth and Cash 1997; Pliner, Chaiken, and Flett 1990), and that rates of body dissatisfaction are increasing among women (Feingold and Mazzella 1998). Weight dissatisfaction is particularly central to assessments of body satisfaction. Dissatisfied women almost always want to lose weight, whereas a substantial number of men who are dissatisfied with their weight wish to gain (Cash and Roy 1999). Weight gain is one of the most important factors in decreased body satisfaction, especially for women. And although limited evidence suggests that losing weight can improve body image, the high failure rates of diet plans and the high likelihood of regaining weight suggest that the effects may be short-lived (Cash and Roy 1999). Not only do women and men feel differently about their bodies, but their experiences of being overweight are different. Overweight women are more highly stigmatized than are overweight men (Rodin 1992; Wadden and Stunkard 1985). Although the size and restrictiveness of Millman's (1980) male sample preclude drawing strong conclusions, she finds provocative indications that relative to women, men who are overweight encounter less prejudice, suffer fewer negative social consequences, and do not feel as negatively about themselves.

It is not surprising that women are less satisfied with their bodies than are men. Girls learn at an early age that they are evaluated on the basis of their physical appearance (McKinley 1999). The severe prejudice toward overweight women is in part the product of a persistent dualism between mind and body that characterizes much of Western thought (Williams and Bendelow 1998). Women are associated with the potentially unruly body, governed by drives, instincts, desires, and emotions; men are associated with the mind, guided by rationality and logic (Bordo 1993; Chernin 1981). The overweight female body is especially threatening, as it represents a body that has run out of control, unable to restrain and limit its appetites. McKinley (1999) argues that ideologies about ideal weight are intricately connected to ideologies about ideal womanhood, including conceptions of femininity, presentation, maternity, and sexuality. Common to both sets of ideologies are a continual focus on the body, a "demand for containment and control," and the difficulty of meeting the ideal (McKinley 1999:107).

Attitudes toward overweight and obesity vary substantially across cultures. The relationship between gender and attitudes toward obesity also vary cross-culturally:

> In more gender egalitarian cultures, we find either no information about body standards, or we find the same standards for both men and women. . . . Neither group [Melanesian peoples in Kalauna and Polynesians] holds different standards for men and women as do many western societies, where observers have noted more stringent standards of thinness for women than for men even

though women have greater biological propensity to be fat (Beller 1977). For Western women, dissatisfaction with their body size and shape is yet another expression of and contributor to their subordination, whereas in more gender equal cultures, women as well as men can find self-satisfaction through the body. (Counihan 1998b:8)

Even within the United States attitudes toward gender and overweight have varied historically and subculturally (Counihan 1998a, b). Among groups that do not value thinness in women, or at least have standards that are more realistic, such as Puerto Rican and African American communities, women may experience less dissatisfaction with, and express fewer negative feelings toward, their bodies (Akan and Grilo 1995; Brown et al. 1995; Hesse-Biber 1996; Rucker and Cash 1992). At the same time it appears that ethnic differences are beginning to diminish (Hesse-Biber 1996). The strength of the cultural ideal of thinness, accompanied by higher levels of education, affluence, and acculturation among ethnic minorities in the United States, suggests that the ideal of thinness is spreading.

Bodies

As is evident from an examination of gender, the stigmatization of obesity, and dieting, attitudes toward the human body run deep: "The body is presented as haunting us with its passive materiality, its lack of agency, art, or even consciousness. Insofar as the spirit's motive is the guiding force, clarity and will dominate; the body, by contrast, simply *receives* and darkly, dumbly responds to impressions, emotions, passions. This duality of active spirit/passive body is also gendered, and it has been one of the most historically powerful of the dualities that inform Western ideologies of gender" (Bordo 1993:11). Some feminist scholars argue that this gendered dualism explains the inordinate attention paid to controlling women's bodies by the medical sciences, the beauty industry, and popular media (Balsamo 1996; Bartky 1988; Bordo 1993).

Many feminist scholars have examined and deconstructed representations of women's bodies (see, for example, Bordo 1993; Macdonald 1995). Advertising, filled with images of the ideal female, is a rich source of material for determining the demands placed on bodies by contemporary societies (Holmlund 1989). According to Bordo (1993), representations of women's bodies in advertising reflect and reinforce changing norms. Until the 1980s excess weight was the problem, but currently it is the flabby body (even if thin) that provokes the greatest wrath. Working out and food restriction are now jointly held to be the tools necessary for achieving the bodily ideal. The slender, ideal female body that populates advertising is intricately associated with control, willpower, discipline, autonomy, and liberation (Bordo 1993; McKinley 1999). Through her body, the slender woman demonstrates her ability to restrain her appetites and to transcend the threatening, material body.

Significant feminist scholarship focuses on the body itself as a site of control, domination, and struggle. Foucault's (1979) analyses of power and discipline are the starting points for much of this work. Foucault argues that modern bodies are subjected to pervasive, continual, and minute disciplinary practices that attempt to ever more closely control the body's comportment and movement through space and time. Increasingly in modern societies, control is exercised not through formal disciplinarians or public sanctions but via numerous discursive and cultural practices, which Foucault calls "technologies," diffused throughout society. Several Foucauldian concepts are at the center of recent feminist analyses of the control and discipline directed at women's bodies, including self-surveillance, panopticism and the gaze, the confessional, and the omnipresent potential for resistance.

Drawing on the work of Jeremy Bentham, Foucault (1979) offers the panopticon, a model prison constructed as concentric cells around a central observation tower, as a metaphorical solution to the problem of social control (Germov and Williams 1999). Assuming they are subject to constant surveillance, prisoners of the panopticon continually police themselves. Foucault suggests that modern subjects similarly participate in the operation of power in the form of surveillance, by closely monitoring themselves for increasingly minute transgressions.

Much like the prisoners of the panopticon, dieters and indeed women in general police themselves (Bartky 1988; Germov and Williams 1999). As women internalize the critical gaze of others, they subject themselves to careful self-examination. Parents, friends, medical practitioners, diet organizations, and even strangers participate by monitoring the food intake and bodies of dieting women (Hesse-Biber 1996). Germov and Williams (1999) argue that women help perpetuate the thin ideal not only by subjecting themselves to constant scrutiny but by closely inspecting the bodies of other women. In this context, hiding food and eating secretly are not manifestations of disordered eating, but are rational responses to nearly continual surveillance by others, whether actual persons or a more generalized, unbound cultural gaze (Bartky 1988; Spitzack 1990).

Confession is closely related to surveillance. Body monitoring may be an important ritual in and of itself in the culture of weight loss (Hesse-Biber 1996), but it is most effective when tied to confession. The good dieter not only watches herself carefully but willingly confesses her transgressions, for it is through the admission of guilt that redemption is made possible: "Telling the truth about oneself, to oneself, is a pervasive cultural activity, legislating morality and working to 'normalize' individuals who transgress the laws governing numerous institutions and practices. . . . Speaking the truth about oneself, to physicians, clergymen, lovers, teachers, among others, underscores the power of normative bases of judgment, for implicit in the act of confession is a promise to realign thoughts and actions with predominant social values" (Spitzack 1990:60). The centrality of confession to the storytelling that dominates 12–Step recovery groups (Kurtz 1994; Lester 1999), self-help literature that encourages readers to confront their defects and failings (Simonds 1992; Spitzack 1990), and the popularity of daytime television talk shows (Shattuc 1997) attest to the significance of confession as not only a pervasive form of discourse but a powerful tool of social control.

While accepting the insights of Foucault's analysis, feminist scholars are quick to point out that he pays far too little attention to the relationship between gender and technologies of the body (Bartky 1988). Arguing that "an apparatus of gender organizes the power relations manifest in the various engagements between bodies and technologies" Balsamo (1996:9) suggests that we specifically attend to "technologies of the gendered body." Similarly, Bartky (1988:27) argues: "Foucault treats the body throughout as if it were one, as if the bodily experiences of men and women did not differ and as if men and women bore the same relationship to the characteristic institutions of modern life. Where is the account of the disciplinary practices that engender the 'docile bodies' of women, bodies more docile than the bodies of men? Women, like men, are subject to many of the same disciplinary practices Foucault describes. But he is blind to those disciplines that produce a modality of embodiment that is peculiarly feminine." Bartky (1988:27) identifies three categories of disciplinary practices that produce the docile female body, "those that aim to produce a body of a certain size and general configuration; those that bring forth from this body a specific repertoire of gestures, postures, and movements; and those that are directed toward the display of this body as an ornamented surface."

Dieting and exercise undertaken in pursuit of the ideal female body are dramatic examples of Bartky's first category of disciplinary practices. There are no diet police who enforce food restriction and exercising, nor are there formal schedules of punishment for women who refuse to or cannot conform. But there are costs. Women diet and exercise relentlessly "against the background of a pervasive sense of bodily deficiency" (Bartky 1988:33). And as the research on antifat prejudice attests, women who do not cooperate and fully participate in the disciplining of their bodies face a variety of sanctions, including ostracism, public harassment, and job discrimination.

Examining dieting and exercise from the perspective of gender technologies yields a number of useful insights. First, it becomes clearer why so many women, from such a young age, seemingly voluntarily invest huge amounts of time, energy, and money into an apparently useless enterprise. Even though the ideal of the slender female body is ultimately impossible to achieve, and despite strong evidence that diets do not work, a majority of women in the United States continue to diet. Morgan (1991:151) argues: "Practices of coercion and domination are often camouflaged by practical rhetorical and supporting theories that appear to be benevolent, therapeutic, and voluntaristic." Especially significant in this regard are medical discourses that link body weight and health and diet industry discourse that presents dieting as a concrete way in which women can exert control and take care of themselves. The issue is not whether the medical and diet industry arguments are ultimately true or false. The relationship between body weight and health is complex (Cogan 1999), and in some individual cases weight loss may be prescribed. The point is that these perspectives are pervasive, rarely challenged, and internalized throughout the population, not just by those persons with clear medical indications.

Second, by looking at dieting as only one of a number of gender technologies directed at women's bodies, it becomes possible to link dieting to such diverse practices as cosmetic surgery and bodybuilding. It is well to remember that in the contemporary United States, the ideal body is not simply slim, it is toned and tight (Bordo 1993). Dieting by itself is insufficient. Taken to an extreme in bodybuilding, exercise and working out promise to tame the unsightly flab. And if that is not enough, the body can be literally chiseled into shape with the aid of cosmetic surgery. Dieting, body building, and cosmetic surgery share a marked propensity to treat the body as sheer physical matter that, with the right tools, techniques, and discipline, can be molded into the desired shape.

At the same time, weight loss and particularly bodybuilding differ in one significant way. The bodybuilder's ultimate goal is to build body mass, and thereby construct a body that takes up space and evinces power (Bolin 1997). But the weight-loser seeks to diminish the body, and to do so not so much by doing something to it, as by depriving it, in this case, of food. The experiences of female bodybuilders demonstrate that gender greatly colors this process. Despite the emergence of a more muscular ideal body type for women, the association of muscularity with women continues to be culturally problematic (Holmlund 1989; Schulze 1997). Female bodybuilders, particularly in the competitive arena, are placed in a double bind, as they try simultaneously to achieve the ideal body as defined by the standards of bodybuilding and retain their femininity. Although both female and male bodybuilders hope to achieve a high degree of muscular definition, women bodybuilders are also subject to gender norms that define the ideal female body as at least lean, if not thin (Bolin 1997). Among the competitive bodybuilders observed by Bolin (1997), bigness carried positive connotations for the men, but was viewed more negatively by the women. Balsamo (1996:49) asserts, in fact, that "judges are instructed to look for certain faults in women that are not usually seen in men: stretch marks, operation scars, and cellulite; they are also directed to observe whether female competitors walk and move in a graceful manner, which seemingly is not a concern with male competitors." Similarly, Bolin (1997:189) suggests that "in contrast to the male competitor, whose masculinity is unmarked, the female competitor is required to display femininity combined with muscularity. This quality defined for frontage presentations is interpreted by contestants to mean decoration of the body with traditional symbols such as long nails, fluffy hair, hair ornaments, and the like." Even as female bodybuilders challenge definitions of the ideal female body, they are caught in the trappings of traditional femininity.

Dieting, cosmetic surgery, and bodybuilding differ both in the specific tools and techniques used and in their ultimate goals. But at the same time, in their shared objectification of the body and their ultimate hope of transforming it, all subtly question and blur the meaning of the "natural" body (Balsamo 1996). An ad in a local newspaper for a plastic surgery center exhorts readers to "Uncover the Beautiful You With Plastic Surgery," and claims that these surgeons "have been discovering beauty for over 20 years." The ad implies that there is "natural beauty" hidden in every body, but the raw material of the body is *not* naturally beautiful. Indeed, the body hides the real beauty that can only be discovered by a surgical expert. Operating here is what Adams (1997:60) calls the "surgical aesthetic," that is, "the theory and practice that deals with the surgical transformation of women's bodies from a 'natural' state of inadequacy and ugliness into a potentially 'ideal' state of beauty and perfect functioning." The ad clearly targets women. It pictures a young, thin, naked woman, and the words "beautiful" and "beauty" are themselves gendered, more often associated with females than males. Messages about aging are joined with messages about gender. Balsamo (1996) argues that the most frequently requested cosmetic surgery procedures are those that counteract the effects of aging, namely, face lifts, nose reconstruction, tummy tucks, liposuction, skin peels, and hair transplants. In 1998 facelifts and chemical peels were among the five cosmetic surgery procedures most frequently requested by women (American Society of Plastic Surgeons 1998).

Added to the philosophical understanding of the relationship between gender, control, and bodies is the gender-based, social construction and distribution of power. Despite recent inroads into significant societal institutions, women in the United States continue to be disadvantaged with respect to control over valued societal resources. But one arena in which women have not only been allowed but expected to demonstrate control is in the physical appearance of the body, more specifically, body weight. With other avenues for exercising power effectively closed off, weight control represents a particularly feminine/female outlet for self-control. The potential for real self-control and self-determination through weight control, of course, is illusory. Rather, as an effective gender technology for producing specifically female, docile bodies, weight control further shackles women (Bartky 1988).

Sociologists have recently paid increasing attention to the relationship between real, lived-in bodies and social structure. In calling sociologists to shift from a sociology of the body to an embodied sociology, Williams and Bendelow (1998:23) argue: "Whilst [a sociology of the body] translates, in corporeal terms, into a treatment of the body as simply one amongst many topics which sociologists can study from 'outside' so to speak, [an embodied sociology], in contrast, refuses to slip into this deceptive Cartesian view of the world—one which treats mind and body as distinctly separate entities—taking the embodiment of its practitioners as well as its subjects seriously through a commitment to the lived body and its being in the world, including the manner in which it both shapes and is shaped by society." Dieting reminds us in no uncertain terms of the actual materiality of the human body. Women's dieting experiences are not simply a function of cultural notions of thinness and ideal weight. The operation of bodily "set points," or the body's tendency to gravitate toward a particular weight, below which it is difficult to stay for any length of time (Rothblum 1994), provide at least partial evidence of a genetic role in body weight. In addition, as biological organisms, humans have to eat. It is possible to abstain from alcohol or cigarettes; it is impossible to abstain from food. Hunger as both a physiological response to food deprivation and a socially constructed response to desire for food is central to our understanding of dieting. Consequently dieting is an especially promising arena in which to explore the relationship between the body as material organism and the body as cultural object.

Food

If dieting lies at the intersection of material embodiment and cultural discourses and practices, so does food. Consuming food represents in no uncertain terms the actual lived experience of the material body, as food is taken in from the outside, tasted, chewed, digested, and through processes mysterious and hidden but no less real, incorporated into the body itself. At the same time, food is not consumed solely for its nutritional value. Food preparation and eating are not only physiologically motivated activities but cultural enterprises. What we find appetizing and appealing, as well as rules for preparation, including which foods are eaten raw and which foods are cooked, and how, is a function of culture (Lupton 1996).

Anthropologists have amply documented the significance of food and eating for a wide variety of cultural practices and functions (Counihan 1998a; Lupton 1996). In many societies food and eating are tied to power relations as they are used to mark and maintain boundaries among social classes, regions, genders, life-cycle stages, religions, and occupations (Lupton 1996). Furthermore, food and eating are often central components of important cultural rituals and traditions (Lupton 1996). Building on Mauss's (1967) analysis of the gift as a powerful means to establish reciprocal exchanges between people, anthropologists have noted the pervasiveness of sharing and exchanging food as strategies to build and maintain interpersonal connections (Counihan 1998a, b). In addition to connecting people, gifts of food are frequently used to ensure good relations with the gods.

Food and eating are central to the construction of gender in the United States, as is reflected in and reinforced by their representation in popular culture. An examination of magazine advertisements related to women, food, and eating reveals a mixed bag of contradictory messages (Bordo 1993). Control and restraint are common themes, particularly in ads for diet foods or aids. At the same time ads exhort women to indulge, but within limits, and preferably in private. According to Bordo (1993), it is taboo in advertising to show women indulging freely and openly in food. A recent television ad for potato chips is thus particularly striking. In the ad, several supermodels are stuffing potato chips into their mouths. But this is unlike other ads that allude to binge eating in which women appear desperate and overwhelmed by food, and the eating is private, isolated, and secretive. These women are having a good time. They are in a group, out in the open, and enjoying themselves. But not to worry—these are no ordinary potato chips. They are fat-free. Consequently the ad assures us, you "can eat like the boys, and still look like the girls." Go ahead and eat like the boys, the ad urges, but if you eat regular potato chips that way, you will surely pay a price. Those chips will soon show up as unsightly flab and bulges. Under normal circumstances, the cost of eating like the boys is high indeed—you may end up looking like them.

In the potato chip ad, the solution to the tension between restraint and indulgence is to go ahead and indulge, even voraciously, but in safe foods, that is, those for which you won't pay a price. A related but somewhat different approach is to show women indulging, but in small, limited portions. A magazine advertisement for miniature candy bars reads "God's Gift to Women," sandwiched between a picture of three somewhat comical looking musketeers at the top and a photograph of the candy below. Should there be any doubt whether God's gift is the men or the candy bars, the ad exclaims, "Big on Chocolate, Not on Fat!" But the caption is misleading. These candy bars are not reduced-fat or fat-free. They are low in fat only if you consume just one or two.

The relationship between gender and actual attitudes and activities centered on food is complex. As is true in many cultures, in the United States exchanging and sharing food build and maintain relationships and connections between people. But unlike the situation in many traditional societies, food exchange between women and men is not reciprocal. In advertising, women are much more likely to appear preparing and serving food for others than consuming it themselves (Bordo 1993). Giving food to others is a concrete way to demonstrate love and experience pleasure. But when women do indulge themselves, food is often represented as a suspect substitute for other needs, motivated by desperation or loneliness. A television advertisement shows a woman fantasizing about the Red Baron, but despite the romantic backdrop, clearly it is not the aviator, but his pizza, that sends her into a swoon. In reality, as primary nurturers of others, women prepare and serve food to their husbands and children while simultaneously restricting their own consumption. Giving food to others is a token of love; restricting your own intake is a sign of self-control. To the extent that planning menus, purchasing food, and preparing and serving meals provide some degree of control over other people's food consumption, women may gain some small degree of power (Counihan 1998b). But, these activities also support women's subordination as they reinforce the expectation that women nurture and serve others. I have heard more than one woman comment, "I like to cook, *when I don't have to.*" Similarly, Bordo (1993:124) says, "Despite the pleasure I take in cooking, in relationships where it has been expected of me I have resented it deeply."

Reacting and Resisting

Cultural representations of women and their bodies, food, eating and dieting are powerful, acting to homogenize and normalize (Bordo 1993). And as we have seen, technologies of gender directed at women's bodies are strong and pervasive (Balsamo 1996; Bartky 1988). But Foucault (1979) reminds us that where there is power, there is resistance. In the case of women's bodies, Bartky (1988:43) argues:

Historically, the forms and occasions of resistance are manifold. Sometimes, instances of resistance appear to spring from the introduction of new and conflicting factors into the lives of the dominated: the juxtaposition of old and new and the resulting incoherence or "contradiction" may make submission to the old ways seem increasingly unnecessary. In the present instance, what may be a major factor in the relentless and escalating objectification of women's bodies—namely, women's growing independence—produces in many women a sense of incoherence that calls into question the meaning and necessity of the current discipline. As women (albeit a small minority of women) begin to realize an unprecedented political, economic, and sexual self-determination, they fall ever more completely under the dominating gaze of patriarchy. It is this paradox, not the "libidinal body," that produces, here and there, pockets of resistance.

As examples of oppositional discourses that have recently emerged, Bartky (1988) goes on to cite female bodybuilding, attempts in radical feminist communities to develop a new female aesthetic, a popular literature of resistance, and a mass-based feminist movement.

Recognizing the power of the forces of control and domination should not blind us to the many ways that women act individually and collectively to resist. Women are not simply passive recipients of the messages sent their way. We can take a lesson from critical cultural studies, which has moved from the view of audiences as passive absorbers of media messages to the view of audiences as active interpreters and users of those messages (Croteau and Hoynes 2000). This perspective leads to an examination of women as active, interpreting, critical participants in cultural practices related to eating and dieting. To be sure, antifat prejudice and negative attitudes toward overweight people are strong and pervasive in the United States. For many persons, especially women, decreased body satisfaction and lowered self-esteem are the results. But there is accumulating evidence that some individuals are actively resisting stigmatization by rejecting negative labels and attempting to construct new, more positive identities as overweight people.

Drawing on interviews with overweight women, Cordell and Ronai (1999:31) define narrative resistance as "the narrative strategies subjects use to create and manage their own identities and to defy the power of discursive constraint." They identify three strategies for resisting negative and constraining identities.

First, some women use exemplars to actively contrast themselves with the negative identities associated with overweight individuals. Exemplars are "negative labels that are typically applied to overweight women" (Cordell and Ronai 1999:31). Overweight women distance themselves from the exemplars of overweight persons as unattractive, sexually undesirable, exploited, self-loathing, and jolly. Second, women construct continuums on which they can place themselves favorably, compared with other women, along dimensions of degree of obesity, sloppiness, and health. Finally, women refer to a number of loopholes that relieve them of responsibility for their obesity, including personal illness, genetics, and poor socialization.

In a study of large Canadian men and women, Joanisse and Synnott (1999) identify three categories of strategies that people use to respond to and resist the stigmatization of obesity. The first category, which the authors term passive resistance, includes internalization and anger. Internalizers accepted the negative view of being overweight and continued to try to lose weight, while the angry respondents rejected the negative view, but rather than fight back, tended "to seethe internally" (61). Second, respondents used four techniques of active resistance, including verbal assertion, physical aggression, flamboyance, and activism. Verbal assertion involved responding verbally to others' prejudice and discrimination, while physical aggression usually consisted of minor acts of vandalism. Respondents who used flamboyance proudly and flagrantly displayed their size, for example, by wearing brightly colored clothing. Activism involved joining advocacy groups. Finally, respondents described two strategies of reflective resistance, self-acceptance and enlightenment, whereby they realized they could still live happy, productive lives despite their weight.

In response to pressures to conform to ideal standards of thinness and physical attractiveness, some women are changing their behavior as well as their attitudes. Some women refuse to diet. Honeycutt (1999) describes two groups of diet-resisters. The equivocators are ambivalent about their ability to lose weight and frequently express negative feelings about their size, but have nonetheless stopped dieting, in part due to a long history of dieting failures. The fat boosters reject dieting and join formal organizations that fight to promote size acceptance and advocate for the rights of obese individuals. In recent years collective movements organized around issues of obesity and dieting have become more visible and influential. The National Organization to Advance Fat Acceptance (NAAFA), established in 1969, focuses both on political activism and on providing social support for overweight persons (Sobal 1999).

Resistance can take a number of forms, whether one acts individually or collectively. McKinley (1999:110–111) suggests: "A fat body, especially when the woman refuses to apologize for her size, can also embody protest against the control and limitations of the female gender role. . . . Rather than arguing that fatness can be attractive or sexual or healthy, when a fat woman refuses to watch her body and refuses to apologize for her nonconformity to ideal weight, she challenges constructions of the ideal women as bodies, as contained, and as subject to male approval. She also resists labeling herself and other women as deviant." In this view, resistance is actually embodied in the obese woman. These varied analyses of resistance share the view that women who diet and otherwise attempt to lose weight have bought into cultural ideals of thinness and physical attractiveness. They are nonresisters. Joanisse and Synnott (1999:60) define "*internalizers* as those who agree with the norms of the majority culture and constantly engage in weight loss attempts." In contrast, resistance involves some combination of self-acceptance and refusal to diet, whether undertaken individually or collectively. As reasonable as this formulation may appear, it is problematic. Conceptualizing resistance as a dichotomy defined by the presence or absence of dieting behavior implies that all weight loss efforts represent misguided attempts to conform to societal standards, and that all members of a weight loss group are non-resisters by definition. Surely the situation is more complex. How do women interpret and act on cultural messages regarding body size and attractiveness? How do women, as embodied individuals, actually experience eating, hunger, and dieting? Under what circumstances, if any, might weight loss be appropriate? Are losing weight and dieting synonymous? Are there any ways in which resistance can be practiced even within the confines of a commercial weight loss organization?

Participating/Observing

Compelled by these and similar questions, I joined a commercial weight loss group, intending both to fully participate as a paying member and to systematically observe the group as a feminist scholar.

Locating the Research:
The Group and Its Members

The group I joined is part of a large, international, commercial weight loss organization. I have chosen not to name the organization for two reasons. First, I am committed to maintaining the confidentiality of participants. Revealing the organization would increase the likelihood that individuals could be identified, particularly in the case of group leaders, since there are so few of them. Second, in many ways, the identity of the organization is irrelevant. Certainly the organization, through its philosophy of weight loss, written materials, and employees, exerts considerable influence over what goes on in its groups. But this research is not primarily about a particular weight loss organization. Rather, the focus is on the many and sometimes conflicting ways in which the meanings and experiences of weight loss are continually constructed and reconstructed. The organization is thus only one site of many where people come together to talk about weight loss in an environment of acceptance and support. As they do so, they develop mutual understandings of what it means to try to lose weight.

This organization focuses on lifestyle modification, with group support and education its primary concerns. Members do not have to buy prepackaged food or drugs, but once they become paying members, they receive a specific weight loss plan to follow. As members arrive at the meeting, they pay the weekly fee and weigh in. Most members stay for the formal meeting, during which they celebrate accomplishments, receive educational information, and discuss the trials and tribulations of weight loss. It is not known, nor is it particularly relevant, whether this weight loss group is representative of other weight loss groups or programs. In fact, I assume that this group is probably not representative of weight loss programs in general. Programs vary widely in their philosophies of and approaches to weight loss, their costs, and in the types of members to whom they are accessible, affordable, and attractive. Lifestyle modification groups differ in numerous ways from medically oriented programs or 12-Step programs such as Overeaters Anonymous (Lester 1999; van Wormer 1994).

But even if the organization is not representative of other weight loss programs, its influence is likely to be large. Founded in 1963, it is the oldest and largest commercial weight loss organization in the United States. Since then the group has gone international, and an estimated one million members attend approximately thirty thousand weekly meetings in twenty-four countries worldwide, including Canada, Mexico, Brazil, Sweden, Great Britain, Poland, France, Israel, South Africa, Australia, and Hong Kong. Most members in the United States attend traditional meetings at various sites, some owned or leased by the organization for the sole purpose of holding meetings and others borrowed or rented from other organizations, such as churches, schools, or community centers. In a midsize city there may be a dozen or more sites, each of which is likely to hold several meetings every week. In recent years the organization has instituted programs at work sites, making it possible for employees to attend meetings immediately before or after work or during their lunch hour, thereby greatly increasing the convenience. In addition, the organization can reach even nonmembers through its magazine, website, and the large variety of food products bearing its name not required for following the program but widely available in grocery stores.

Because lifestyle change is a relatively ambiguous and open-ended goal, lifestyle modification groups may be relatively less limited by a specific model of obesity and weight loss. And due to the broad appeal of self-improvement, lifestyle modification groups may attract somewhat heterogeneous members, at least in their degree of overweight and their perspective on weight loss. At the same time, both leaders and members are highly homogeneous in their social characteristics. Of the six leaders observed, all are Caucasian, in their late thirties to early fifties, and all but one are female. Group members are also homogeneous, though somewhat less so than leaders. It is harder to describe members, partly because they are far more numerous, and they attend different meetings. Most important, member turnover is rapid and high. It is not unusual in a meeting with an average attendance of fifteen to twenty members for a core of four to five regular attendees to be there nearly every week, while the remaining members come for a while and then drop out, only to be replaced with new members. Furthermore, since meeting attendance is not mandatory, it is not unusual for members to come early to weigh in and then leave before the meeting starts. Nonetheless, some general observations on member characteristics can be made.

In contrast to leaders, members' ages vary widely. While the typical member is between thirty and fifty years old, members as young as twelve and as old as seventy are not unusual. Otherwise, there is little demographic variation among members. The vast majority of members are white, with fewer than a dozen African Americans attending during the two years of the research. In addition, most members are middle class, and the great majority are female. There are rarely more than one or two men at a meeting, and meetings with no men at all are common. It is possible that more men join the group but do not attend meetings, but there may have been even fewer males had it not been that men sometimes join and attend with their wives.

Several factors contribute to the high degree of homogeneity in the group. Its social class composition is partly a function of both location and cost. The organization has multiple meeting sites in a variety of neighborhoods in the city, and most people are likely to attend meetings fairly close to their homes. I attended meetings at a busy shopping center in the middle of a large and growing middle-class neighborhood. Furthermore, the cost, though not prohibitive, can add up quickly. Promotions to attract new members are common, especially after holidays and prior to swimsuit season, when the registration fee is reduced to fifteen dollars, half the standard fee. Subsequent meetings cost eleven dollars each, although prepaid packages can save members a dollar or so per week. At the recommended weight loss rate of one to two pounds per week, and assuming a steady rate of loss, someone desiring to lose twenty-five pounds can expect to attend meetings for at least twelve to twenty-five weeks, at a total cost of $150 to $300. Food scales, cookbooks, and other optional materials entail additional costs.

The more weight you want to lose, the longer it will take, and the higher the expense involved.

There is another reason that the group attracts middle-class members. In her personal account of her decision to stop trying to lose weight, Sallie Tisdale (1994:28) argues that the ways people choose to diet, in other words, the ways people choose to not eat, are highly affected by social class: "Even the ways we *don't eat* are based in class. The middle class don't eat in support groups. The poor can't afford not to eat at all. The rich hire someone to not eat with them in private. Dieting is an emblem of capitalism." There is something almost inherently middle class about support groups. The philosophy of self-help that characterizes many support groups resonates with cultural values that emphasize individual solutions to social problems. Rather than critiquing or changing the larger political, economic, and social context that spawns certain problems, individuals are encouraged to find personal strategies for coping with the environment. Support groups provide a comfortable, relatively nonthreatening atmosphere in which to do so. Increased attention to the value of communication and talking about one's problems with sympathetic others has contributed to the proliferation of self-help support groups in recent years (Wuthnow 1994).

The overrepresentation of women in the group in part is due to the greater emphasis placed on physical appearance and weight for women than for men, as we have seen. Despite its official gender-neutrality, the group itself is clearly directed at women. Because discussions focus on questions and issues of particular concern to women, men who join may feel less comfortable, or at least may find that their issues are less likely to be addressed. The assumptions underlying many discussion topics imply that members are female and, in particular, are females in fairly traditional roles. It is generally assumed that women do the majority of cooking in their households, and that members themselves are cooking. How to cook appropriate foods for yourself while simultaneously pleasing your family is a frequently voiced concern. How to manage the program if someone else is cooking is rarely discussed.

The weight loss group described here, then, is not representative of all weight loss groups, nor are group members assumed to be representative of some larger population. Men do join the group at times, and several African American women have joined and attended regularly. The voices and experiences of men and African American women are included here. But the fact remains that members are predominantly middle-class, Caucasian women.

The nonrepresentativeness of the group and its members raises questions about the relevance of the findings. Does it matter that group members are not representative of some larger population, and specifically that the group is largely populated by middle-class, Caucasian women? On some levels it does. Substantial research suggests there are significant gender differences in body image, body satisfaction, and dieting. If women and men are situated differently in relation to issues of weight, and if they differ substantially in their likelihood and experiences of dieting, then we would expect to find differences in their perspectives on weight and dieting.

There are also racial differences among women in body image and attitudes toward weight. That African American women and girls tend to be more satisfied with their bodies (Akan and Grilo 1995; Brown et al. 1995) and express less negative attitudes about being overweight (Rucker and Cash 1992) certainly does not mean that African American women are immune to cultural pressures regarding body size. But subcultural norms may interact with, temper, or even subvert dominant cultural norms. If this is the case, it is likely that African American women hold different attitudes toward dieting and weight loss.

Given gender and racial differences in body images and the experiences of dieting and weight loss, it would indeed be hazardous to generalize the findings described here to men, or to women from social classes or ethnic groups other than middle-class Caucasians. In this sense the nonrepresentativeness of the group and its members is a concern. In some ways, however, the homogeneity in membership is less problematic. The point of the research described here, as is true of most qualitative, participant-observation research, is not to draw statistical generalizations from a sample to a larger population. Nor is the point to make systematic comparisons between different groups, such as men and women or Caucasians and African Americans. Rather, the point is to come to some greater theoretical understanding of the various ways that people, particularly women, talk about weight and dieting.

From this perspective, a specific weight loss group is a very rich site, albeit only one site of many, in which people talk about losing weight. The organization that sponsors this particular group clearly favors some definitions and understandings of weight loss rather than others, and thus is likely to favor certain ways of talking about weight loss. Consequently the group may attract or at least retain members who are predisposed to think and talk about weight in similar ways. But the group is not closed. Members come and go, frequently and regularly, and they bring to the group different perspectives and experiences. Some of these perspectives and experiences are a function of sex, ethnicity, and social class, but others are rooted in specific relations with family and peers, differential exposure to and interpretations of mass media messages, unique health histories, and so on.

Locating the Researcher: Feminist Scholarship and Participant Observation

When I decided to participate in the weight loss group as both a paying member and a researcher, I chose a stance that raises numerous issues concerning values in the research process and the appropriate distance between researcher and research participants. Sociologists, from the very beginning of their discipline, have debated, sometimes heatedly, the role of values in research. Marx has been roundly criticized for letting his passion interfere with his scholarship, and even Weber, a strong proponent of value-free sociology, argued that value relevance should guide sociologists in choosing research topics. However, the positivist stance, emphasizing value-neutrality, objectivity, and distance between observer and observed, has dominated the social sciences. Values and emotions presumably bias all phases of the research process, since they impede the researcher's ability to be objective. Therefore much professional training attempts to socialize social scientists into the positivist stance.

Many feminist scholars strongly challenge positivism. Some, including some physical scientists, question the very possibility of objectivity (Reinharz 1992). They argue that personal bias is inherent in observing a phenomenon from a particular standpoint. Every viewpoint is partial. If it is impossible to achieve objectivity, the only viable solution is for diverse researchers to examine a topic from multiple perspectives and draw on a range of backgrounds, training, and ideologies. In this way "the personal bias that each person brings would cancel out the bias of another person" (Reinharz 1992:261).

Issues of objectivity are particularly acute in participant-observation research, where debates center on the appropriate degree of distance between observer and observed. While recognizing the need to establish rapport, mainstream researchers advocate appropriate distance from research subjects to avoid bias and enhance objectivity (Reinharz 1992). In contrast, feminist researchers argue that closeness is necessary to truly understand one's research participants. Reinharz (1992:69) states, "Feminist ethnographers who emphasize closeness rather than distance in fieldwork relations believe that understanding based on participant observation is enhanced by total immersion in the world one is studying. Total immersion comes about when the researcher begins to share the fate of those she is studying." The implication is that one can only fully understand a phenomenon by experiencing it, and this is done at least in part by minimizing, if not eliminating, distance between researcher and research participants, implying some degree of mutuality and reciprocal giving. This contrasts with more exploitative relations in which the researcher receives (or takes) data from the subjects while providing little or nothing in return (Reinharz 1992).

Closeness obviously has its risks, not the least of which are the sometimes uncomfortable, even painful emotions that can be aroused. If research participants have been traumatized or are otherwise suffering pain, identification surely entails sharing in their suffering. Rothman (1986) eloquently describes the tremendous stress she experienced while interviewing women who had undergone amniocentesis, and similarly Gordon and Riger (1989) speak of the personal pain involved in interviewing rape survivors. Other painful emotions can occur if we fail to identify with participants, particularly if we feel that we should identify with them. While studying women in a countercultural setting, Kleinman (1991) describes her anger, lack of empathy, and anger at herself for not feeling empathetic toward the women. Sociological researchers do not commonly admit feeling deep emotions during their research. In part as a result of their professional training, when researchers do respond emotionally in the course their work, they are likely to actively work on their emotions to bring them into line with normative expectations, that is, to do what Hochschild (1983) calls emotion-management.

Maintaining some distance between researcher and participants is not a bad thing, and may be necessary to see a phenomenon, if not more accurately, then from different perspectives. Fully seeing a physical object requires both distance and closeness. Moving back from an object provides an angle of vision otherwise impossible to achieve. To see the details, however, we must move closer. Only when we continually manipulate our distance from the object, moving alternately closer and farther away, do we get a clearer picture, and then only if we also repeatedly change our angle of vision. Conceptualizing distance between researcher and participant as a unilinear continuum ranging from near to far may be inaccurate, or at least incomplete. A more fitting analogy may be an enlarging spiral around the object viewed.

Debates over the place of researchers' personal experiences in the research process are related to issues of distance. Positivist scholars advocate the separation of the scientist from the object of study, a stance that feminists charge is patriarchal. In contrast, Reinharz (1992:258) argues that the inclusion of the researcher's personal experiences is a distinguishing mark of feminist scholarship:

> Feminist researchers generally consider personal experiences to be a valuable asset for feminist research. To the extent that this is *not* the case in mainstream research, utilizing the researcher's personal experience is a distinguishing feature of feminist research. Personal experience typically is irrelevant in mainstream research, or is thought to contaminate a project's objectivity. In feminist research, by contrast, it is relevant and repairs the project's pseudo-objectivity. Whereas feminist researchers frequently present their research in their own voice, researchers publishing in mainstream journals typically are forbidden to use the first person singular voice.

That is, the researcher is consciously and recognizably present in feminist research, although feminist scholars vary in their approaches. Some base their research entirely on their own experiences, including Macdonald and Rich's (1983) study of homophobia and lesbian aging, and Paget's (1990) research on confronting death as she faced her own terminal cancer. Other researchers begin with personal observations but go on to collect data from others for comparative purposes, as in Reinharz's (1988) study of miscarriage. Others begin by researching other's experiences and only later recognize themselves as part of the group being studied (Rush 1980).

Issues of researcher location also relate to discussions of the extent to which work can be separated from other areas of your life. Normative expectations emphasize compartmentalizing the different components of your life, thereby temporally and spatially separating roles from one another. Feminist criticism challenges both the wisdom and the actual viability of compartmentalization. Reinharz (1992:260) suggests that in feminist critiques of role separation, we see a "new 'epistemology of insiderness,' that sees life and work as intertwined." This intertwining is seen in Ruzek's (1978) ethnography of the women's health movement, as her research quickly spread beyond given research settings and included subscribing to relevant periodicals, gathering information in her personal travels, and soliciting friends to gather information. Brown (1985) took this a step further in her study of a Haitian Voudou cult, fusing herself and her work as she became deeply involved in Voudou interpretation and healing.

Not all feminist scholars reject positivism and the ideal of value-free science, and some researchers who do not identify themselves as feminists nonetheless reject some tenets of positivism. Nonetheless feminist scholarship is a major arena in which these debates have unfolded, and it has deeply influenced my research. From the very beginning, I confronted issues of distance, personal experience, and role compartmentalization. I did not ask permission from the weight loss organization to conduct my research. The group is open to anyone willing to pay, and so I simply joined. But being cognizant of ethical issues surrounding distance from and potential exploitation of research participants, I wanted to be as open as possible with participants, both leaders and members, about my dual role as group member and researcher. Given the high membership turnover and erratic meeting attendance, a general public announcement of my role would have been useless unless repeated at every meeting. Instead, as I met and spoke with individual leaders and members, whenever possible I mentioned that in addition to being a group member, I was doing research on women's experiences of dieting and weight loss. No one seemed to care much. To be sure, many people expressed interest in what I was doing, but no one voiced concern.

Participant observation rests on recording fieldnotes that are sufficiently detailed to provide a rich description of the setting and persons observed. Because I was not trying to hide my researcher status it was possible to record some fieldnotes while at meetings. Many members took notes or jotted things down, so note taking provoked little attention. But other factors related to distance and personal experience impeded my ability to take detailed notes at meetings. Because I was committed to minimizing distance between myself and other members, and because I considered my own experiences as valid data, I was obligated to participate in meetings as fully as possible. This meant attending to what leaders were saying and engaging in group discussions and activities. These activities precluded detailed note taking. My solution was to jot down as much as possible during meetings, and then write detailed notes as soon as I could after the meeting ended.

When I joined the group, I expected the bulk of my research to be confined to the weekly meetings. For the first several weeks, my note taking was confined to the meetings, and for the most part my observations were restricted to exactly what occurred and only secondarily to my responses and reactions. A subtle shift took place after a couple of months, as my notes increasingly included experiences outside the meetings. Conversations with friends about their own weight struggles, interaction with family members, chance encounters in grocery stores and restaurants, and a wide variety of other experiences began making their way into my fieldnotes. The boundaries between my work and the rest of my life began to blur, until they were, for all intents and purposes, indistinguishable. I subscribed to periodicals focused on weight loss, bought dozens of magazines because of cover stories related to dieting and weight loss, and watched hours of television shows that seemed somehow relevant. Even television shows, movies, interaction with friends, and conversations with colleagues that seemingly had little to do with weight loss began to be viewed through the lens of my research. Distinctions between being in the setting and out of it, as well as between working on my research and not working on it, became virtually meaningless.

I began analyzing my data almost as soon as I began collecting it, and again issues of distance and personal experience were relevant. Despite my commitment to minimizing the distance between myself and the research participants, and my conviction that my personal experiences were valid data, including myself in the research turned out to be no easy feat. Even including excerpts from my fieldnotes where I was clearly present and participating caused some degree of discomfort, if not embarrassment. Furthermore, I was conflicted. As a critical, feminist observer, I was deeply aware of the sexist culture that glorifies thinness and objectifies women and their bodies. But as a person who was overweight, I also knew that I didn't feel well, had little energy, and had great difficulty buying clothes that were comfortable and attractive. It took me some time to see that both of those systems of knowledge are valid. Once I began to recognize, take seriously, and respect the active negotiation process that I was going through to somehow reconcile and balance these ways of knowing, I was forced to rethink my theoretical stance. I began to accord much more credit to the participants, and gained a greater appreciation and respect for their struggles. A view of society and culture as exerting far-reaching, overarching, and insidious control over women gave way to a view of a more dialectical process of active and ongoing resistance and negotiation by individual women who not only listen to their culture but listen to themselves.

The shared meanings that are constructed, interpreted, rejected, and reconstructed in the process of conversation and discussion are the focus of my analysis. I argue that it is in people's language and talk that we see meaning-making unfold. Both my sociological training and my feminist convictions motivated my decision to actively participate in the group as a paying member. As a feminist scholar, I am convinced that understanding women's experiences requires closeness between researcher and research participants. Similarly, from a sociological perspective, participant observation is a primary tool for gaining insight into how individuals actively construct meaning. Furthermore, as an active participant in a weight loss group, my personal embodiment was keenly apparent. My actual, lived experiences in the group deeply inform my interpretations.

In chapter 2, I provide a detailed description of the organization, including the six meeting leaders, group members, and the weight loss plan. After discussing members' justifications for and feelings about joining the group, I introduce the major concepts of weight loss that emerge as group members talk about dieting and losing weight: self-help, work, religion, addiction, and feminism. These frameworks or metaphors, all tied to broader historical and cultural trends in the United States, provide language and perspectives that leaders and members draw on to describe and explain their weight loss experiences.

The following five chapters discuss in detail each of the concepts in turn, beginning with the two most strongly endorsed and employed by the weight loss organization, self-help and work. In chapter 3, the organization's approach is placed in the context of the larger self-help movement in the United States. The weight loss group actively promotes a view of itself as a self-help group through the arrangement of its meeting space, the structure of meetings, leaders' roles, and a number of factors that promote cooperative and supportive relations between group members. In this chapter I also consider factors that diminish the group's capacity to act as a self-help group. Ultimately the assumptions that underlie the self-help model, namely, that being overweight is unhealthy that body weight is subject to individual control, and that diets don't work, reflect and reinforce members' views on the meaning of health, good food, and exercise.

Chapter 4 focuses on the other major point of view endorsed by the organization, that of weight loss as work. Clearly compatible with emphases on self-improvement, self-help, and a strong work ethic, the work model operates in two ways. First, it reflects members' views on what personal characteristics are necessary to succeed at weight loss. Hard work and discipline emerge as by far the most important requirements, and people who fail to lose weight are assumed to be lazy and undisciplined. Second, the perspective focuses attention on the nature of the work itself. It emphasizes the structure and precision of the weight loss plan, and considers the payoff of weight loss for members. Viewing weight loss as work highlights the contemporary objectification of the body and the overriding trend toward increased rationalization in the larger society.

Chapter 5 describes a metaphor that is not as obviously endorsed by the organization, but that nonetheless emerges as members explore their ongoing struggles. By turning weight loss into a battle between good and evil, the concept of religion moralizes weight loss, which is most obvious in discussions of temptation, sacrifice, guilt, and the need for surveillance. This framework highlights the tension in the group between the potential for recognizing the importance of ritual and community and pressures toward isolating and individualizing the weight-loser. Furthermore, a religious outlook, by incorporating the inexplicable, magic, superstition, and taboo, can potentially release the deep emotions evoked by weight loss. But this potential is largely diminished as weight loss is subjected to larger forces of rationalization, commercialism, and the spread of a scientific perspective.

Chapter 6 focuses on addiction, a view of weight loss that the organization consistently downplays. I begin by examining Overeaters Anonymous, a group that embraces and reinforces the view of compulsive overeating as an addiction. The contrast between this group and the observed weight loss group is most obvious when we consider three areas in which we might expect an addiction model to have some influence: in discussions of hunger as a physiological response of the material body, in considerations of control and loss of control, and in definitions of normal and disordered eating.

In chapter 7, I consider whether it is possible to identify a feminist concept of weight loss that operates in the group. In many ways, this seems unlikely. Feminist scholars and activists have been visible and vocal critics of the weight loss industry and the obsession with thinness that fuels it. Nonetheless, in discussions of self-care, self-acceptance, and the effects of gender roles on weight gain and loss, we catch glimpses of a pseudo-feminist language of individual liberation. In contrast to the addiction perspective, the weight loss organization does not suppress or resist a feminist metaphor. Instead, it uses a highly selective, watered-down version of liberal feminism to promote itself. In effect, feminist language is co-opted, as liberation is conflated with traditional understandings of individualism and self-reliance. The potential for truly feminist weight loss remains latent, at best.

In the final chapter, I begin by considering what the concepts of weight loss have in common. All five frameworks share explicit emphases on control and surveillance and are relatively silent on issues of hunger and the social construction of ideal weight. But the perspectives also differ, most notably in their views of the body and food. Depending on the approach, the body is seen as a symbol of health and virtue, an object to be shaped and worked on, or a problem to be transcended. Similarly, food is variously defined as relatively unimportant, potentially dangerous, or a source of bodily fuel. The organization accommodates the differences and conflicts between the concepts by largely translating the metaphors of religion, addiction, and feminism into the metaphors of self-help and work. Food and eating are desensualized, weight loss is rationalized and de-emotionalized, and the causes of and solutions for obesity are individualized and depoliticized. I end by reflecting on whether it is possible to conceptualize truly feminist weight loss.

2 | In the Beginning

When I attended my first meeting, I had little idea of what to expect. I did remember that my grandmother had joined this same group when I was a child, and I had vague recollections of her recounting the tribulations of public weigh-ins and having to eat liver every week. The latter prospect didn't especially bother me, but the idea of being publicly weighed was enough to keep me in the parking lot. But, determined to see the research through, and convinced that probably much had changed since my grandmother's time, I entered the organization's suite and immediately confronted the commercial side of the group. Behind a counter at the front, a very large woman whom I came to know as Eileen sat and greeted people as they arrived. When I told Eileen I was interested in joining, she launched into a rapid and highly confusing explanation of my payment options. I was totally baffled and Eileen wasn't much help. At this point a man walked behind the counter and Eileen said, "Now, Richard, tell me again what the special is going to be next week." Abruptly, he said, "It's all tied to the prepaid plans." "But won't it be cheaper to join next week?" asked Eileen. Richard impatiently replied, "I told you, it's all tied in with the prepay packages," and the two of them launched into a long and involved conversation concerning registration fees, prepaid packages, and having to pay for missed meetings. Still somewhat confused, but guessing I would be more likely to return if I paid in advance, I purchased a four-meeting package for forty-five dollars and proceeded to the weigh-in area at the back of the suite.

The commercial elements of the program were obvious here as well. Off the main meeting room three small cubicles were lined up, open at the front, and separated only by flimsy, movable dividers. A scale, similar to those in doctors' offices, stood in the middle of each cubicle. A large display of organizational paraphernalia for sale stood in the area right before the cubicles. Cookbooks, exercise videos, water bottles, food scales, inspirational materials, and a variety of other diet aids were prominently displayed, with prices clearly marked. Not only was it impossible to get to the scales without passing the display, but members frequently had to stand here, waiting in line to be weighed. As members waited they often leafed through the cookbooks and examined the other merchandise.

By the time I got back to the cubicles, five people were waiting in line. Two people were weighing members; a woman named Ann, and Richard. Mercifully, weigh-in was relatively private. On each scale the mechanism showing the weight was turned so that no one, including the person being weighed, could see the actual weight, except for the person doing the weighing. At the top of each scale a sign reading "No Bare Feet on the Scale" further obscured the weight from viewers. When it was my turn I stepped into the cubicle where Ann was weighing and told her I wasn't entirely sure what I was doing. She said, "Don't worry, we're going to help get you on the right track." She told me to step on the scale, she adjusted it, and then, rather than telling me what I weighed, she wrote it directly into my membership booklet and then pointed to it with her pen so that I could see. Ann then asked how tall I was and showed me the weight range appropriate for my height. She said that was the range I would be working toward. I would eventually have to set a specific goal weight within that range, but not until I was closer to, or even within, the range. Ann handed me several pamphlets and told me to be sure to stay after the meeting so that Richard could explain the program to me.

I left the cubicle and found a seat in the main meeting area. Four rows of chairs were arranged in an elongated U-shape, facing the front of the room. A blackboard hung on the front wall, on either side of which sat videocassette recorders, with a flip chart off to one side. One of the organization's exercise videos was playing on the VCRs. About twenty people were scattered about the room, mostly seated in small groups of three or four, laughing and chatting. Several people weighed in but didn't stay for the meeting, and a few left before the meeting was over. The vast majority of those present were women. Of the three men who weighed in, only one stayed for the meeting.

At about seven o'clock, Richard ran to the front, clapping and encouraging others to do so, shouting, "Remember, applauding burns calories!" He spent several minutes animatedly working the room, applauding, greeting members by name, and asking people how they were doing. Eventually the noise subsided, Richard calmed down, and we moved into the formal meeting, which fell into three main parts. First, the motivational section of the meeting focused on what it means to be "on program," and what happens if you go "off program." At the end of this discussion, Richard showed a brief video focused on the role of protein in the diet. The final part of the meeting was celebration. As members applauded and shouted words of encouragement, Richard ran around the room handing out small, colorful stickers to new members and to returning members for coming to the meeting, losing weight or exercising in the previous week, and other personal accomplishments. My sticker said, "I did it!" and Richard said, "That means I turned myself in." Richard closed the meeting by exclaiming, "I'll see less of you next week!"

In the hour I spent at this first meeting I witnessed a basic routine that varied from week to week only in the minutest of details. Members who stayed for meetings quickly became familiar with the pattern, sometimes keeping leaders on track when they strayed. The few times that leaders forgot to do celebration or were close to running out of time, members were quick to remind them. On another occasion Richard said he would save time by skipping the educational video, but members protested and ended up staying almost fifteen minutes later to watch it. As a result of the routine, a high degree of familiarity and predictability characterized the meetings, further reinforced by the relative homogeneity of organizational employees and group members.

This chapter begins with an overview of the weight loss organization—group leaders, members, and the weight loss plan espoused by the group. Leaders and members share many characteristics; most notably they are predominantly middle-class, Caucasian females. But there are differences as well. Leaders vary widely in personality, leadership style, and approach to the group, and these characteristics interact with and influence their organizational roles. Members, despite homogeneity in social characteristics, vary widely in how overweight they are and how much weight they hope to lose. The group's basic weight loss plan, despite several changes in recent years, strictly but implicitly controls calorie intake, and relies heavily on weighing and measuring food and on keeping detailed records of what one eats. Next, we examine members' reasons for joining the group, first by considering the explicit justifications members provide and then by considering members' thoughts and expectations as they began the weight loss program. Here we begin to see the tensions between members' previous experiences with diets and the organization's presumed focus on lifestyle modification. The chapter ends by introducing the major concepts of weight loss used by members to describe and explain their experiences. In the course of group discussions, members draw on a number of common languages to make sense of their experiences. The concepts of self-help, work, religion, addiction, and feminism resonate with values and trends deeply embedded in United States culture. Applied to dieting and weight loss, these frameworks provide a language that both reflects and reinforces the ambivalence, conflict, and contradictions of losing weight.

The Organization: The Routine, the People, and the Program

To gain a better understanding of how the weight loss organization operates, I begin by describing employees of the organization, group members, and the weight loss plan advocated by the group.

Employees

Group leaders and receptionists, the majority of whom are part-time, make up the organizational staff. Receptionists staff the front desk, register new members, and weigh members as they arrive. Receptionists here are all Caucasian females who are group members. Some have reached their weight loss goals; others are close to goal; and a few, like Eileen, have met it at one time and are trying to reach it again. In exchange for their services, receptionists can continue as group members and weigh in weekly at no cost.

At the location I attended, seven meetings are held weekly, and one day each week, walk-in service is available so that members can get weighed without attending a meeting. During the two years I belonged to the group, I attended various meetings and observed six different leaders. As the official representatives of the organization, leaders conduct the formal meetings. Members set their individual weight loss goals in consultation with leaders, and members are encouraged to go to the leaders with individual questions or concerns. The six leaders differ in personality, interactional style, and approach to leading meetings, but all share certain key characteristics by virtue of their organizational roles.

Richard is unique for a number of reasons, not least of which is that he is the only male leader and one of only a very few male members in the group as a whole. Richard dresses very casually, often in khakis or jeans and a sweatshirt, and his style and approach match. Richard's exuberance and energy level are frenetic at times. Rarely standing still, Richard continuously roams the room. He speaks loudly, frequently almost shouting, and repeatedly encourages members to clap and shout back at him. Richard pays little attention to the meeting outline provided by the organization, and it is frequently difficult to follow his logic since he ad-libs freely and jumps from topic to topic, depending on what suits him. None of this bothers members who attend his meetings. Richard's energy and enthusiasm are contagious. His meetings are casual, bantering and teasing are common, and the noise level can be deafening.

The first time I observed Cheryl's meeting, the contrast with Richard's was jarring. Dressed in a suit, hair styled, and meticulously made up, Cheryl exuded professionalism. Cheryl conducts the only daytime meeting designed for mothers with young children. Attendees at Cheryl's meeting rarely surpass six or seven, but despite the low number and the frequent presence of small children, Cheryl always stands in the front of the room, lecture-style, draws heavily on the meeting outline, and maintains a generally formal approach throughout. Overall, Cheryl is subdued, tending toward quiet support in contrast to Richard's energetic encouragement.

I first observed Linda when she substituted for a vacationing Richard, but subsequently observed her on numerous occasions conducting her own meetings. Quite tall, perhaps six feet, and very thin, Linda stands in stark contrast to the "before picture" that she prominently displays at the front of the room. She is the only female leader who frequently emphasizes the amount of weight she has lost on the program, reminding members often that she has weighed well over two hundred pounds at various times in her life. In some ways, Linda resembles Richard. She moves around the room freely, speaks loudly and energetically, and maintains a casual, joking relationship with members. At the same time, Linda evokes a degree of professionalism almost entirely lacking in Richard's presentation. She nearly always wears suits, and is more likely than Richard to use the official meeting outline, if not stick to it faithfully.

Debbie is the leader I observed most frequently. Debbie is in her late thirties, lost twenty-five pounds on the program, and has maintained the loss for ten years. Debbie is the only leader who is a full-time employee of the organization, not only leading weekly meetings but also working in the office. Debbie dresses professionally and relies heavily on the organization's weekly outlines for her material, but more than other leaders, she takes a personal approach, actively cultivating socioemotionally oriented relationships with members. Debbie greets members by name as they arrive, and while other leaders frequently help weigh members in, Debbie often uses the time before meetings to approach members individually, ask them how their week has gone, and talk about particular issues they have encountered. Toward the end of my research, Debbie lost her job as a result of organizational downsizing, a traumatic experience that she frequently talked about during meetings. Debbie continued to lead meetings on a part-time basis, but eventually announced that she needed to commit full-time effort to finding a new job, and was leaving the organization. Debbie's departure was difficult for her regular attendees, partly due to the disruption in meeting routine but especially because of the close personal relationships that she had formed with members.

Ruth was a receptionist for several meetings and occasionally substituted for the regular leaders. When Linda left the organization to get married and move to another state, Ruth stepped in as a temporary substitute, but soon became Linda's permanent replacement. The contrast between them was dramatic. Where Linda was outgoing and exuberant, Ruth was subdued and quiet, speaking at times in a voice that made it difficult to hear her. In contrast to Linda's and Richard's casual, joking relationships with members, and Debbie's close, personal relationships, Ruth's relations with members were professional and formal. Ruth was the least likely of the leaders to incorporate her personal experiences into her presentations. While conducting many meetings over several months, Ruth never revealed her marital status, whether she had children or another job, or any other details of her personal life, information frequently and routinely shared by other leaders.

Shirley led the only two weekend meetings, which met on Saturday mornings, and conducted the walk-in service on Friday. Shirley always dressed professionally, even on Friday, and her leadership approach, like Ruth's, was relatively formal and quiet. At the same time, Shirley casually incorporated personal experience into her presentations and often talked about her husband, two children, and part-time job as a secretary in a nonprofit agency. What distinguished Shirley most clearly from the other leaders was her body type. She was a lifetime member of the organization and fell within the weight range recommended for her height, but Shirley was not thin. Rather, her body type was what some might call big-boned or stocky. By example, Shirley provided at least some members with a model of successful weight loss other than thinness.

Despite the differences among them, as lifetime members of the weight loss program, leaders have all met and maintained their weight loss goals. At the start of every meeting, leaders introduce themselves to the group and inevitably mention how much weight they lost and how many years they have kept it off. Richard and Linda had lost large amounts of weight, over two hundred and nearly one hundred pounds respectively. Both leaders prominently display before-and-after photographs of themselves at the front of the room, and occasionally Debbie passes around a picture of herself before her weight loss. The photographs serve a dual purpose. First, the photos are strong motivational devices. They are visible proof that the program works. Second, the photos are a bonding device between leaders and members. By displaying the photos and frequently incorporating personal experiences and anecdotes into their discussions, leaders continually remind members that they can empathize, having been there themselves. Indeed, by reminding members that leaders too have to weigh in monthly and continue to maintain their goal weights, they emphasize the similarities between themselves and the rest of the group.

Members

Although they are largely homogeneous in social characteristics, members, like leaders, vary widely in how overweight they are when they begin the program and consequently in how much weight they hope to lose, a fact that was obvious the first time I went to a meeting. Standing in line to be weighed, I was immediately struck by the wide range of body weights and types around me. There were many individuals who weighed considerably less than I did, but there were also many who weighed more. When members met their weight loss goals, they were always asked by the leader to tell the group how much total weight they had lost. Here too a wide range was observed. The six leaders experienced weight losses ranging from a low of fifteen pounds to a high of over two hundred pounds. Members displayed similar variations. The diversity of body weights displayed was increased somewhat by the occasional presence of lifetime members. Individuals who reach their goal weight become lifetime members, and to maintain their status they must weigh in once a month and stay within two pounds of their goal weight. As long as they do so they can attend meetings at no cost, although many come simply to get weighed and then leave before the meeting begins.

Very few men joined the group, but among the few male members as a whole, the range in how overweight they were was considerably more narrow than that of the female members. As a group, the men who join are considerably more overweight and have more weight that they want to lose, compared with women who join. While some women intend to lose very large amounts of weight, many have as few as ten to fifteen pounds to lose. In order to join, individuals must be at least ten pounds over the upper limit of the ideal weight range for their age and height, and many women join who have little more than this to lose. I never observed a new male member this close to his ideal range, and an educated estimate is that the average man intended to lose around fifty pounds. Men who join with their wives are somewhat less overweight than other men in the group, but on average they too are more overweight than many women who join.

The gender difference in ranges of overweight suggests that women and men may differ in how much extra weight they can tolerate. It is not hard to understand why many group members, female and male, have large amounts of weight to lose. Diets are notorious for their failure rates. Members who are greatly overweight have in all likelihood experienced years of dieting and gaining back even more weight. But if women are likely to join a weight loss program with very little weight to lose, why don't men do so? The answer may lie in gender differences in the cultural ideal. If the cultural ideal for men is more broadly defined and overweight men are less likely to be stigmatized, then they are likely to more accurately judge their own weight and may be more tolerant of a few extra pounds than are women. Men may thus be less likely to join a weight loss group until they deviate greatly from the ideal range, or face a specific health problem. Conversely, given the narrow ideal for women, the greater stigmatization of overweight women, and the greater likelihood that women overestimate their actual weight, it is not surprising that women may be less tolerant of gaining even small amounts of weight. This may explain why a majority of American women are almost continuously dieting, why women are more likely to join weight loss groups than men, and why many women join such groups with relatively little weight to lose.

In sum, this particular group, both in membership and in leadership, is largely populated by middle-class, Caucasian females who vary widely in the amount of weight they hope to lose. As a result, it is not surprising that the organizational philosophy both reflects and reinforces values and assumptions common to this segment of the population. The organization emphasizes self-help and mutual support, and does so in an environment particularly conducive to focusing on women's concerns.

The Program

A careful examination of the weight loss program demonstrates the ways in which the organizational philosophy meshes with members' characteristics and values. When I joined the group in 1994, the cornerstone of the program was a fairly simple eating plan. Foods were divided into six major categories: bread, milk, protein, fruits, vegetables, and fat. Members were limited to a specified number of selections from each category per day. Foods were translated into selections on the basis of volume or weight. For example, eight ounces of skim milk or one cup of nonfat yogurt was one milk selection, one ounce of meat, two ounces of fish, or three-quarters of an ounce of cheese was one protein, and one teaspoon of olive oil was one fat selection. If members felt that the amount of food in the basic plan was insufficient, they could use up to twenty-one additional personal selections and seven hundred optional calories per week. To make it easier to learn and follow the plan, mix-and-match meal menus were included in the written materials given to new members. By choosing meals from those provided, members were guaranteed to consume the minimum number of selections in each category.

Leaders emphasized that if followed faithfully, the basic program guaranteed nutritional variety. Emphasizing the plan's nutritional value serves a dual purpose. First, the organization counteracts charges that diets are unhealthy. Second, by linking the plan to the basic food pyramid recommended for everyone, the organization argues that this is not a diet at all, but simply the way everybody should be eating. This argument is crucial for an organization purporting to encourage lifestyle change as opposed to dieting.

Although the program was not very complicated, not all members grasped its logic. Peggy was a member who didn't fare well on the program. She didn't consistently lose weight and she encountered frequent difficulties following the plan. One night Peggy told the group that one of her problems is that she loves bread, and eats far too much, maybe seven breads a day. In response, Debbie asked the group whether seven breads are too many on the program. Several members shook their head, and one said, "You get four to six every day. And you can just use personal selections if you want more." Peggy looked doubtful and asked, "Well, what about potatoes? Aren't they really high in calories?" Peggy didn't see that as long as she followed the portion specifications, a potato counted as one bread selection.

Much of Peggy's confusion relates to the usual association of dieting with calorie counting. For most people, losing weight means reducing and counting calories, an activity that females in particular learn to do at a relatively early age. When a random sample of full-time students at a small, private midwestern university was surveyed, 75 percent of the females, compared with 28 percent of the males, said they are at least sometimes aware of the calorie content of the food they eat (Stinson 1992). Some group members are baffled by the apparent absence of calorie counting. Actually, calories are controlled on the program, but they are counted implicitly rather than explicitly. Within each category, foods are divided into portion sizes so that no matter what food one chooses in that category, on average the calorie content will be similar. One-half cup of nonfat cottage cheese, one ounce of chicken, or two ounces of tuna each counts as one protein selection, and all have a similar number of calories. The net effect is that by following the basic program, daily calorie consumption is automatically kept within certain ranges, even though members do not directly count calories.

Disguising calorie counting promotes the perception that this is a different way of eating, not a diet. At the same time, two components of the program become extremely important. First, weighing and measuring food is crucial since calorie control is achieved by controlling portion size. Second, tracking, or the scrupulous recording of everything you eat, is integral to the program. Every week members receive a weekly tracker, a small pamphlet in which they record everything eaten each day, and check off the appropriate number of selections in each food category. Members stay within the appropriate calorie range only by staying within the specified limits for each category of food. Trackers also provide spaces for marking off the six to eight glasses of water that members must drink daily.

Exercise, divided into fat burners, lean builders, and stretches, is also an important element of the program. Members are supposed to do thirty minutes of fat burners, three different lean builders, and three different stretches daily. New members receive a pamphlet describing the different types of exercises, and leaders periodically show a videotape with examples of each type. Leaders frequently tell members that no matter how busy their lives are, they can easily incorporate exercise into their daily activities and don't need expensive gym memberships or equipment. Fat burners can include parking your car further from the office and walking, using the stairs instead of the elevator, or gardening. The message is clearly that physical activity should be a part of everyone's life, and increasing one's activity level requires only a little effort and creativity. Trackers provided spaces for recording the amount of time spent on fat burners, and the number of lean builders and stretches completed daily.

When I first joined I didn't learn the basics of the program immediately, nor did I have to track what I ate. New members routinely spent one to two weeks on an initiation program, Faststart, during which they chose meals and a snack from a predetermined list. Members learned the program gradually, and most important, since choices were limited to a few specified meals and substitutions were kept to a minimum, members automatically conformed to the basic plan. After my first meeting, Richard explained the logic by saying, "It's not a quick weight loss plan. We just choose the meals for you so that you don't have to keep track of everything." Whether Faststart was intended as a quick loss plan or not, not surprisingly, many members lost large amounts of weight during their first week, averaging about five pounds, and sometimes surpassing ten pounds in a single week. The menus were based on the minimum number of selections allocated in each category, and a maximum of 100 additional optional calories. Anyone who strictly followed the initiation plan consumed 1,000 to 1,200 calories daily, presumably a substantial decrease for many. New members frequently complained about being hungry on Faststart. During my first week on the program I was almost continuously hungry, and consequently felt edgy and highly conscious of food. Between the hunger and the time I spent cutting vegetables, preparing meals, and measuring and weighing food, I felt that food occupied more of my time and energy than it had before I joined.

The organization benefits from the fact that Faststart frequently results in large weight losses, although as a retention strategy, it is not without risks. On the one hand, rapid weight loss is a good hook to bring members back. Immediate gratification is a strong reinforcement. Members may be more likely to return when they see dramatic effects, especially in the face of any inconveniences or discomforts encountered. Yet there is a risk. For a number of reasons, many of them physiological, maintaining this rate of weight loss is highly unlikely. The organization endorses a weight loss rate of one to two pounds per week, a substantial loss, but one that pales in comparison with the dramatic losses of the first week. Members may be disappointed and frustrated after following the plan and not seeing the kind of results they have come to expect after the first seven days. During my week on Faststart I lost five and a half pounds. Buoyed by my success, I set aside the hunger and discomfort of the first week and committed myself to sticking to the plan for another week. When I weighed in at my second meeting I was sorely disappointed to find that I had lost only one more pound. Rationally I knew I couldn't expect to lose five pounds every week, but the contrast between the first and second week was dramatic. Not surprisingly, member turnover is rapid and high.

Since 1994 the organization has revised the basic program several times. In the fall of 1994 it launched an advertising campaign that promised a new plan for 1995. Leaders assured members that the basic plan would remain in place, but they would have an alternative plan to follow if they chose to do so. As the new year approached, leaders teased members by alluding to the new plan and suggesting how exciting it was going to be. One night Debbie told the group, "I've seen the new plan and I think you're going to like it." At a meeting not long after, Debbie said, "All the girls in the office are doing the new plan. You know, we have to learn it so we can teach it to you guys, and we all love it!" The plan was finally unveiled in January, just in time for the postholiday rush of new members. Tuned into the cultural obsession with fat and fiber, the new plan involved keeping daily fat intake within a specified range and consuming at least a specified number of grams of fiber. The plan took advantage of the increasing popularity and availability of low- and nonfat foods, and was significantly easier than keeping track of selections. But unfortunately the plan had a major flaw. Quite simply, it lacked the built-in calorie control at the heart of the basic plan. The results were predictable. When Debbie asked members what they liked about the new plan, Estelle quickly and enthusiastically responded, "I can eat all the fat-free frozen yogurt I want!" Heidi, too, had problems with the plan. After following the new program for several weeks, Heidi was consistently gaining weight rather than losing it. Sensing that Heidi was frustrated and about to drop out, Debbie asked to see her tracker, and immediately realized that Heidi was drinking five or six cans of regular soda everyday. Heidi said, "But I thought that's OK because they don't have any fat." Debbie said, "Yeah, but they still have calories." The organization was in an odd position. After spending much time and effort distancing itself from diets, it now had to remind members that calories matter. By the end of the year the organization had dropped the plan.

Over the course of 1995 and into the next year, the organization also modified the basic plan. First, Faststart was dropped and new members learned to track selections immediately. Second, the basic selection plan was simplified. The milk and protein categories were combined into one, as were fruits and vegetables; personal selections were dropped and optional calories changed from 700 per week to 250 per day. Third, different minimum and maximum ranges for each food category were given, based on current weight. The more a person weighed, the higher were his or her minimum and maximum ranges. As members lost weight, they moved into lower ranges. Finally, the organization tried to give members greater freedom and better accommodate the contingencies of everyday life. Members could partake of indulgences, and compensate for them by reducing the number of selections consumed during the rest of the week. Indulgences were typically high-fat, high-calorie foods such as barbecued spareribs or an ice cream sundae. All the changes were meant to increase the plan's attractiveness by not requiring members to follow predetermined menus, simplifying tracking, and making it easier for members to integrate the plan into their lives. None of the changes modified the underlying logic of the plan.

Recently the program changed again. The organization substantially revised the basic plan, although it continued to rely heavily on counting and tracking. The notion of selections was done away with, and all foods were assigned a point value, based on a combination of fat, fiber, and calorie content. All members had to do was to record what they ate and the food's point value, and keep their total points within a specified range, based on their current weight. The point system harks back to the discarded fat and fiber counting plan, but with built-in calorie control. The formula used to calculate point values means that members are subtly encouraged to eat foods that are high in fiber and low in fat, since they carry relatively fewer points. While one cup of vegetarian baked beans has three points and a cup of nonfat yogurt has two points, a small, one-half cup serving of premium ice cream has seven points. Depending on your weight, the latter could constitute one-fourth to one-third of your total daily point allowance. The point system has a major advantage over the earlier selection plan. In that plan, dining out or eating convenience foods made tracking very difficult, since it was not always clear how the foods fit into the selection categories. With the advent of the point system, members received a cardboard slide rule that they could use to calculate the point value of any food, as long as they knew the fat, fiber, and calorie content, all of which is now standard information on package labels.

During a two-year span the basic program thus underwent various modifications. At its core was a relatively strict regulation of calorie intake, albeit disguised as tracking food selections or point values. At the same time, fueled partly by the need to respond to members' needs and complaints and partly by the desire to capitalize on new cultural fads and obsessions, the organization experimented with a number of options and additions. Some of the changes were quickly dropped; others were incorporated into the basic plan.

"What Brought You in the Door?"

People join a weight loss group because they want to lose weight. But many people, particularly women, want to lose weight and attempt to do so without joining a formal group. Reasons for joining are frequently discussed at meetings. Debbie commonly began her meetings by introducing new members and saying, "So tell us, what brought you in the door tonight?" Reasons for joining are also talked about when members discuss such topics as the difference between realistic and unrealistic weight loss goals, or the relationship between life events and weight gain or loss. Examining these reasons provides insight into the sorts of public justifications that are given and accepted for joining a weight loss group.

Justifications fall into three major categories. First, a number of reasons for joining the group are *future oriented.* Members often join because they want to lose weight for an upcoming event. Emily and Jennifer joined together in anticipation of being bridesmaids in a mutual friend's wedding. Toni, one of the few African American members, joined a few months before her own wedding, and drew audible gasps from those present when she announced, "I just bought my wedding dress and I got it a size below where I am now. So I gotta lose the weight so I can get into it!" Weddings, class reunions, or a child's graduation are all future events that provide a specific, time-sensitive goal for weight loss, implying a specific time frame for losing the desired weight. Consequently, a certain rate of weight loss *has* to be maintained to reach the goal. This in turn means that members who join in anticipation of a future event frequently begin with relatively unrealistic goals, thereby increasing both the pressure they feel and the potential for frustration.

Future-oriented justifications are notable in two respects. First, they are frequently *other directed.* Even when members do not explicitly say so, they imply that these events are significant precisely because at them they are going to be seen by others. Second, these justifications are often *appearance related.* Members rarely mention physical appearance explicitly when they talk about why they joined the group. But when members join in anticipation of future events at which they will be seen by others, they are at least in part motivated by the importance of physical appearance and, particularly, appearing thin.

The second category of justifications for joining is *past oriented.* Most prominent in this category are holidays, especially Thanksgiving, Christmas, and New Year's. Consonant with the societal tendency to define the entire period from mid-November to early January as a holiday season, members most commonly join after the entire season has passed. In these months wide fluctuations in both the number of new members and meeting attendance occur, and the winter holiday season is the most obvious correlate. Both membership and attendance drop substantially during the holidays and then rise rapidly in early January. In some ways this explanation is future-oriented, tying in with New Year's resolutions and making a commitment to future changes. And the organization capitalizes on this by working New Year's resolutions into its advertising and running various promotions and membership specials near the beginning of the new year to make it easier for people to act on their resolutions. But the future orientation should not be overplayed. In most instances, even if there is an element of orienting yourself to new ways of eating and acting in the future, most of these explanations emphasize joining a weight loss group to make up for previous excesses, especially those associated with the holidays. Joining the group is a form of penance, offered in repentance for the splurges of the past.

The final category of reasons for joining includes a somewhat less consistent and cohesive set of explanations that are more personal or *self-oriented.* Some of these explanations relate very explicitly to losing weight per se, such as when a new member stated that she had "tried everything else," or when another new member, who had previously belonged to the group, said that her weight "began creeping up. I want to see if I can keep it off this time." Similarly, Connie stated, "I know how to eat. I gravitate toward good foods, like fruits and vegetables, but I need the structure." These explanations are focused on losing weight as a goal in and of itself. The members want to lose weight, they realize they need help to do so, and they view the weight loss group as able to provide the help.

Other explanations in this category privilege the self more than weight. Now in her early fifties, Connie said, "My youngest child left for college this year. Now it's time for me," implying that she is doing something specifically for herself, rather than for others. Faye, an African American member in her forties, worked in a nursing home.

She said, "I'm tired all the time. Taking weight off might help." Connie and Faye imply they will personally benefit from losing weight, independent of appearance. Connie suggests that joining a weight loss group is one way of taking care of or attending to herself, as opposed to nurturing others. Faye emphasizes the personal health and energy benefits that might be gained by losing weight. Both women contextualize their explanations by referring to their family and work roles. However, neither woman fully sees the connection between her roles and her feelings about herself. Connie recognizes the time she has invested in caring for and nurturing others, and now intends to do the same for herself. It is not clear, however, why Connie sees losing weight as a way to care for herself. Likewise, Faye suggests that losing weight might enable her to cope better with the physical demands of her job, but it apparently does not occur to her that her chronic fatigue is related as much to the conditions of working in a nursing home as it is to her weight. Both women frame their explanations in terms of the potential benefits to themselves that might come from weight loss, and neither explanation directly focuses on physical appearance. Nonetheless, both Connie and Faye ultimately decontextualize their experiences and miss the connections between their individual experiences of weight, on the one hand, and structural contingencies encountered via their family and work roles, on the other.

That explanations for joining fall into three major categories, and are frequently repeated, implies that diverse individuals may be motivated to lose weight by a limited number of widely shared factors and, more important, that there are culturally acceptable reasons for wanting to lose weight. Physical appearance underlies a large number of the explanations and yet is rarely mentioned explicitly, mirroring cultural ambivalence in the United States concerning physical appearance. Physical attractiveness is highly valued and thinness is a central component of physical attractiveness, particularly for women, but at the same time people who seem particularly concerned with physical appearance are viewed with suspicion, if not condemned for their self-absorption and shallowness.

Perhaps the most striking feature of the explanations is that they are highly rational, belying the strong emotions frequently associated with weight loss. Certainly individual members vary in their degrees of self-consciousness regarding their motives for joining. Members often cite multiple factors, and at times note that their motives have changed over time. Wendy was a Caucasian member in her late twenties, who joined not long after giving birth to her first child. When I first met her, Wendy had lost twenty-five pounds before joining, over sixty pounds since, and by the time she reached her goal weight, had lost about one hundred pounds. Reflecting on why she joined the group, Wendy stated, "I admit when I first joined I did it for my husband. You know, I was really fat, and I was like worried that he might leave me for someone who was like, thinner. But now I'm doing it for myself. I want to get to my goal for me." Wendy recognizes the tension between being other- and self-motivated, and in some ways resolves the tension by suggesting that her motives have changed over time. In other instances as well, the tension between motives is apparent. Members frequently attempt to reconcile health-oriented and appearance-oriented motives by arguing that when you look better, you feel better, and vice versa. The tension between health- and appearance-related justifications parallels the tension between seeing the program as a diet and seeing it as lifestyle change.

Despite the organization's concerted efforts to present the program as lifestyle change, new members commonly refer to the program as a diet. In many cases, it is the newest in a long line of diets previously tried and abandoned, as when a new member admits, "I've tried everything else." Even though members who have been coming for sometime less frequently refer to the plan as a diet, this notion is hard to shake. Nowhere is this clearer than in members' explanations for the timing of their first meeting and in their descriptions of how they acted once they decided to join the group.

Since many new members assume the program is another diet, not surprisingly they consider the contingencies of everyday life in deciding when to join. It is largely a question of "how will I do this?" Members may wait to join until after specific events, such as a family reunion, a holiday, or a scheduled picnic or ballgame. Not only are events of these sorts associated with overeating, but they present very real challenges related to having or not having control over what food is served or available. Members also consider practicalities related to time and money as well as family issues, including concerns over having to cook different meals for themselves and for their families.

These concerns have several significant implications. First, by suggesting that following the plan will be easier once certain events have passed or practical problems have been addressed, members ignore the fact that eating is always intricately interwoven into our lives, and social occasions in most cases do not just stop. Second, the concerns suggest that eating and not eating can be, and perhaps should be, highly conscious and planned events. Finally, members clearly assume that the way you eat after joining the program will differ substantially from the way you ate before.

This assumption is apparent in members' descriptions of how they acted once they decided to join the group. At one meeting Cheryl moved into the motivational part of the meeting by asking people to describe the last meal they ate before their first meeting, what she called "last supper stories." Sandy replied, "I made sure I went out and got a large order of fries." Corinne responded, "I knew I was going to come after the holidays, so I really binged. I figured it would be my last chance." Darla concurred, saying, "Oh yeah, I ate everything in sight." The day I planned to attend my first meeting, I took my son out to a local restaurant for lunch. I hadn't planned to, but I figured it would be a while before I ate out again, so I had a fried fish sandwich with a trip to the salad bar, light on the lettuce, heavy on the potato salad. Cheryl went on by asking members what they thought they would have to give up when they began the program. The list included French fries, pizza, cheeseburgers, candy bars, cake, and potato chips.

The fact that members can so easily recount not only what they ate at their "last supper," but exactly what they were thinking at the time, indicates that new members assume that the plan will require vast changes in their eating habits. The theme of "giving in" in anticipation of "giving up" runs throughout the stories. Operating on the assumption of future deprivation, members make sure they indulge one last time. Members also distinguish between "good foods" and "bad foods." Good foods are those you will have to eat after joining and bad foods are the ones you will have to give up. Since bad foods are those that are most enjoyed, it is apparent throughout the entire discussion that members expect to give up not only specific foods but pleasure itself.

This is not, however, the intended moral of the story. After soliciting last supper stories and lists of foods to be given up, Cheryl asked members to share their "fast food success stories." Members responded by describing how they incorporate fast food into the program. Sandy's family orders pizza for dinner every Sunday. So Sandy bought one of the organization's booklets that translates foods from popular fast food restaurants into program selections. After examining the breakdowns on pizza restaurants, Sandy chose the one that allowed her to eat the most pizza and still stay within her daily limits. Sharon said that when she takes her children for fast food, "I eat a plain hamburger. Sometimes I eat just half the bun. I might eat half of a small order of fries, but it still fits in." Sandy noted that a fast food seafood restaurant is another good place, since "you can have three of their chicken pieces, rice instead of fries, and green beans instead of cole slaw." Cheryl said she was recently in Minnesota for a vacation, and went to the Mall of America. While there she ate at a restaurant famous for very large burgers served with big plates of French fries. Cheryl said, "It was a good choice for me to split one of the hamburger platters with my grandmother. That way I only ate half of the burger."

The explicit moral of the discussion is that there are no forbidden foods. The message is not that you have to give up fast food, but that fast food can actually be incorporated into the program. Counter to members' assumptions that deprivation is a central component of weight loss, the organization goes out of its way to communicate that nothing has to be given up in order to follow the program and lose weight. In this way the organization attempts once more to disassociate itself from diets. But the message serves an additional purpose. Leaders stress that, as long as you keep track of what you eat, it is impossible to go off the program. Since any food, even fast food, can be translated into selections, there is no food you cannot eat. If internalized by members, this message is a useful antidote to the all-or-nothing thinking that frequently undermines weight loss efforts. Indulging in high-fat, high-calorie food is not a sign of failure, that is, a sign of going off your diet.

At the same time, it is quite obvious that you can't eat the same way or eat the same foods that you ate before joining and still lose weight. Underlying the message that deprivation is not necessary is the subtler message that this is nonetheless a turning point. It is true that any food can be tracked, but it is also true that there are limits built into the program, and choices have to be made. Discussions focused on the absence of deprivation in the program are inevitably paired with discussions of strategies for eating what you want when you want, but doing so in such a way that it can be incorporated into the program. Fast food can still be eaten, but some choices are much better than others. You can still eat at a restaurant, but portions will need to be downsized or the food somehow doctored. You can enjoy a family reunion, but only as long as you track everything you eat. There is a significant tension between the message that you will not have to give up anything and the implication that you will be eating differently, which expresses, in fact, an ongoing tension between the meaning of diets and deprivation on the one hand and lifestyle change on the other. Lifestyle change is open-ended, never-ending, while diets last for a finite time period. Diets start when you want to lose weight, and end once you have lost the desired weight.

Despite members' relatively rationalized explanations, joining a weight loss group usually evokes a range of emotions. At times members express positive emotions, but these are often tempered by more negative ones. Members who have tried everything else before joining the group are likely to hope that this program will actually work. But if all else has failed, this may truly be a last resort. And so, even in the midst of hopefulness, members are likely to fear that this attempt too is doomed to fail. The association of fear with dieting may seem strange. After my first meeting, Richard explained the Faststart program to me and two other new members. He went through the written materials quickly, and I was rather overwhelmed. He looked at me and asked, "Besides being totally scared, are you doing OK?" At the time I thought his question was odd. Although I was confused, and very uncertain of what I was getting into, I'm not sure I would have said I was scared. But fear does play a role, even though it takes different forms. Fear of the unknown is common, and individuals joining for the first time experience not only the program as an unknown but the group as well. Members may also fear committing to the program. New members occasionally admit that even during their first week, they have not stuck to the program completely. Finally, members are very likely to fear failing, an anxiety exacerbated by the individualization of weight gain and loss. Not only are individuals blamed for being overweight, they are blamed for not being able to lose weight.

Speaking of Weight Loss

Persistent themes of ambivalence, inconsistency, and contradiction pervade the language of members as they struggle to lose weight and, significantly, as they struggle to talk about dieting. Losing weight is difficult, physiologically and psychologically. Particularly for women, dieting arouses a range of strong emotions and strikes directly at issues of self-identity. In a weight loss group, people are expected to talk about losing weight. And as they do, it becomes apparent that individuals draw upon different and sometimes conflicting models of weight loss to explain their experiences. I refer to these models as *concepts of weight loss*. Members use them to make sense of the contradictory and conflictual processes of dieting and weight loss. At times the concepts work as metaphors, whereby a multiplicity of sometimes contradictory meanings are reduced to a unitary analogy (Geertz 1973). They provide a common language that members can use to communicate to themselves and to each other what it means to be a woman trying to lose weight.

These frameworks emerge from the language of the participants themselves, both group members and organizational leaders. At the same time, the labels for the concepts are mine. Participants do not refer to them as such, nor are they necessarily conscious at all times that they are using them. Rather, the concepts or metaphors are implied in members' speech as they talk through their feelings and experiences. Since all the metaphors are culturally sanctioned to some degree, even though they vary in acceptability and frequency of use, individuals combine them in a variety of ways and draw upon different ones at different times, depending on their needs.

The most common concepts of weight loss are found when members explain why they have joined a weight loss group. First, the *self-help* model sees the decision to join a weight loss group as a turning point. Before joining, members have a number of bad habits that lead to weight gain, some of which result from simple ignorance of the correct way to eat. Members come to the group for both education and support in their efforts to rectify the situation. The goal is to replace bad habits with good ones. Ultimately members are motivated by a desire for enhanced health and self-improvement.

The perspective of self-help resonates with the cultural values of individualism and self-improvement, and is the concept most strongly employed and reinforced by the organization. There is little doubt that individualism is a core value in the United States (Williams 1965), and is closely related to values of freedom and privacy (Wuthnow 1994). In addition, a newly emerging value cluster that emphasizes leisure, physical fitness, and self-fulfillment (Henslin 1975) further reinforces and enhances the popularity of self-help. Added to this is the long tradition of voluntary, mutual-aid associations in the United States (Wuthnow 1994). The spirit of self-help was already deeply embedded in the culture by the time that Tocqueville produced his analysis of American culture and society in 1848, and has only grown stronger since then.

There is ample evidence of the popularity of self-help as an approach to numerous personal problems and issues. Recent decades have witnessed an explosion in the number of self-help books that are readily available in bookstores, supermarkets, and drug stores (Simonds 1992). Indeed, self-help literature is only one manifestation of the growing market for advice targeted specifically at women. Others include women's magazines, soap operas (Modleski 1982; Rosen 1986), romance novels (Radway 1984), and television talk shows (Shattuc 1997). Not only are people buying more self-help books, they are joining more self-help groups, which is itself part of a broader small group movement in the United States (Wuthnow 1994). Wuthnow (1994) estimates that perhaps 40 percent of the adult population belong to small, supportive groups of some sort, and that there are possibly half a million groups targeted specifically at self-help. Other observers note the rapidly growing number of self-help groups concerned with health issues (Checkoway, Chesler, and Blum 1990). Even when people join small groups, the value placed on individualism is evident. The most common reason for joining a small group among Wuthnow's (1994:84) respondents was "the desire to grow as a person."

The second concept sees weight loss as analogous to *work*. Laziness or a lack of discipline and hard work results in weight gain, whereas a desire to work harder motivates people to join a weight loss group. From this perspective, the keys to losing weight are commitment, renewed effort, and discipline, and members view the group as a significant source of motivation. The work ethic has long been highly esteemed in the United States. Even as leisure has ascended as a significant cultural value (Henslin 1975), it has not supplanted the work ethic as much as it has interacted and intertwined with it, so that leisure time is as rigidly scheduled and regimented as work time (Freund and McGuire 1999). This tendency has been exacerbated by the larger trend of increasing rationalization, as the principles most clearly evident in the fast food industry—efficiency, predictability, calculability, and automation—are increasingly applied to diverse areas of life, including education, medicine, religion, and recreation (Ritzer 1996). Furthermore, in a capitalist economy, productivity is closely tied to consumption. We have seen the unprecedented spread of commercialism and the growth of consumerism at the center of the culture (Ritzer 1999).

These trends are evident in the application of the work ethic to the development of both the self and the body. A large portion of self-help literature rests on the assumption that the self is a product that can be endlessly changed, corrected, and improved with hard work and the proper tools and techniques (Simonds 1992). In his research on the small group movement, Wuthnow (1994) finds that the seemingly secular value of hard work influences respondents' understanding of a spiritual journey as requiring commitment and a strong work ethic. As noted earlier, in the United States the body is increasingly viewed as a material object that can be consciously and actively shaped and molded via such practices as bodybuilding (Heywood 1997; Schulze 1997) and cosmetic surgery (Adams 1997). Despite clear differences among them, what dieting, bodybuilding, and cosmetic surgery share is an unwavering belief that the body can be molded into the desired size and shape, if you only spend enough time, use the right tools, apply the correct techniques, and work at it hard enough. In no small part because it resonates with emphases on individualism and self-help, the work analogy is strongly evident in the weight loss group.

The third concept of weight loss is that of *religion*. Here it is giving into temptations of the flesh and indulging in costly pleasures that lead to weight gain. Weight loss comes through personal transformation from sinner to one of the faithful, as you come to see the error of your ways. Members come to the group to confess their sins and renew their faith. Concomitantly, deciding to join a weight loss group is conceptualized as a sort of conversion experience. The religious metaphor is clearly present in the weight loss group, but because weight loss is not literally a religion, and because religion itself has changed in recent decades, this perspective is not as evident as those of self-help and work. Although the group emphasizes notions of temptation, sacrifice, guilt, and surveillance, it simultaneously downplays ritual, community, and emotion.

Religion has been a central value in the United States since its founding. Survey research continues to document the importance of religiosity and spirituality in individuals' lives, as evidenced in high rates of church membership and attendance and in the large number of people who profess a belief in God (Wuthnow 1994). But at the same time, religion has changed as it has interacted with and been affected by a number of other societal trends. The spread of rationalization and commercialism has not left religion and churches untouched (Ritzer 1996, 1999). In addition, churches have had to contend with increased secularization and growing disillusionment with both church and clergy (Wuthnow 1994). Furthermore, religion has had to engage and interact with science as the scientific perspective has become ever more entrenched. The results of these trends have included an increased emphasis on individual spirituality rather than organized religion, the growth of the New Age movement, and changing views of God (Simonds 1992; Wuthnow 1994).

These changes in religion are evident in numerous ways. Recent decades have witnessed the growth of "mega-churches," which increasingly market themselves to potential members, offer many more individually oriented small groups than they do church services, and in incorporating bookstores, restaurants, exercise classes, and multimedia presentations, come to resemble shopping malls more than traditional churches (Ritzer 1999). In addition, the interaction between religion and science/psychology is evident in self-help literature, where religious concepts infuse seemingly secular approaches, and even authors of explicitly religious self-help draw on science to back up their claims (Simonds 1992). Finally, but more subtly, we see the interaction between the religious and the secular in the pervasiveness of the confessional mode of speaking in diverse areas, including self-help literature (Simonds 1992), daytime television talk shows (Shattuc 1997), and proliferating therapy groups, especially those modeled on the 12-Step approach of Alcoholics Anonymous (Kurtz 1990; Lesieur 1990; Lester 1999).

The fourth significant way in which individuals speak of weight loss uses the concept of *addiction.* A total loss of control over eating leads directly to weight gain, and despair is the most important motivator for seeking help. The tendency to define more and more dysfunctional behaviors as addictive is related to many of the broader trends already described. Simonds (1992:225) argues: "Addiction presents a convincing image of our problems because it recognizes the salience of disguised yet uncontrollable consumption in American culture. If addiction means insatiability, then addiction is the goal of consumer-oriented culture." Furthermore, our views of addiction are affected by a larger trend of medicalization, whereby a broad range of previously nonmedical conditions come to be understood as medical problems, subsequently to be diagnosed and treated by medical practitioners (Riessman 1983). In recent years a vast array of behaviors, conditions, and events have been medicalized, including alcoholism, drug addiction, child abuse, attention deficit hyperactivity disorder, depression, childbirth, menstruation, and menopause (Freund and McGuire 1999). The popularity of the addiction model is evident in the growth of 12-Step groups that began with Alcoholics Anonymous in 1935 and rapidly spread to other addictions, including drugs, gambling, and compulsive overeating (Kurtz 1990; Lesieur 1990; Lester 1999). The addiction model also spread rapidly in the self-help field, where it was first applied to adult children of alcoholics, then to codependents, and subsequently to "women who love too much" (Simonds 1992). The self-help editors interviewed by Simonds (1992) predicted that the application of an addiction perspective to a wide range of individual and relational issues would continue to increase throughout the 1990s.

The weight loss group observed here is not a 12-Step group, nor does it subscribe to an addiction model of overeating. The most critical way in which the weight loss group differs from 12-Step groups is in its attitudes toward self-control and willpower. Because the group is explicitly based on the assumption that weight can be individually controlled, self-control and willpower are by far the most important keys to successful weight loss. This view stands in stark contrast to the position of 12-Step groups, such as Overeaters Anonymous, which believe that the only way to arrest addictive behavior is to surrender control to a higher power (Lester 1999). The contrasts between the weight loss organization and groups based on an addiction model of overeating are most obvious in discussions of hunger, control, and disordered eating.

The concepts of self-help, work, and religion represent the most common ways in which members of the weight loss group speak about losing weight. In contrast, the organization downplays the concept of addiction, in large part because it conflicts with the group's emphasis on willpower and self-control as the keys to weight loss. Another, more subtle perspective also informs and reflects members' understandings of the weight loss process. It is a concept of *feminism* or more accurately, a kind of pseudo-, liberal feminism. In some ways, a feminist metaphor of weight loss is odd, considering the strong and highly vocal feminist criticism of the weight loss industry. And yet it is not so odd, given the organization's position vis-à-vis women. Despite pretenses of gender neutrality, the organization is highly dependent upon women, who make up the vast majority of its membership. The organization's very existence depends on its ability to continually attract new female members. But the women it is trying to attract are not the same women it was trying to attract thirty or even twenty years ago. The feminist movement has greatly affected today's women. Although feminist protest may be less visible today, and despite a concerted backlash and resurgence of conservative politics (Faludi 1991), the feminist movement has had a significant impact on society as well as on the consciousness and life situations of individual women (Taylor and Whittier 1993). Even those who do not personally identify themselves as feminists have adopted many of the assumptions and guiding ideas of the movement. As a result, women today think about themselves, their bodies, and their lives in different terms than did women a generation ago. It is these contemporary women that the organization must attract, and to do so it must speak to them in a meaningful way. At the same time, the feminist critique of the weight loss industry and of the cultural obsession with thinness has the potential, if taken seriously by enough women, to undermine the organization's very existence.

One solution is to adopt some of the language and general themes of feminism, but simultaneously to co-opt, subvert, and twist them to suit the organization's purposes. This approach is widely used in the popular media. Self-help books in recent years have been affected by both the mainstreaming of liberal feminism and the resurgence of conservative politics, and the result of this rather peculiar mixture has for the most part been an emphasis on individualism and rational personal action (Simonds 1992). In advertising, liberation takes the form of self-indulgence, self-assertion, and achievement, as women are urged to purchase a vast array of consumer products to demonstrate self-care (Macdonald 1995). Similarly, television programming can be read as a complex struggle between feminism and antifeminism that simultaneously provides models of empowerment and traditional notions of femininity (Douglas 1994). The weight loss organization uses a similar approach. Weight loss and gain are placed in the context of women's family and work roles, and discussed in the languages of self-care and self-acceptance. To the extent that a feminist approach to weight loss is apparent, it is highly mediated by the organization. At the same time, limited as it is, a feminist framework provides some potential for conflicting perspectives on weight loss, and even resistance.

All five concepts are apparent in varying ways and to different degrees in the weight loss group. Individuals are more or less likely to use particular metaphors to explain their personal experiences, but members are to some extent familiar with all the perspectives. Members can use different models at different times or combine them in unique ways, depending on the circumstances. A close examination of the five concepts yields insights into how women in the United States today talk about and understand dieting and weight loss.

I make no claim that the concepts described here constitute the only ways in which people talk about weight and dieting in the United States. Some individuals or groups may employ different metaphors to describe and understand weight loss. Even within this group, the frameworks vary in strength and in frequency of use. At the same time, the concepts of self-help, work, religion, addiction, and feminism clearly resonate with some people, at least in part because they are also present in the popular media. These concepts, and possibly others, provide a sort of "raw material" out of which individuals can construct and reconstruct a personal understanding of weight loss. Individuals can creatively combine elements of various perspectives to meet their own needs or at the very least, can position themselves in opposition to the dominant models of weight loss. The latter course brings with it the possibility of resistance.

The nonrepresentativeness of the group makes it impossible to argue that these are the only or the most common ways in which even white, middle-class females talk about weight, let alone men, or women from other social classes or ethnic groups. However, the five concepts described here do represent possible ways to talk about losing weight. The value in closely examining the talk in this specific group is not due to its representativeness. Rather, the group provides a setting rich in detailed talk about weight and dieting. And it is here that we begin to see glimpses of the complex, sometimes contradictory ways in which weight loss is constructed in the United States.

3

"I Couldn't Have Done It Alone"

As a profit-making enterprise, the weight loss group has a clear stake in continually attracting new members and retaining old ones. This is easiest when members see results from their efforts. The group thus benefits when it offers members a plan that they can understand and commit to, and that increases the likelihood of losing weight. To this end, the group devotes much effort to giving members insight into the process of weight loss and the group's role in that process in particular ways. Although the group supports or at least tolerates a number of different perspectives, the organization promotes weight loss as a form of self-improvement that comes from lifestyle modification, and fashions itself as a support group.

At a meeting not long after the Christmas holidays, close to thirty members were present, including ten or twelve who had recently joined. Before the meeting Debbie drew a small bull's eye on the flip chart in the front of the room. After greeting new members and celebrating achievements, Debbie moved into the educational portion of the meeting and asked for a volunteer. Joyce was an enthusiastic regular attendee who usually brought her eight-year-old daughter, Carrie, with her. When no one else volunteered, Carrie raised her hand. Debbie handed Carrie a ball and directed her back to the scales and told her to stand behind the wall separating the weigh-in cubicles from the meeting room. Debbie said, "OK, Carrie, I want you to throw the ball and hit the bull's eye." When Carrie peeked around the corner looking quite puzzled, everyone laughed. Debbie asked the group, "Was what

I was asking Carrie to do realistic?" Members shook their heads in response, and Debbie continued, "Of course not. If we're going to do something we have to have a realistic goal. But lots of times, when we want to lose weight, we start with unrealistic goals. Those of you who have been around a while, what kinds of unrealistic goals did you have at first?" Wendy responded, "I expected to lose four or five pounds a week. At first I did. I was so fat, and I was eating a lot less, and I started walking, so I did lose a lot. But there's no way you can go on like that. And the first week I didn't lose that much I was devastated!" Jill, who had just joined the previous week, said, "I wanted to lose twenty pounds by the first week in February," implying a weight loss rate of six to seven pounds per week. Debbie emphasized, "These kinds of goals lead to a lot of frustration, and set us up for failure. We want you to have realistic goals, and that's what we're going to talk about tonight." She pointed to the chalkboard, where she had written, "I will walk for ten minutes three times a week," and said, "This is a realistic goal. Realistic goals have an action word and a time frame. Here the action word is 'walk' and the time frame is 'ten minutes three times a week.' " She turned to the second page of the flip chart. "SMART" was written at the top of the page in large bold letters, and underneath, "Specific," "Measurable," "Achievable," "Relevant," and "Trackable" were listed down the page. Debbie asked, "How can we make our unrealistic goals more realistic?" Dawn, a young African American woman who had joined very recently, replied, "We can measure our progress with something instead of pounds, like inches." It was clear that Debbie was looking for goals not directly related to weight, but she said, "That's right, set goals that don't necessarily have to do with pounds." As the discussion progressed, Carolyn and Brenda had been whispering to each other. Finally, Brenda frowned and raised her hand. Her tone of voice and facial expression communicated her frustration as she asked, "Well, what *is* realistic? I thought five pounds a week is realistic." Debbie hesitated and answered, "We recommend one to two pounds a week. We consider that a safe weight loss." Brenda appeared incredulous. She shook her head, whispered something to Carolyn, and Debbie continued the discussion with the group. Not surprisingly, Brenda dropped out a couple of weeks later.

    To place the concept of weight loss as self-help in a societal context, this chapter begins with a brief description of the development of the self-help movement in the United States. Of the five concepts that animate discussions of weight loss in the group, the one most frequently employed by the organization is that of self-help. This chapter explores the ways in which the self-help framework is reflected in and reinforced by the physical arrangement of the meeting location, the content and structure of meetings, and the roles played by group leaders. Group members also use the self-help metaphor and commonly conceptualize the weight loss group as a support group. The chapter therefore examines the factors that promote supportive relationships among members and between members, leaders, and receptionists. Those factors include shared experiences of stigmatization, group norms that encourage the mutual sharing of experiences and expertise, the friendship bonds that develop as people interact over time, and concerted efforts by group leaders to instill a supportive, group orientation in members. At the same time, the weight loss group is not purely a support group. The chapter next considers factors that diminish or impede the group's capacity to be a self-help support group, including the organization's profit-making orientation, the relatively scripted interaction between employees and members, the optional nature of meeting attendance, high member turnover, and various pressures toward conflict and competitiveness between members. The chapter concludes by discussing the key assumptions underlying a self-help concept of weight loss, namely, that being overweight is unhealthy, that body weight is subject to individual control, and that diets are unhealthy and ineffective. These assumptions have significant implications for how health is defined, understood, and assessed, the emergence of new discourses of healthy eating, perspectives on food and exercise, and the individualization of social problems.

The Self-Help Movement

The group's emphasis on education permeates discussions. Leaders often use acronyms to help relay information to members. In the meeting just described, the acronym SMART explicitly connected the discussion to education. With the frequent reminder that weight loss is secondary to the primary goal of long-term lifestyle change, the group promises to give members the tools and techniques they need to help themselves. Strategically, the group positions itself solidly within the self-help movement.

Organized self-help groups are only one manifestation of a wider interest in self-help and mutual support. Individuals who do not join a group may purchase any of the thousands of self-help books widely available in bookstores, supermarkets, or drug stores, or obtain self-help advice from magazine articles or television talk shows (Simonds 1992). Wuthnow (1994) suggests that self-help groups are only one component of a much more extensive small group movement in the United States that also includes adult Sunday school classes, Bible study groups, and special interest groups. Self-help groups can be defined as "experiential learning communities that create, apply, and disseminate an experiential perspective and knowledge to members and to other people" (Borkman 1990:23). Groups vary widely along a number of dimensions, including size, affiliation with national or local associations, the role and professional experience of the leader, and the particular condition or situation that they address (Powell 1990b; Schopler and Galinsky 1995; Wuthnow 1994). But whatever their focus and specific structure, self-help groups have a common goal of bringing people together to share information based on experiential knowledge and to provide mutual and multidirectional support (Powell 1990a). Storytelling is a key activity in many self-help groups (Wuthnow 1994). Through storytelling, members share personal experiences, reveal coping strategies, identify both common and unique features of their experiences, and begin to reflect critically on their situations and responses (Borkman 1990).

Although the number of self-help groups in the United States, focused on a vast array of personal problems and medical conditions, has increased greatly in the last few decades, the roots of self-help extend deeply. Strongly held cultural values such as individualism, freedom, and privacy promote self-responsibility and have contributed to an environment conducive to the growth of the self-help movement (Williams 1965; Wuthnow 1994). During the mid-nineteenth century, Tocqueville (1848) recognized the democratic spirit of self-help characterizing United States culture, rooted in part in seventeenth-century Puritan beliefs about self-improvement (Starker 1989). Simultaneously, a long tradition of voluntary action has often manifested itself in voluntary, cooperative, mutual-aid associations (Checkoway, Chesler, and Blum 1990; Wuthnow 1994).

As United States society and culture have changed over time, so have the forms and functions of self-help. Small, supportive groups played significant roles in the earliest American settlements, and as new groups have immigrated to the United States, mutual-aid associations have played important roles in their economic, political, and cultural adjustment (Wuthnow 1994). Reflecting societal emphases and concerns of the time, early eighteenth- and nineteenth-century self-help efforts focused on financial success, achieved with a strong work ethic, but by the end of the nineteenth century, spurred by new psychological theories and perspectives, self-help turned more and more attention toward the individual psyche (Simonds 1992).

Societal developments since the 1960s have further encouraged the growth of self-help, as well as contributing to changes in its forms and functions. The civil and other human rights movements have had far-reaching impacts. Significant for many movements, particularly the civil rights and feminist movements, was the development of an experiential frame of reference, which developed as participants shared, discussed, and reflected on their personal experiences with racism and sexism (Borkman 1990). At the same time, a growing distrust of societal institutions and leaders further reinforced a reliance on the personal, experiential perspective (Borkman 1990). Also important were increased knowledge about and interest in group dynamics and processes that affected the structure and direction of many self-help groups (Wuthnow 1994).

As the self-help movement has grown, it has carried on a long tradition of voluntary, mutual support, but has adapted it to new issues and concerns. A key development came in 1935 with the birth of Alcoholics Anonymous (AA) (Withorn 1980). Conceptualizing alcoholism as an addiction with physical, psychological, and spiritual components, AA has as its cornerstone the 12 Steps, which provide a path for members to follow, with sobriety as the final goal (Kurtz 1990). The 12 Steps have subsequently been adopted by a large number of new groups and organizations that have modeled themselves on AA. The first to follow AA's model was Al-Anon, formed in 1951 by the spouses of alcoholics, and the first 12-Step group not related to alcoholism was Narcotics Anonymous, founded in 1953 (Kurtz 1990). It was not long before the 12-Step approach was applied to conditions not previously thought of as physiological addictions. Gamblers Anonymous started in 1957 and within thirty years had approximately one thousand chapters worldwide, about six hundred of which are in the United States (Lesieur 1990). Since the establishment of Alcoholics Anonymous, over eighty new fellowships based on the 12-Step program have been founded, and over time, these have become increasingly specialized (Kurtz 1990; Wuthnow 1994).

The rapid growth of 12-Step groups is only one component of broader changes in the United States that have contributed to the spread of a self-help orientation. Simonds (1992:7) observes, "Self-help books must be studied as ideologically powerful instruments of cultural commerce that are linked both with the proliferation of buyable therapy, in which assistance comes to be seen as a purchasable commodity, and with the increasing volume of the marketplace for leisure consumption." Although Simonds focuses on books, her insights are applicable to the broader self-help movement. Two cultural trends are particularly significant. First, individuals are increasingly encouraged to seek the advice of experts and, more specifically, to seek therapeutic remedies for a wide range of personal problems (Simonds 1992; Wuthnow 1994). Central to the therapeutic outlook is a strong cultural belief in the curative value of talk, whether it takes the form of heart-to-heart talks, therapeutic talk, or television talk shows (Simonds 1992). Second, a deeply entrenched capitalist culture promotes consumption of a wide variety of products and services as the route to self-improvement and happiness (Ritzer 1999; Simonds 1992). Although many self-help groups are located outside the capitalist marketplace, we have witnessed, in recent years, the proliferation of self-help products and services available for purchase, including self-help books, lectures, classes, and retreats, not to mention products such as aroma-therapy candles, fragrances, body-care products, and vitamin and herbal remedies for stress. Women may be especially susceptible to the appeal of self-help, as they have traditionally been urged to care for themselves by purchasing products, including cosmetics, clothing, household products, and food (Bordo 1993; Simonds 1992).

The need to cope with the everyday aspects of living with an illness or other health-related condition, combined with the changing context of medical care in the United States, has also enhanced the attractiveness of self-help groups. Two relatively recent developments are particularly important. On the one hand, a burgeoning patient and consumer rights movement has simultaneously resulted from and reinforced declining faith and trust in the medical profession (Checkoway, Chesler, and Blum 1990). The media have further reinforced increased public skepticism by frequently reporting changing and sometimes contradictory medical research and advice. Add to this an increasing dissatisfaction with the costs of medical care and the apparent unavailability and inaccessibility of health services for many people, and the result has been a growing interest in alternatives to the traditional medical care system (Checkoway, Chesler, and Blum 1990). On the other hand, with medical costs skyrocketing, cost containment is the new buzzword, and insurance companies, the government, and other interested parties have actively sought supplements for and alternatives to the professional medical system for providing patient education and support (Borkman 1990; Checkoway, Chesler, and Blum 1990). Indeed, the search for alternatives became even more imperative throughout the 1980s and into the 1990s as funds were cut for numerous social programs, including neighborhood health centers,

Medicaid, and food stamps (Checkoway, Chesler, and Blum 1990). Furthermore, related to deeply embedded values of individualism, hard work, and self-improvement, United States culture increasingly emphasizes personal responsibility for individual problems and well-being (Borkman 1990; Crawford 1979). Compounding the situation are changes in families and communities that have undermined traditional support systems (Wuthnow 1994). One consequence has been an explosion in the number of health-related self-help groups (Checkoway, Chesler, and Blum 1990), intended to support persons dealing with a wide variety of medical and health-related conditions, including bereavement (Videka-Sherman 1990), sickle cell disease (Nash and Kramer 1994), mental illness (Kurtz 1994; Noordsy et al. 1994), lupus (Katz and Maida 1990), and compulsive overeating (Lester 1999; van Wormer 1994), to name just a few.

Not to be overlooked in the growth of self-help is the practical support provided by both religious organizations, including churches, and secular organizations, such as hospitals, schools, and community centers (Wuthnow 1994). In many cases these groups provide meeting space, resource materials, leaders, and motivated and interested participants (Wuthnow 1994). Self-help groups are increasingly easy to find owing to a growing number of clearing houses, directories, and worldwide web–based information (Meissen and Warren 1994; Wuthnow 1994). A fairly recent development has been the use of computer-based self-help groups to supplement more traditional groups and to reach individuals for whom groups are not available or accessible (Finn 1995). In the area of weight loss, NutriSystem has instituted an at-home, computer-based program, through which members can use the Internet to order food and supplies, ask questions, and even receive one-on-one support from a weight loss counselor (Nutrisystem, Inc. 2000).

The self-help movement, along with the values underlying and supporting it, has been criticized on numerous grounds. Most generally, critics argue that rampant individualism and a focus on self-sufficiency and self-improvement promote overwhelming self-indulgence, and concomitantly contribute to the diminishment of a collective mind-set, the undermining of traditional family, religious, and economic institutions, and community breakdown (Bellah et al. 1985; Etzioni 1982; Lasch 1979, 1984; D. Rieff 1991; P. Rieff 1966; Toffler 1970; Yankelovich 1981). Ironically, even when individuals join together in small, mutually supportive groups, group norms that emphasize emotional support, tolerance, the unwillingness to criticize others, and the respect for private space may ultimately reinforce individualism

(Wuthnow 1994). Wuthnow (1994:6) argues: "Some small groups merely provide occasions for individuals to focus on themselves in the presence of others. The social contract binding members together asserts only the weakest of obligations. Come if you have time. Talk if you feel like it. Respect everyone's opinion. Never criticize. Leave quietly if you become dissatisfied. Families would never survive by following these operating norms. Close-knit communities in the past did not, either." Other critics charge that in the philosophy of self-help, individual behavior is assumed to be the cause and cure of nearly all that ails society (Simonds 1992). Individuals are held solely responsible for their health and well-being, societal contributions to illness and other social problems are downplayed if not ignored, and the potential for social, political, and economic change is muted (Checkoway, Chesler, and Blum 1990; Simonds 1992; Wuthnow 1994).

Other criticisms have been leveled at self-help groups that address health and illness issues. Medical professionals have raised concerns that fall into two broad categories (Chesler 1990). First, professionals worry about the potential dangers to members, such as the negative emotions that may be aroused when difficult issues are discussed, as well as the possibility that misinformation will be shared (Chesler 1990). If in fact group members hesitate to criticize one another and strive for tolerance of all opinions, these concerns may indeed be valid (Wuthnow 1994). Second, professionals see in self-help groups a potential threat to their own authority (Chesler 1990).

Even those observers who see potential benefits in self-help groups question whether they meet the needs of ethnic minorities and social classes other than the middle class. The limited evidence available suggests that mainstream self-help groups, especially those concerned with mental health and well-being, are predominantly populated by middle-class Caucasians (Chesler 1990; Lieberman and Snowden 1994). Specifically, African Americans appear to be less likely than Caucasians to participate in self-help groups related to mental health and substance abuse problems (Snowden and Lieberman 1994). Similarly, Latinos may be less likely than Caucasians to join mainstream self-help organizations (Gutierrez, Ortega, and Suarez 1990). At the same time, this does not mean that self-help is irrelevant in African American and Latino communities. Just the opposite may be true. Latin American communities in the United States have frequently participated in their own forms of self-help through churches, mutual-aid associations, and political organizations (Gutierrez, Ortega, and Suarez 1990). In the African American community, the roots of self-help are found in black churches and fraternal organizations, and currently self-help encompasses groups focused on a broad spectrum of individual and community issues, including coping with illness, strengthening families, and community development (Neighbors, Elliott, and Gant 1990).

Despite sometimes harsh criticism, self-help in its many forms appears to be deeply entrenched in United States culture. In part this is because self-help rather easily meshes with strongly held values of individualism and personal responsibility. But it is also due to the fact that self-help holds potential benefits for individuals, communities, and perhaps society as a whole. First, if self-help groups counter the isolation experienced by some individuals and provide the sort of psychological and emotional support that persons may find lacking in their work, neighborhood, and even kin relationships, they can provide some sense of community, even if it differs substantially from traditional notions of community (Simonds 1992; Wuthnow 1994). Second, self-help endeavors may nurture and enhance members' self-esteem as they learn successful coping strategies and receive positive reinforcement and support from one another (Wuthnow 1994). Third, self-help groups in many instances can provide practical advice and assistance to individuals facing a variety of illnesses and other individual or family problems and issues (see, for example, Galinsky and Schopler 1995; Powell 1990b, 1994). Finally, self-help groups may hold at least some potential for providing a basis for societal change. Many self-help groups clearly focus on individual change. But at the same time, groups vary widely in the extent to which they address broader social, political, and policy-related issues (Powell 1990a). For example, the women's health movement has emphasized not only empowering individual women through self-help but working toward broad-based change in medical and other societal institutions (Simonds 1992; Withorn 1980). It appears that even in individually oriented groups, some members may be prompted to become more involved in larger social and political issues by virtue of their group participation (Wuthnow 1994).

Helping Them Help Themselves

The weight loss group examined here builds on the growing popularity of the self-help movement and models itself after a typical self-help support group, although there are important differences. Many self-help groups emphasize lifestyle modification. The weight loss organization says its central concerns are increased health and well-being, and it focuses on individual goals like feeling better or fitting better in your clothing. Lifestyle modification, however, is the key to achieving these goals. Debbie's analogy between the program and a three-legged stool captures the group's approach: "If one of the legs is missing or broken, the stool won't work. It's the same with the program. The three legs are food, activity, and behavior, and if any is missing, it won't work." Like the approaches of other self-help groups, the organization's emphases fit with society's increasing health consciousness, but do so by individualizing health issues. The group focuses on individual lifestyle choices and their effects on health, and virtually ignores environmental, political, social, or economic contributions. As a result, the group pays a great deal of attention to how members feel, both physically and psychologically. Leaders frequently associate weight loss with increased energy, the ability to ride a bike, walk long distances, or accomplish some other physical feat, or with just feeling better. Similarly, leaders often imply that weight loss will lead to greater happiness, in part as a direct consequence of enhanced health but also as a result of greater self-assurance and higher self-esteem.

From the organization's perspective, the key to feeling better is education, since it is through education that members learn to make smart choices. When Cheryl asked group members to share "fast food success stories," members enthusiastically responded. Several members provided the names of fast food restaurants that are particularly accommodating, and others suggested specific fast foods that can easily be incorporated into the plan. Leaders frequently make these sorts of comparisons, both between different foods and between different varieties or brands of the same food. Debbie was fond of comparing two brands of cereal. Although both are fat free, one has only one or two grams of fiber, whereas the other has nearly twenty grams. Whenever these kinds of comparisons are made, the assumption is that if members simply know better, they will choose more wisely. Eating some foods consequently makes more sense than eating others, and strategizing is the major tool of smart eating and weight loss.

As with other self-help groups, the organization ultimately focuses on long-term change and downplays the significance of weight loss per se. The overriding goal is to change the way you eat, an ongoing process that never ends. Weight loss, rather than a goal in and of itself, is simply the visible and physical indicator of the real goal, establishing a healthier way of eating and living. Group meetings, leader roles, and interaction between members consistently reflect the group's focus on self-help.

Meetings: "And Tonight's Topic Is . . ."

The physical arrangement and décor of the meet-
ing room support the organization's manifest educational function.
Leaders often use a large chalkboard and flip chart to display discussion topics, post reminders of things such as changes in meeting times
or special promotions, and to solicit and record information from
members. Up front on either side the two televisions, elevated for
easy viewing and connected to VCRs, are frequently playing exercise
videos as members arrive. Leaders also use videotapes to explain the
program to new members and occasionally to start and inform group
discussions. The names and total amount of weight lost by members
who reach their goals are written on colorful pieces of paper and
prominently displayed on a large bulletin board hanging on the back
wall. Colorful posters that attractively portray healthy foods in a
whimsical manner, such as bright purple grapes in a pea pod, hang
throughout the room. As I found at my first meeting, a wide variety of
merchandise is alluringly displayed where members can't miss it,
right in front of the scales. Chairs are arranged in four sections of rows,
all facing forward. The chair arrangement and the placement of the educational paraphernalia focus members' attention on the front of the
room, where leaders spend most of their time. In a traditional support
group, chairs are usually arranged in a circle, and leaders and members are virtually indistinguishable from each other, but here the classroom setting physically distinguishes the leader from the rest of the
group. The room arrangement highlights the leader's special status and
makes it difficult for members to interact with one another without interacting through the leader.

Despite the organization's best efforts, neither leaders nor members
entirely share the view that the primary concern is education. Indeed,
members and leaders like the educational component the least, and the
meeting structure reflects these preferences. Meetings typically last one
hour, although there are two or three per week that are streamlined and
last only half an hour. Theoretically, meetings are divided into education, motivation, and celebration, which at times merge into one
another. In fact, the educational component is expendable.

Leaders use the *educational* segment to relay information to members, who presumably translate it into smart choices and behaviors.
Topics often relate to the basics of good nutrition, and cover such things
as the importance of proteins, the different types of fat found in food,
or the benefits of nutritional variety. On some occasions leaders use
short, informational videotapes to communicate educational infor-

mation. At one meeting we watched a videotape that provided examples of easy ways to incorporate exercise into one's daily routine. But the information relayed is often available in the written materials members receive when they join, and consequently members need not depend on the meeting for pertinent information. At times the factual material is dry and relatively boring, and at other times it is ambiguous or even contested, as with the ongoing debate over the relative merits of margarine and butter. A presumably unintended consequence is that if members ask questions that go beyond the information in the written material, leaders have a difficult time answering. Because some leaders cover educational material last, it is frequently shortened or dropped. The fun, celebration-oriented parts of the meeting can easily expand to fill available time. Some leaders allow members to exert considerable control over meeting content and pacing. Although Ruth and Shirley move directly into the discussion topic, other leaders chat informally with the group about how the week has gone, their accomplishments, obstacles, and successful coping strategies, and any questions or issues that members raise. Depending on the number of members present and their responsiveness, a considerable amount of time can pass, and consequently the educational component can be shortened or dropped.

The second major component of the meeting is *motivational.* Topics may include taking care of yourself, overcoming plateaus in the weight loss process, developing positive self-images, or navigating places, occasions, or situations that make it difficult to stick to one's food plan. Videotapes might depict a discussion-provoking scenario, or leaders might describe a problematic situation and ask members to respond. Although education and motivation frequently overlap, ultimately leaders use the motivational segment to renew members' effort and commitment, and to help them overcome common stumbling blocks.

The final segment of the meeting, *celebration,* reinforces motivation, as the group visibly recognizes, rewards, and celebrates members' accomplishments and successes. Members often announce how much weight they have lost that week, but they might also announce that they exercised, coped successfully with a difficult social situation, fit into a smaller size of clothing, or simply that they came to the meeting despite having had a bad week. As members share, leaders roam the room, pass out colorful stickers as rewards, and prompt members to applaud and show their appreciation for and encouragement of others' achievements. Celebration is the most energetic, participatory, loud, and fun segment of the meeting. Nearly anything can be rewarded, so celebration not only buttresses the group's motivational efforts but bonds the group. While leaders readily shorten or drop the education segment, they rarely do so with celebration, preferring to run late, if necessary, to fit it in.

The room arrangement and meeting content express the organization's concern with lifestyle modification through education. Members and leaders, however, do not entirely share the organization's relative emphases. While the organization prioritizes education, leaders and members downplay education and instead prioritize mutual support, encouragement, and celebration. Leaders' roles further reinforce the different concerns.

Leaders: "If I Can Do It, You Can Do It!"

The six leaders differ in personality style, leadership techniques, and the types of relationships formed with members. Yet leaders are employees of the organization and thus are constrained at least within certain broad limits by its needs and agenda. Leaders must play roles largely organizationally defined and constrained by the meeting structure; typically, they play four different, though overlapping and interdependent, roles. The six leaders vary in their emphases and apparent comfort with some roles, but all can play any of the roles as the occasion requires, sometimes shifting between roles multiple times within one hour-long meeting.

Because the organization focuses on education, leaders are most obviously expected to be *experts*. But although they provide members with factual information and answer members' questions, leaders only reluctantly play this role and, at times, actively downplay their expertise. Being an expert is not as fun as some of leaders' other activities, but this is only part of the story. Despite the organization's clear focus on education as a vital part of lifestyle change, leaders are not always well prepared to be experts. Even though leaders get background material on the meeting's topic, such as fats or proteins, the information they receive frequently includes only the basics. In addition, members can often find the same information in other forms, particularly in the organization's videos and informational pamphlets. Providing accurate, up-to-date information is also problematic because information changes over time, sometimes rapidly, or is debated even within the medical and scientific fields.

Leaders become visibly uncomfortable when members ask specific questions that go beyond the organization's basic information, and they use various techniques to deal with such problems. Most commonly, leaders direct members to their written materials to see if the answers can be found there. This strategy is useful for two reasons. First, because members' questions are rarely very technical or complicated, the answers are indeed frequently found in their materials. But second, and more important, this strategy diverts attention away from the leader as expert and redirects responsibility for finding the answers back to the member and to the group as a whole. A related strategy, used more sparingly, is to direct the question to the group at large. Although this approach also shifts responsibility away from the leader, it is riskier, because it affords leaders much less control over the kinds and quality of responses. As a result, leaders ultimately defer to medical experts and may go to unnecessary lengths to avoid providing expertise, sometimes with amusing results. One evening as I arrived, Debbie was examining Carolyn's food tracker. Carolyn was a new member who was counting fat and fiber grams. Debbie pointed to the tracker and said, "See, you didn't get in enough fat here." Carolyn appeared puzzled and replied, "You mean I have to have a certain amount?" Debbie reminded her that she shouldn't go below the minimum fat requirement. Debbie used this conversation to begin the meeting and reminded members that it's important to have some fat in the diet. After asking members what the minimum fat and fiber daily requirements were, Debbie stated, "If you don't get enough fat, that's when you're going to have your gall bladder problems. And it leads to constipation. It's a lubricant." Carolyn thought this peculiar and said, "That's strange, because usually I have a problem that way, but not this week." Debbie said, "Eventually it'll be a problem. And fat's good for your hair. If you don't have enough fat your hair will fall out." Barb incredulously responded, "Really? Your hair falls out? That's funny, because our doctor put my husband on a nonfat, low cholesterol diet and since then he's gone completely bald! Do you think that if he went back to eating fats his hair would come back?" I thought this unlikely, since Barb was probably in her fifties. If her husband was of a similar age it's likely he would have gone bald anyway. In any event, Debbie backed down and said, "Your doctor is always the final authority, not me or the group." Although Debbie didn't have to give very technical or complex advice, she ultimately avoided playing the expert and explicitly deferred to a medical authority.

To the extent that leaders do consider themselves experts of sorts, it is largely because they have succeeded in doing what members are trying to do—lose weight. Thus leaders are more willing and able to be *role models*. Leaders virtually always introduce themselves to begin each meeting. They tell the group their name and then enthusi-astically state how much weight they have lost on the program, and how long they have kept it off. On one level the weekly introduction is a practical strategy. High membership turnover means that leaders can-not assume that everyone present knows who they are. But at the same time, through the standard introduction leaders easily and nat-urally reassert themselves as role models. Before-and-after photo-graphs, displayed prominently or passed around during the meeting, reinforce the introduction and provide visible and sometimes dra-matic proof that the program works.

Leaders play a third role, that of *socioemotional support-provider.* Because the organization promises not only to educate members but to provide them with support throughout the weight loss process, leaders continually attend to members' feelings. The organization opens its doors a half hour before the meeting begins to avoid overly long lines at the scales. Most leaders, but especially Debbie, use this time to approach individual members and chat about their progress and problems. Debbie stands near the coffee table so she can talk to mem-bers as they get something to drink, or she sits down next to someone who has already been weighed. During these informal chats Debbie not only encourages individual members, but also encourages them to support one another. Often Debbie begins her meetings with a direct reference to one of these conversations. She might reiterate informa-tion she relayed if she thinks it might be relevant to others, or raise an issue that came up in the conversation and solicit suggestions from the group. Leaders frequently emphasize that the group is there to provide support, and continually interweave "feeling talk" into group discus-sions. "How did it go this week?" is the question leaders ask most fre-quently. Members often respond with accounts of weight gains or losses, but they also recognize that leaders are soliciting not just quan-titative reports of success but qualitative, feeling-based assessments of how the week has gone. This is especially obvious at Cheryl's meet-ings, where members rarely report how much weight they have lost and instead focus on their responses to and feelings about their various chal-lenges and accomplishments.

Leaders are effective sources of socioemotional support not only because they have succeeded on the program in the past but because they are also continuing members. Leaders empathize with members on a number of levels. Leaders have personally experienced being overweight and the struggles involved in trying to lose weight. They have "been there." But perhaps more important, leaders are still there.

Like members, leaders must stay on the program and maintain their weight loss, a requirement that they emphasize. On the few occasions when this has been problematic, leaders shared their struggles with the group. At one point Richard gained back enough weight to move out of his goal range. He lost his lifetime-member status and began to attend meetings as a paying member again. After a week-long vacation, Richard told the group that he had to weigh in on Friday and that he feared he had gained weight while away. At the following week's meeting, Richard reported, "You know I was on vacation. Well, I went to my meeting Friday and I stayed exactly the same!" Members greeted Richard's announcement with applause and enthusiastic cheers, which obviously pleased him.

Finally, leaders act as coaches, cheerleaders, or *motivators.* Their primary task is to consistently communicate the message, "You can do it!" Just as an athletic coach has to pump up team members for the big game, weight loss leaders pump up members for the coming week and get them into the right frame of mind before they leave. Richard and Linda are motivators par excellence. Richard begins his meetings in exactly the same way, week after week. Seemingly appearing out of nowhere, he bounds to the front of the room, greets members vociferously, and enthusiastically urges them to applaud. Richard's energy, style of presentation, and manner of dressing strongly support his role as coach. Unlike the other leaders, who show a marked preference for variations on the business suit, complete with stockings and heels, Richard looks like he belongs in a gym, usually appearing in sweat pants and athletic shoes. Although Linda dresses more formally, she also relies heavily on playing the role of motivator. Once Linda substituted for Richard while he was on vacation. As she moved to celebration, Linda told the group, "For the celebration, I like to give stickers. Does anyone get their ten-pound ribbon, for losing their first ten pounds?" No one said anything. She said, "What about 'breaking a zero'?" There were many people who seemed uncertain, so she asked, "Do you know what 'breaking a zero' is?" After several members shook their heads she explained that the goal weight range appropriate for her height was 122 to 141 pounds. When Carol reached 141 she fell within the range, but had to set a specific weight as her final goal. Her leader asked her, "Do you want to set 141 for your goal?" Carol told her, "I don't want to weigh one-forty anything. How about 139?" Carol explained that breaking a zero meant moving from one ten-pound range into the one below, as in going from 140 to 139 pounds or 130 to 129 pounds. Jean happily said, "Oh! I did that!" Linda gave her a sticker and then moved around the room and asked each person how much weight he or she had lost. After each announcement she repeated it loudly, and encouraged everyone to clap.

Although leaders play the role of motivator in varying ways, they all use stickers as small, tangible rewards for various accomplishments. The stickers are similar to those that elementary school teachers affix to students' homework assignments to praise them for work well done, and presumably to motivate them to achieve further. The stickers are colorful, frequently depicting balloons, bears, animals, or other cartoonlike graphics, and say, in bold letters, such things as "WOW!" "I did it!" "More! More!" or "Keep Going!" Stickers are given for almost anything. When leaders ask members what they have to celebrate, or what they feel good about, they most commonly state how many pounds they lost in the previous week. Leaders always respond enthusiastically to the announcements, no matter how small they are, encourage other members to applaud or otherwise recognize the accomplishment, and then give the member a sticker to affix in the membership booklet. But weight loss is not the only accomplishment that can be rewarded, and, as we have seen, leaders frequently encourage members to share other things they feel good about, such as taking a walk or successfully handling food in a difficult setting, such as a business trip or holiday. One aspect of a leader's role as motivator is to teach members to redefine, or at least widely broaden, their notions of what constitutes success, which then broadens the realm of accomplishments that can be recognized, rewarded, and reinforced during celebration. Linda explicitly prompted members to share their successes by asking whether anyone had accomplished specific sorts of tasks, such as losing his or her first ten pounds. In addition, Linda promoted diffusion from one meeting to another by introducing members at Richard's meeting to the notion of "breaking a zero," which presumably is recognized and rewarded at Linda's meetings. Subsequently members at Richard's meeting reported breaking a zero as a notable accomplishment and simultaneously socialized new members into understanding its meaning.

It is tempting to see the roles as personality types. Certainly personality has something to do with the way that individual leaders define their role and whether they emphasize some aspects of the role as opposed to others. Richard is well suited for the role of motivator. His enthusiasm and energy are infectious, and his meetings are by far the liveliest and loudest. But Richard cannot rely solely on being a coach. By virtue of his official position, Richard, like the other leaders, must also play the roles of expert, role model, and support provider. As employees of the organization, leaders face relatively clear role expectations, and are constrained in how creative they can be with the material they are given.

The Group: "I Couldn't Have Done it Alone"

People who join self-help and support groups often face problems that provoke some degree of anxiety. Because groups are usually specialized, members are currently dealing with the same stressor or have dealt with it in the recent past. Members can expect to share both practical and emotional support. Considerable research suggests that when individuals experience anxiety due to a stressful situation, they prefer to be in the presence of others, rather than alone (Gerard and Rabbie 1961; Rofe 1984; Schachter 1959; Suls and Miller 1977), and preferably with others who are undergoing the same stress (Schachter 1959). Given a choice, people prefer being around others who have already encountered a similar situation and thus can provide information on the nature of the stressor and what to expect (Kirkpatrick and Shaver 1988; Kulik and Mahler 1989; Kulik, Mahler, and Earnest 1994; Shaver and Klinnert 1982). This is true even if the people present are prohibited from speaking with each other, partly because others can provide a measuring rod against which one's own emotional reactions can be gauged (Schachter 1959). Experimental research also identifies several factors that promote cooperation in small groups. Cooperation and cohesiveness increase when group members face a shared threat or common enemy (Lanzetta 1955; Sherif 1966) and when there is a superordinate goal that requires a cooperative effort to achieve (Blake and Moulton 1979; Sherif 1966). To the extent that group members can develop a "we-feeling" and define themselves as a group, the likelihood of cooperation is increased (Brewer 1979, 1987; Brewer and Kramer 1986; Kramer and Brewer 1984; Orbell, van de Kragt, and Dawes 1988). Something as simple as having a few minutes for discussion, or just believing that one is similar to others in the group, can enhance feelings of group belonging.

Many conditions that lead to cooperation in small groups operate in the weight loss group. Above all, members define themselves as overweight, a stigmatized status in the United States. In addition to providing a basis of similarity among members, this fact intensifies pressures toward cooperation by providing the group with a common "enemy." In some cases, a specific person, such as a critical family member or co-worker, poses problems. Lois evokes tremendous sympathy from the group as she describes her landlord's refusal to install a ramp so she can more easily leave her house to exercise. Similarly, it is heart-wrenching when Justin, a twelve-year-old who joined with his mother, Rose, tells the group he wants to lose weight because "I get teased a lot at school." More commonly, the enemy is a culture that stereotypes and discriminates against people who are overweight. Even members who have not faced the blatant prejudice described by Lois and Justin can easily identify with the hurt and shame they feel. Thus members frequently share their experiences in dealing with an antifat culture. It is significant, however, that members all choose to deal with the stigmatization and discrimination by changing themselves to conform to societal norms. Members join the group to lose weight, not to learn how to resist or change society. Those who describe experiences of discrimination receive sympathy and empathy from other members, but they also receive concrete suggestions to fortify their efforts to conform to societal standards. More than anything else, members are expected to share with one another the expertise that they have gained through experiences many are familiar with. It is information to which most members have reasonable access, including how to incorporate dining out into the program, how to resist tempting foods, and how to deal with the weight gain that frequently comes after vacations, what members call "vacation blues." Leaders frequently prompt members to share stories and helpful hints, which bolsters members' views of themselves as competent sources of information and enhances mutual sharing.

The common stigmatization and the sharing of mutual expertise, support, and motivation promote strong bonds between group members and organization employees as well as among members. Leaders make a point to introduce new members by their first name, and address members by name whenever possible. A relatively strong "we-feeling" develops over time, particularly between leaders and regular attendees. This is especially apparent when a leader is absent and a substitute is brought in to run the meeting. One evening when Linda was substituting for Richard, the topic of discussion was "food secrets." Near the end of the meeting, Linda asked members to share their secrets. But she barely paused long enough to let anyone reply and said, "Why should you tell me anything? You don't know me! My Thursday class will probably tell me all kinds of good stuff." Although Linda may have reacted too quickly, her point was valid. At the very least, relations between leaders and members are often comfortable. Members get used to a leader's style, and over the course of time leaders come to know something about the personalities and needs of individual members. Eventually a high degree of trust characterizes the relationship.

Trustful, supportive relationships also develop between members and receptionists, the other major role players associated with the organization. A receptionist's major responsibility is to weigh members as they arrive for the meeting. Although leaders sometimes help weigh in, it is usually receptionists who actually see and interact with members at their most anxious and vulnerable moment, as they step onto the scale. Receptionists know what members weigh, and exactly how much they have gained or lost in a given week. While leaders certainly have access to this information, and while members can choose to share it with leaders, it is knowledge routinely available to receptionists.

Leaders primarily interact with members in a public, visible arena in front of the entire group. Receptionists, in contrast, interact with members on a one-to-one basis in a comparatively more private setting. As I have described, members are weighed in three cubicles located at the very back of the suite of rooms, off the main meeting room. As members arrive they form a line near the opening of the first cubicle, and then move to the appropriate one as a scale opens up. Privacy is clearly more illusion than reality. There are no doors, the walls are thin, and receptionists frequently talk to each other through small windows in the walls between the cubicles. At the same time, the semblance of privacy affects interaction between members and receptionists in a number of ways. In a context of pseudo-privacy, some members are more open and feel more comfortable sharing personal information. Receptionists are often the first persons to ask members how their week has gone and how they are doing. Members who are not comfortable speaking and sharing personal information in front of a large group are likely to find it easier to share concerns with receptionists in the cubicles.

This certainly doesn't mean that member-receptionist interaction is entirely informal and unrestrained. Receptionists, if at all possible, need to move everyone through the line before the meeting begins. They cannot spend much time chatting with individual members. Furthermore, weigh-in is one of the most routinized parts of the meeting. Members receive a small pamphlet to take home with them in which they record their weight loss and place the stickers received during celebration. But their official membership book is kept at the meeting site. The books are filed in alphabetical order and placed on a table near the front counter. As members arrive they must stop at the table, find their book, and take it with them to the scales. If they don't automatically hand their membership book to the receptionist, she asks, "Did you pick up your book on the way back?" The receptionist then takes the booklet, stamps it, and collects the fee. Next she turns to the scale and adjusts it. As the member steps onto the scale the receptionist usually asks, "How did your week go?" or "Did you have a good week?" She records the weight in the member's book and tells her or him how much weight was lost or gained (without disclosing the actual weight). Receptionists give members the appropriate pamphlets or other meeting materials, and end the interaction by saying, "OK, you're all set!" Clearly receptionists follow a script with very few and relatively minor variations. However, since the script is not written down and is delivered in the relatively private cubicles, receptionists and members interweave a good deal of informal, personal interaction throughout the scripted conversation.

Receptionists are also in a good position to form supportive relationships with members because they carry on individually oriented interaction. While leaders frequently greet and chat with members as they arrive, and are available after the meeting for individual questions and consultation, they spend most of their time interacting with the group as a whole. Receptionists *only* interact with members one-on-one. As a result, receptionists are likely to know members' names and to address them by name. Although leaders do attempt to learn names, an easier feat when members attend regularly, I overheard leaders ask receptionists a particular member's name on numerous occasions. Furthermore, while leading and facilitating group discussions, leaders have to balance individuals' needs against each other. Leaders must not allow any single person to dominate the group's time or devote an inordinate amount of time to a specific individual's concerns. Although receptionists do face time constraints, because they interact with one member at a time, they are more flexible than leaders in this regard.

Group leaders and members, especially regular attendees, clearly form personal bonds. However, since most leader-member interaction occurs during the meeting, members can determine how much personal disclosure occurs. Leaders make concerted efforts to create a supportive climate in which members can contribute to the discussion. But despite these efforts, some, perhaps many, members are not comfortable sharing personal information with the group. Some meetings are very large, with as many as fifty or more members attending at one time, and turnover from one meeting to the next is high, making it difficult for members to become familiar with one another. Because receptionists, in contrast, interact with members one at a time and in a relatively more private context, members may thus be more likely to disclose personal details to them. In turn, they are in a position to be able to, if not have to, respond to members' individual needs and concerns. On one occasion I was very close to losing my next ten pounds. I hadn't had a terrific week and I was fairly certain it would be very close. Ruth, then a receptionist, was doing weigh-in and when she told me how much I lost, I knew I had missed it by half a pound. I groaned and Ruth looked at my booklet. She realized how close I was and said, "Let's do it again." She noticed I was wearing my shoes, so she said, "Take your shoes off." When I placed a paper towel on the scale and got back on, barefoot, it made a one-pound difference, which put me over the ten-pound mark. Ruth could see the psychological and motivational benefits of reaching a particular benchmark. Leaders can easily sympathize with a member's frustration at narrowly missing a goal, but as the receptionist, Ruth could manipulate the situation to ensure that the goal was reached.

Personal, supportive relationships also form among members. At times, competition and jealousy occur between members, and these experiences will be discussed below. But several factors promote close relationships among members and between members, leaders, and receptionists. Although members have individual goals, neither resources nor rewards are limited. One member's success does not depend on or imply another member's failure. Thus the potential for overt conflict is decreased. In addition, leaders try to enhance bonds between members. Most commonly, leaders encourage members to share expertise, encouragement, and support.

Occasionally, however, leaders try to institute group-oriented goals to further strengthen bonds between members. A simple way to do this is to announce at the end of the meeting how much weight the group as a whole lost during the previous week. Leaders might also try to persuade members to work toward a common goal that is easier to achieve if everyone cooperates. For example, Ruth not only defined a collective goal that was not directly related to weight loss, she extended the goal across different meeting groups. Early in the summer of 1995, Ruth announced that all the groups meeting at that location were going to "walk across America." Ruth calculated how many miles it is across the United States in a straight path, posted a large map of the country on the back wall, and purchased little stickers in the shape of tennis shoes. Each shoe represented a set number of miles walked or minutes spent in other kinds of exercise. Each week as members arrived, they stopped at the front desk and recorded the number of miles they had walked or how long they had exercised during the previous week. During the meeting receptionists added the numbers and at the end of the meeting the appropriate number of tennis shoes were added to the map. At other times, members worked together on community-oriented goals. Leaders often encourage members to participate in walks to raise money for charities, or at least to pledge monetary support to other members or leaders who were walking. When the local area was struck by devastating floods, leaders informed members that there was a particular need for large-size clothing. Big bins were placed near the front door and members were encouraged to donate clothing they could no longer wear.

The fact that friends and family members often join at the same time enhances the growth of cooperation and mutual support. In effect, small primary groups come to the organization preformed, and preclude the necessity to form bonds where none previously existed. Sharing personal accomplishments, setbacks, and discouragement may be considerably easier when the audience is not entirely composed of strangers. At the same time, close bonds do develop even between members who began as strangers, sometimes between otherwise unlikely persons.

Wendy was a young, vivacious member who was very successful on the program. In her twenties, married, with two young children, Wendy lost a hundred pounds by the time she met her goal, twenty-five pounds of which she lost before joining the group. To say that Wendy was bubbly is a gross understatement. Her enthusiasm, openness, and friendliness were hard to contain, and her sincere concern for and encouragement of others made her a favorite among members. And no matter how hard it was to get a response from the group, leaders could always count on Wendy to respond to questions and keep the conversation moving. In contrast, Betty was a seventy-year-old widow who attended the same meeting. Over the course of nearly two years Betty struggled to lose fifteen pounds and was still about five pounds from her goal. Betty was virtually stuck at her current weight, repeatedly losing then regaining a pound or two from one week to the next. Betty was quiet, subdued, and reluctant to speak during meetings. But despite dramatic differences in age, personality, and success with the program, Wendy and Betty grew quite close. The two always sat together and spent the time before the meeting animatedly chatting. Wendy often brought new pictures of her children to show to Betty, and although Betty rarely spoke during meetings, she easily shared her frustrations with Wendy. No one was prouder than Betty when Wendy met her weight loss goal. At Wendy's last meeting the two shared a tearful farewell and promised to stay in contact by phone.

Even if members don't form close friendships, they are likely to become comfortable with one another and, over time, form bonds of varying strength. When members reach their goal weights they almost always attribute part of their success to the support and encouragement received from the group. On the evening Joyce was recognized for reaching her goal, she emotionally told the group, "I know I couldn't have done it alone. I tried lots of times. But this time, I did it and you know, it's because of you guys!" The sentiment was widely shared.

A Support Group (Sort of)

Although the organization goes out of its way to promote itself as a self-help group that depends strongly on mutual support for its success, it is not purely a support group, for a number of reasons. Most important, the organization is a profit-making enterprise. The first and clearest reminder is that members pay to join, and must pay each week before getting weighed. Two bodies of research suggest that charging a fee is not all bad. First, research on the foot-in-the-door technique of persuasion demonstrates that once individuals make even a small commitment, they are more likely to comply with a larger request at a later time (Beaman et al. 1983; Dillard 1991; Greenwald et al. 1987; Lipsitz et al. 1989; Pliner et al. 1974; Schwarzwald, Bizman, and Raz 1983). Second, cognitive dissonance research suggests that once individuals make a decision, they attempt to reduce potential dissonance by rating more positively the choice they made and devaluing the alternative (Brehm 1956; Knox and Inkster 1968; Younger, Walker, and Arrowood 1977). Together, this research implies that, on the one hand, members' commitment to the group may increase if they have to invest not only time and energy but money. On the other hand, since members pay for missed meetings, they may be more likely to quit if they're not seeing clear progress. But the important point is that as a profit-making business, the organization has to promote itself for its own survival. The commercial elements of the enterprise are always present.

Each week, in addition to paying membership fees, members confront a prominent display of weight loss aids available for purchase, including food scales, recipe books, water bottles, electronic food trackers, and exercise videos, to name just a few. Explicit sales pitches are rare, but small products are sometimes given as door prizes, and leaders frequently work endorsements of various products into the discussion. One evening, as we have seen, Debbie compared the program to a three-legged stool that needs all three legs to work. The three legs are food, activity, and behavior. Debbie had taped three sheets of newsprint to the wall, and labeled each with one leg. Debbie asked, "What sorts of things does the group give you to help you with the legs?" As members responded she wrote their suggestions on the appropriate sheet of paper. For food, people named the food trackers, food companion booklets that give the point values of various foods, food scales, recipe books, and the recipes on the backs of the leaflets handed out at meetings. Related to activity, members suggested the exercise booklet and the "slide guide" that calculates the number of calories burned while exercising. Debbie reminded members of the organization's exercise videos. Regarding behavior, members reiterated the importance of attending meetings, and Debbie noted that the group sells a number of inspirational books and tapes. With very few exceptions, the products and services described had to be purchased. In effect, the meeting was one long advertisement.

Tension between the organization's business and service elements is omnipresent and affects the roles of both receptionists and leaders. Receptionists' positions facilitate a moderately high degree of personal interaction with members. At the same time, receptionists are closely aligned with the business aspects of the organization. One evening I arrived for the second of two meetings held back to back. When I got there, Debbie was still doing the initiation for ten to twelve new members from the first meeting. Ruth was the only receptionist working and when I got to the scale, she complained that Debbie was taking too long. I said, "It's more complicated now that there are the two different plans to choose from." Ruth agreed but said, "She still needs to speed it up." We were interrupted by a new member, who wanted to join. Since Debbie was still talking there was no one to meet and register new members at the front desk. Ruth weighed me and ran up front even though a line was rapidly forming at the scales. The meeting started late.

If meetings are to start on time, which is especially critical when they are scheduled one after the other, receptionists must move people through the lines at the scales as rapidly and efficiently as possible. Ideally, all members will be weighed and seated before the meeting begins. This rarely occurs in actuality, partly because members often arrive late, but largely because lines quickly form at the scales, and since individualized interaction frequently occurs in the cubicles, slowdowns are inevitable. Leaders often must start the meeting while members are still in line waiting to be weighed. This situation is less than ideal for both leaders and receptionists, not to mention members. Members standing in line chatting with each other often distract leaders and make it difficult for seated members to hear what leaders are saying. In turn, receptionists feel particularly pressured to move quickly under these circumstances, and must cope with members who are impatient and frustrated at not being seated for the start of the meeting. Although the division of labor between leaders and receptionists is intended to maximize efficiency, it is also ambiguous enough to contribute to confusion and conflict, as receptionists expect leaders to help register new members and weigh old members whenever possible. When there are multiple receptionists working, or the number of members present is relatively low, covering both the front desk and the scales is less problematic. It is harder when a limited number of receptionists have to deal with a large number of members. In this case, receptionists' needs to maintain organizational efficiency impede their ability to carry on individualized interaction with members and are likely to conflict with leaders' desires to provide individual and group support.

Leaders' abilities to maintain the aura of a support group are also impeded by the fact that much of their interaction is, to at least some extent, scripted by the organization. Leaders do not choose weekly meeting topics for the educational and motivational segments of the meetings. They are determined by the organization. In any given week the same topics will be covered no matter where the meetings occur or who leads them. Leaders receive an outline of the information to be covered, along with suggested activities or discussion techniques that they can incorporate into the meetings. But the script is flexible, and leaders vary considerably in their reliance on or deviation from the script. Richard ad-libs and is so frenetic in his delivery that it's not always obvious he has a script. Conversely, Debbie highly depends on the script, carries it with her throughout the meeting, refers to it often, and frequently incorporates activities it suggests. Regardless of how strictly individual leaders follow the script, its very existence places certain restraints on all leaders. Leaders are not free to discuss whatever topics they want to with members, nor can they allow members' needs or interests to entirely determine the discussion's content or direction.

The weight loss group differs from other support groups in another significant way. In traditional support groups, the entire point of joining is to attend meetings, since it is here that members receive emotional and practical support. In the weight loss group, however, mutual support is not the only commodity purchased. Meeting attendance is optional or even entirely dispensable if members assume they are purchasing a diet. Although members must weigh in once a week and pay for missed weeks, they are not obligated to stay for meetings. Even though many members do stay, more than a few members come in, get weighed, and leave. The result, exacerbated by an apparently high dropout rate, is two groups in one. There is a relatively large group with an unstable and frequently changing membership, and a smaller, fairly stable core group of regulars. Mutual support, concern, and friendship characterize the bonds between leaders and regular attendees, but this is less true of the large group as a whole.

Pressures toward competitiveness and conflict between members, some of which stem from the relative and ambiguous nature of physical attractiveness and thinness, further complicate the organization's role as a support group. Building on small group research finding that individuals affiliate with others for reasons of comparison, Festinger's social comparison theory (1954) argues that people evaluate their thoughts and actions by comparing them with those of others. People prefer to compare themselves with others with whom they are similar (Festinger 1954; Miller 1984), and are most likely to use social comparison to evaluate themselves when they are uncertain about a relevant aspect of themselves (Festinger 1954). Because the definition of thinness is ambiguous and changing, individuals look at others to measure their thinness as well as their success at losing weight. As I stood in line to get weighed at my first meeting, observing those around me, I admit that I was somehow heartened to see several women who obviously had more weight to lose than I did. On another occasion, Linda began the meeting by walking around the room welcoming new members and chatting with others. She came to a mother and daughter, Judy and Kristen, who were sitting in the back row. Linda said to Kristen, "Did that make you feel good when I said I weighed two hundred pounds when I was fourteen?" Kristen was about fourteen years old and clearly did not weigh anywhere near two hundred pounds. Kristen nodded her head yes, and Linda said in the kind of singsong voice that children use when they're showing off to each other, "because I was fatter than you are!" Indeed, leaders rarely make these types of comparisons in front of the group, and there are strong, though unspoken norms against such comparisons. Linda bends the rules in this instance, possibly because the comparison involves herself, and because it is intended to put Kristen at ease. Linda offers herself as a comparison point, assuming that Kristen will judge herself favorably in contrast. Even so, Kristen is obviously embarrassed and the comparison is jarring.

At the same time, members regularly compare how much weight they have lost in a given week, as well as how much total weight they have lost, often during casual conversations before or after meetings. At a meeting not long after I joined, a new member sat down next to me. I said hello and she smiled and said, "Hi! I'm Amy. So how did you do this week?" I said, "Pretty good. I lost two and a half pounds." She said, "That's great!" I asked her how she had done and she replied, "I was really worried. I didn't know. But I lost six pounds!" I responded, "That's really good. I lost five and a half pounds my first week." Amy asked how much I had lost so far and how long I had been coming and I said, "This is my third week. I've lost nine pounds so far." Since pounds lost in a week and total weight lost are easily quantifiable and widely shared markers of success, comparisons are facilitated, if not encouraged. Frequently during weigh-in receptionists equate having a "good week" with a substantial weight loss, as when Ruth told me, "You had a good week—you lost three pounds!" During group discussions, leaders often draw attention to members who have lost substantial amounts of weight, typically in excess of twenty or thirty pounds.

Comparisons do not inevitably lead to competition. However, explicitly recognizing and rewarding large weight losses increases the likelihood of competitiveness between members. During celebration leaders frequently and directly prompt members to report how much weight they have lost. Each announcement of lost weight is greeted with applause, and the larger the loss, the louder is the group's response. Losses exceeding three pounds in a single week are especially likely to get loud reactions. During celebration members receive individual encouragement and reinforcement, but at the same time certain individuals are singled out as particularly successful. As a result, success in the program is equated with the amount of weight lost.

In some ways, strong group cohesiveness militates against, or at least minimizes, competition. But, despite the existence of a small core of regular attendees, member turnover is high. A continually changing membership tends to dampen group cohesion to some extent. More important, strong cultural norms that promote competitiveness between women, especially in the area of physical attractiveness and thinness, may supersede or at least conflict with group norms against explicit comparisons and competitiveness. Recently I spotted a bumper sticker that read, "Lord, if I can't be thin, let all my friends be fat." Indeed, despite strong group norms that militate against negative comparisons between members, such comparisons do occur, and almost always they occur between female friends. Lucy and Eve, two women in their twenties, both weighing well over two hundred pounds, were close friends who joined the group at the same time and consistently attended meetings together. One evening before the meeting started, Lucy and Eve were talking about how they were doing and were comparing their progress. Eve had lost close to two pounds that week, but she said to Lucy, "That's nothing like seven pounds!" implying that's what Lucy had lost. Lucy responded, "Yeah, but I'm probably right now where you were when you started." Eve said, "You just have to catch up."

While this incident is relatively innocuous, and the competition mild and friendly, others are less so. Particularly illustrative is the relationship between two other friends who joined and attended meetings together, Joyce and Peggy. Joyce (who also brought along her young daughter Carrie) was very successful with the program, steadily lost weight, and fairly rapidly reached her goal range. Peggy, in contrast, struggled. She attended meetings irregularly, had more trouble sticking to the plan, and inconsistently lost weight, or even gained weight in a given week. Regularly, although usually when Peggy was not there, Joyce explicitly criticized Peggy's lack of effort and persistence. One evening when Peggy was absent, Joyce referred to her at one point, and said, "Peggy is having a real hard time. I think it's because she's kind of estimating serving sizes, and she's not writing stuff down." The following week Peggy was there with Joyce, and after Debbie started the meeting, she walked over to Peggy and asked, "Do we have something to celebrate over here this week?" When Peggy said she had lost two and a quarter pounds everyone clapped, and Debbie asked what she had done differently. Peggy said, "I used my tracker and wrote everything down. I'm embarrassed to admit it now, but this is the first time I've done it." All the time Peggy was talking, Joyce nodded her head, looked at the group, and made the OK sign with her fingers, seeming to say, "Haven't I been telling her that all along?" A month later Peggy was not at the meeting and Joyce reached her goal weight. Debbie brought her up front. After acknowledging how close she felt to the group and thanking members for their support, Joyce once again compared herself with Peggy. Joyce said, "You have to find what's right for you; what works for you. But Peggy tries to eat what someone else eats, or does what somebody else does. So if Debbie says she eats such and such for breakfast, then that's what she starts eating for breakfast." Despite the fact that Joyce made such comments frequently, and although they clearly violated group norms, Debbie never suggested to Joyce that her remarks were inappropriate.

Ironically, the organization may benefit from some competitiveness between members, and thus is likely to tolerate, if not encourage it. Company profits depend on attracting new members and retaining continuing members. Competition may not help to attract new members, but in a context of high member turnover, it can operate as a cost-free motivational strategy to encourage members to return. The organization officially endorses a weight loss rate of one to two pounds per week, a rate which leaders describe as safe and healthy. However, this loss rate may be unacceptable to new members, who frequently come to the group with unrealistic goals. The messages that members receive about the appropriate rate of loss are, in fact, highly contradictory. Although it may be difficult to maintain a loss of more than two or three pounds per week over any length of time, it is clear from celebration that losses of this magnitude, or even greater, are not only possible, but not uncommon. Despite the organization's official position, leaders call attention to and reward larger losses. Members who actually maintain a steady loss of one to two pounds per week may see their loss as inadequate, and their progress as too slow, compared with reported losses of four, five, or more pounds, and may feel the need to catch up with other members.

The relative nature of thinness and the ambiguity of defining weight loss progress set the scene for comparisons between members. The ease with which progress is quantified, both as number of pounds lost per week and total weight lost, facilitates comparisons, which are likely to become competitive when losses, particularly large ones, are highlighted and rewarded. Additionally, in an economically competitive weight loss market and given high rates of membership turnover, the organization may benefit from competitiveness between members to the extent that it increases member motivation. But simultaneously, the competition between members and the organization's economic concerns undermine the weight loss group's ability to operate purely as a support group.

Speaking of Self-Help

The weight loss organization and its employees make a concerted effort to represent themselves as a support group, and members accept and reinforce this representation. The language of self-help, with explicit references to lifestyle modification, education, changing bad habits, and making smarter choices, permeates organizational materials and meeting discussions. The group's emphases on self-help, lifestyle modification, and mutual support as legitimate routes to weight loss are based on three key assumptions. First, a central assumption is that being overweight is unhealthy. Second, and even more important, is the assumption that body weight is subject to individual control. Finally, and ironically, it is assumed that diets are unhealthy and ultimately do not work. Cultural norms and popular knowledge bolster these assumptions, despite the fact that the first two are highly questionable and the third poses problems of its own.

Employees and members see self-improvement, often defined as enhanced physical health, as a major justification for losing weight. New members frequently cite fatigue, lack of energy, high blood pressure, and a variety of other health concerns as motivating factors in their decision to join a weight loss group. Continuing members and leaders alike often claim that enhanced health is an inevitable outcome of losing weight. Beginning with the premise that being overweight is unhealthy, group participants easily move to the assumption that weight loss is the key to good health, a belief widely promulgated by the scientific and medical communities (Institute of Medicine 1995). Unfortunately, the taken-for-granted link between health and body weight is tenuous at best. Considerable research challenges the view that obesity is a major health risk (Barrett-Connor 1985; Ernsberger and Haskew 1987; Fitzgerald 1981; Keys et al. 1984; Mann 1974). In addition, research continues to suggest that optimal health may be associated with being moderately overweight (Cogan 1999; Ernsberger and Haskew 1987; Keys 1980; Keys et al. 1984; Troiano et al. 1996). But despite mounting evidence that the effects of obesity on health are not as clear and strong as previously believed, the presumed association between health and body weight goes largely unquestioned, both in the wider United States culture and in the smaller confines of the weight loss group.

Closely related to the first assumption is the belief that weight is subject to individual control, primarily through the restriction of caloric intake. Nowhere is this assumption clearer or stronger than in the weight loss group. People join such a group precisely because they believe that if they only do the right thing, namely, change the way they eat, they will lose weight. So strongly is this assumption held that not once in two years did I hear anyone question its validity. Even those members who lose very little weight or lose it very inconsistently continue to believe that they can lose weight if only they are committed and work hard enough. Members are not alone in this belief. One of the most widely accepted beliefs about obesity in the United States is that it results from overeating and consequently is controllable (Cogan 1999). This belief persists despite the fact that research has failed to document clear and consistent differences in the eating habits of obese and nonobese individuals (Coates, Jeffery, and Wing 1978; Garner and Wooley 1991; Institute of Medicine 1995; Wing and Jeffery 1978; Wooley, Wooley, and Dyernforth 1979). Furthermore, a growing body of research, including studies of identical twins, suggests that genetics play some role in body weight (Bouchard et al. 1990; Price et al. 1987; Stunkard, Foch, and Hrubec 1986; Stunkard et al. 1990; Stunkard et al. 1986). This knowledge has had little impact on popular attitudes. Obesity continues to be viewed as a voluntary state that can be altered through individual behavior.

Yet this belief exists alongside the increasingly strong conviction that diets not only do not work but are unhealthy. Group members often discuss their diet histories and ruefully describe the time, energy, and money spent on diets that ultimately fail. Common themes of hunger, deprivation, and poor nutrition pervade the stories. The frustration is palpable as members recount being continually lured into diets that promise large and rapid weight loss, but time and again fail to deliver.

In contrast to the first two assumptions, substantial research verifies the truly dismal failure rate of dieting. Although many people may be able to lose weight and maintain the loss for a year (Miller, Koceja, and Hamilton 1997), as many as 95 percent of weight losers are unable to maintain the loss for five years (Garner and Wooley 1991; Goodrich and Foreyt 1991; Kramer et al. 1989). In addition to the likelihood of regaining weight, dieters are at risk of numerous psychological and physiological ill effects (Berg 1995; Brunner et al. 1994; French et al. 1995; Green et al. 1994; Griffiths and Farnill 1996; Laessle et al. 1996; Patton 1992; Polivy and Herman 1985; Ross 1994). When Chapman (1999) interviewed women about their dieting experiences, they described being obsessed with food, feeling guilty and deprived, overeating, and weight gain as common consequences of dieting. As if this weren't enough, the weight fluctuation frequently associated with dieting is also related to negative health risks (Berg 1995; Blair et al. 1993; Brownell and Rodin 1994; Hamm, Shekelle, and Stamler 1989; Hanson et al. 1996; Iribarren et al. 1995; Lissner et al. 1991).

The assumptions that being overweight is unhealthy, that weight is subject to individual control, and that diets are unhealthy and don't work interact with one another in the weight loss group to affect the ways that weight loss is talked about. On the surface, the association between weight and health seems relatively benign. Even if the health risks of obesity are greatly exaggerated, it is possible that some lifestyle changes, such as improving one's level of physical fitness, may improve one's health. On another level, however, the concern with health and its relationship to body weight is more insidious. An aesthetics of health operates in the United States, wherein people who look healthy, are assumed to be healthy (Spitzack 1990). A century ago, plumpness connoted health, but today thinness is taken as one highly visible indicator of physical well-being (Seid 1994). In their quest for the appearance of health, individuals invest considerable amounts of time, energy, and money. To conform to the current aesthetics of health, a woman must not only monitor her weight but attend to "bulges, muscles, skin tone and texture, 'defective' body parts, fashion, attitudes and behavior, to name only a few dimensions of female wellness" (Spitzack 1990). In the United States the diet, cosmetics, and cosmetic surgery industries enjoy multibillion-dollar profits yearly from individuals' attempts to *look* healthy (Wolf 1991). The association between health, self-improvement, and body weight is even more problematic for individuals in its implications about the self and what it means to improve it. Spitzack (1990:3) comments: "The contradictory forces that underpin discourses of female health are epitomized in strategies designed to aid women in a reduction of the body. Reducing one's body, or becoming less of oneself in order to become more of oneself, pervades health discourses in general, but functions with pronounced blatancy in the domain of weight loss." Like Richard, Ruth customarily ends each meeting by saying, "I hope to see less of each of you next week!" There is a dark side to Ruth's exhortation, despite her intended humor. Successful self-improvement via weight loss does indeed entail a shrinking of the self. Although women are most susceptible to this mode of thinking, men may not be entirely immune. Given the strength of the association between health and appearance, it is not surprising that increasing numbers of men are dieting (Hesse-Biber 1996).

A continuing cultural obsession with health and physical appearance, coupled with a strong belief that individuals can ultimately control their weight, leads easily and naturally to high rates of dieting. But at the same time, greater awareness of the health risks associated with dieting and the abysmal failure rates of most diets have resulted in increasingly negative views of dieting, among both medical professionals and the public. The result has not been a decline in the availability of diet plans, nor does evidence suggest that fewer people are dieting. However, it appears that a new discourse, or a new way of speaking about losing weight, has emerged. In interviews with women about the meaning of dieting, Chapman (1999) found a movement toward a "discourse of healthy eating" in contrast to a more traditional "discourse of dieting." In contrast to the diet discourse, the healthy-eating discourse emphasizes weight control as a route to overall well-being, focuses on permanent lifestyle change, and is more prescriptive than proscriptive in promoting the consumption of healthier foods (Chapman 1999). Diet plans and weight loss groups demonstrate a similar shift in discourse. Ironically, we have witnessed the emergence and growing popularity of what Spitzack (1990) calls the "antidiet," a weight loss plan offered under the guise of a new way of eating. Proponents of antidiets offer particular weight loss plans for sale, yet simultaneously condemn dieting.

The weight loss organization examined here and its employees clearly evince the antidiet orientation. The organization repeatedly asserts that it offers a nutritionally sound plan for lifestyle modification, not a diet. There is something to this. Theoretically, the group's weight loss plan builds in the potential for substantial nutritional variety, written materials attempt to educate members about good nutrition, and leaders emphasize the importance of exercise. Problems arise, however, because in most members' and employees' minds, the ultimate goal is to lose weight. Members occasionally remark that they feel better physically, and every now and then they report specific health benefits, such as lower blood pressure since beginning the program. But most members see these benefits as resulting from weight loss, not from better nutrition or increased physical activity per se. Ultimately, in most members' minds the real indicator of success on the program is the number on the scale.

Antidiet orientations and healthy eating discourses affect the definition of and perspectives on good food. The goodness of food can be judged on numerous dimensions, including taste, cultural or ritual value, nutritional value, freshness, chemical, and additive content, and whether it is organically grown (Lupton 1996). In the United States since World War II the conviction that fat is dangerous, both on the body and in the food we eat, has grown increasingly strong (Austin 1999; Seid 1994). As the cultural emphasis on health has grown, good food has come to mean healthy food, but "healthy" in a particular sense. Currently one of the most important criteria for determining the health value of a food is its fat content, due in no small part to an extensive public health campaign to educate the public about the perils of dietary fat (Austin 1999). The list of problematic food ingredients has grown, and individuals are regularly exhorted to monitor their intake of not only fat but a wide variety of substances, including salt, sugar, and caffeine (Balsamo 1996). The approach is predominantly proscriptive and the aim is to convince people to reduce, if not eliminate, their consumption of certain food substances. Only recently has attention been given to the benefits of increasing consumption of some foods, especially fruits and vegetables (Austin 1999).

The antidiet and healthy eating discourses clearly affect group members' perspectives on food. But in the context of a weight loss group, the primary connotation of good food is quite simple—it is food that contributes to weight loss. The nutritional value of food, while significant, is a secondary concern. Leaders strongly urge members to eat a variety of foods to meet their nutritional needs, and in requiring members to consume at least two servings of dairy products daily, address women's need for calcium. Beyond this, however, little attention is given to the nutritional value of particular foods, and when it is, it is sometimes, though not always, at the expense of any attention to taste. On the one hand, the organization sells a variety of cookbooks and often distributes free recipes to members, and leaders regularly remind members that healthy food can taste good. On the other hand, there is a tendency to downplay issues of taste. Leaders often hold up ground turkey as a low-fat alternative to ground beef even though most members show a marked preference for the taste of ground beef. When Peggy complained of being extremely hungry in the afternoons, Debbie suggested sauerkraut as a high-fiber, filling snack.

Even less attention is paid to the uses of food preservatives, additives, or other chemicals in the growth, production, and processing of food. Although fast food is infamous for being highly processed and nutritionally unsound, members are not encouraged to forgo fast food, but instead are taught how to incorporate it into the weight loss plan. The same is true for most convenience foods, particularly those marketed as light, low-fat, or healthy. As Austin (1999) points out, the launching of the Healthy Choice line of frozen meals in the late 1980s benefited from and subsequently reinforced the cultural obsession with fat reduction. Since that time the availability and profitability of low-fat processed foods has expanded tremendously. Although the weight loss organization does not require members to buy prepackaged, processed foods, it profits from the sale of its line of convenience foods, including frozen dinners. Therefore it is good business to downplay the significance of processing and chemical additives. But the group's acceptance of and support for processed convenience foods extends to other brands. Shirley routinely begins her meetings with a show-and-tell of convenience foods. She encourages members to bring in empty packages or labels of foods they have tried and liked. She displays the packages in the front of the room and usually chooses two or three to highlight, by drawing members' attention to them and asking members to calculate the food's point value using the information on the product label.

Similarly, the tension between a health orientation and a focus on losing weight affects the ways that members and employees speak about exercise. Considerable evidence suggests that regular aerobic exercise has numerous positive effects, both physically and psychologically (Burgard and Lyons 1994). The organization frequently reinforces the importance of exercising, and leaders and written materials offer numerous, seemingly simple ways to increase physical activity. For example, members are encouraged to park their cars farther from their destination, or to use stairs instead of elevators. Nonetheless, the rationale is virtually always that weight loss will be steadier and more rapid if you exercise. Rarely do members or leaders discuss the health benefits of exercise independently of weight loss, and it is unheard of to suggest that exercise can be enjoyable in and of itself. The group speaks of exercise almost entirely in terms of its calorie-burning potential. At one point, members received small cardboard slide rules to calculate how many calories are burned by engaging in physical activities, such as swimming, tennis, or yard work, for varying amounts of time. The organization reinforces this view of exercise by allowing members to trade exercise for more food. Members are supposed to exercise twenty minutes daily. Every twenty minutes above the minimum earns one extra point's worth of food. Even with this incentive, however, members are reluctant to exercise. To the extent that members adopt the group's focus on lifestyle modification, they apparently do not see exercise as an integral component of the plan. During discussions members often complain about the inconvenience and unpleasantness of exercise. And on several occasions, one member or another expressed the misguided view that exercise will actually impede weight loss, since exercise builds muscle and "muscle weighs more than fat!"

Speaking of weight loss in the language of self-help has clear implications for the way in which social problems are perceived and addressed. When self-improvement is emphasized, obesity and weight loss are defined almost entirely as individual problems, not social issues. There is no doubt that a growing skepticism about the relationship between weight and health and a shift in focus from weight and dieting to quality of life and health are positive steps (Cogan 1999). But the continuing individualization of health and health care in the United States limits the benefits of the changing emphasis. The cultural focus is on individual choice and change, specifically lifestyle modification. Societal impacts on health are virtually ignored. In the case of obesity, focusing on the individual obscures societal contributions, including social class differences in the availability and accessibility of nutritional food, changes in work and leisure time, and the profitability of the fast food and convenience food industries in a capitalist economy. Perhaps most important, focusing on the individual doesn't even begin to question and deconstruct the societal stigmatization of obesity.

4 "You Just Have to Keep at It"

Although the language of support and self-help is pervasive, it is not the only way in which members and leaders speak about weight loss. Another model, closely related to that of support, is most obvious when leaders and members conceptualize the process of losing weight, and particularly what it takes to be successful. At the first meeting I attended, the motivational section revolved around the idea of being on or going off the program, beginning with what constitutes a perfect day, and then on to what it means to go off the program. Richard solicited ideas from members about what they would say to someone who said she had three good days and then got totally off the program. People suggested, "concentrate on the fact that three days are better than none, "just start again," and "we're all in this together."

At the end of the regular meeting I had to stay for the orientation for new members. When I weighed in I had received a large packet of information that contained the basics of the program. Richard rapidly ran through the materials with me and two other newcomers. He told us, "For the first week or two it's pretty simple. All you have to do is follow the menus. They're all decided for you." One of the pamphlets had fourteen days' worth of menus, including three meals and one snack for each day. Richard explained that, while one breakfast could be substituted for another, and likewise for the other meals, we had to choose one breakfast, lunch, dinner, and snack for each day. He went on to say, "We've done the work for you! This way when you start, you don't need to worry about learning the program." Lisa, a returning member who had belonged to the group several years previously but had dropped out, sat next to me. Since Lisa had joined before, the program had changed, most noticeably in the inclusion of the preset menus. After Richard finished and left to help set up for the next meeting, Lisa expressed dissatisfaction, and almost impatience, with the new plan. Clearly annoyed, Lisa said, "I want to count things. I want to keep track of everything and write it down." We chatted a few minutes and I asked her whether she weighs all her food. She replied, "Oh yeah! They have scales they sell for twelve dollars. Until you get a feel for how much an ounce is, you need to weigh it."

After my next meeting, one week later, I had to stay again, this time for orientation into the second step of the program. After the meeting I moved up to the front row, right in front of the VCR. Cheryl started a videotape for me and said she would be back to talk to me about it after she completed orientation for a new member. On the videotape, a woman explained the basics of the program. After the tape ended I leafed through the materials I had received and waited for Cheryl. In a few minutes she came over and asked what I thought, and whether I had any questions. I said, "No, I think it's pretty clear." She asked, "Do you think you'll do the mix-and-match menus?" When I said it would probably make it easier, she agreed and pointed out that I could use the food lists to make substitutions. She finished by telling me, "Remember, the mix-and-match menus don't include a snack, so if you think you want one, you need to save something back from the day's meals so you can have your snack. I think you're going to do fine. You seem really focused."

Embedded in these incidents is the idea that weight loss is work. This suggestion contains two major components. First, it implies something about the characteristics of the workers. The value of hard work and discipline is a deeply held, core value in the United States, related to norms of self-sufficiency, achievement, and success (Williams 1965). It is not surprising that when group members suggest that you have to work hard to lose weight, they imply that the good dieter is highly disciplined. That is, dieting, like other work, requires a strong work ethic. But there is a second component of the concept that also applies to dieting. To speak of weight loss as work draws our attention to the structure and organization of the activity of dieting itself. In this way we begin to see that not only does weight loss require members to work hard, but weight loss is hard work.

In this chapter we examine both components of the work metaphor.

We begin with an examination of the work ethic as it is applied to dieting, first by analyzing the meaning of productivity in the context of the weight loss group, and then by considering how laziness is understood by and affects the experiences of dieters. We then move to the second component, related to the nature of the work itself. We examine the high degree of structure and precision that characterize the group's weight loss plan, as well as the nature of payoffs and supervision. The final section discusses the implications of conceptualizing weight loss as work. First, the framework rests on the objectification of the human body, whereby the body is transformed into an object to be molded, shaped, and modified, that is, to be worked on. Viewed from this perspective, dieting is obviously linked to other body-molding/shaping techniques, particularly cosmetic surgery and bodybuilding. Second, the extreme structure and precision that characterize dieting reflect a broader trend of increased rationalization in the larger society.

Keeping at It: Productivity and Laziness

As members recount what they would say to someone who has gone off the program, the language of support and encouragement is clear, but another, more subtle message also emerges. When members and leaders urge one another to keep at it, not to give up, and to be persistent in the face of setbacks, they imply that the person who is most likely to succeed at weight loss is the individual with a strong work ethic. Being goal-oriented is critical, but how long it takes to reach the goal is less important than being persistent. When Jill received a ribbon for losing her first five pounds, she ruefully said, "And it only took me three pages to get there!" She referred to her weight loss record book, in which three pages represent twelve weeks on the program. Ruth immediately responded, "What matters is that you got there!" Emphasizing the work process itself and downplaying the time it takes to reach a goal are clearest when members reach their goal weight. Not long after I joined, Richard began the meeting by walking over to Kathleen and saying, "I saw you dancing off the scale before! What did you do this week?" She said, "I made goal." Members loudly applauded and shouted words of congratulation. Although she hesitated, Richard took Kathleen up to the front of the room and asked her how much she had lost altogether. She said twenty-six pounds, and Richard asked her if she had any words of advice for new people. Kathleen said, "I don't know. I guess I was just two pounds away from goal for a long time, and I kept going up and down. It was frustrating, but I stuck with it, and now I finally made it! You just have to keep at it."

A central concern in this perspective is the pursuit of goal, and the key to success is your attitude. Given the strong organizational emphasis on developing and maintaining high motivation in members, it is not surprising that in practical terms this translates into developing a strong work ethic. In several ways, the concept of weight loss as work is compatible with the concept of self-help and support. The expertise shared by members frequently involves tricks of the trade, or strategies developed by members to get the work of weight loss done. Furthermore, emotional support and encouragement are not given unconditionally. Rather, they are used as rewards for members who demonstrate their willingness to work hard and are withheld from members whose work ethic is questionable.

Productivity: Keeping Up the Good Work

Good workers not only develop good work habits; they are good producers. In the language of weight loss, productivity equals the number of pounds lost. The more pounds lost, the better the worker. After just three weeks on the program, I was at the scales for weigh-in. As I started to step on the scale the receptionist asked, "Good week?" Not knowing quite how to respond, I said, "I think so." She took my weight, entered it in my book, and said, "I can tell!" I had lost five pounds in one week. Almost without exception, the measure of a good week is a function of how much weight members think they have lost. Developing good work habits is important, but they are not sufficient. The work of weight loss is not valued in and of itself. Even though members know that in a given week they might work hard and still not lose weight, or lose very little, they do not consider these good weeks. Indeed, members find these weeks highly frustrating. They feel they did their work, but did not receive the appropriate payoff.

During celebration, as members proudly announce to the group how much weight they have lost, the equation of productivity and weight loss is most obvious. Leaders influence the extent to which weight loss is focused upon and rewarded, demonstrating markedly different approaches. On the one extreme, Linda focused exclusively on weight loss and explicitly prompted members in this direction, while on the other extreme, Cheryl's group constructed a culture wherein weight loss was greatly downplayed. In between these approaches, Richard explicitly rewarded weight loss but also recognized and rewarded a wide range of activities, achievements, and behaviors.

Despite variations in leaders' styles, members tend to focus on amount of weight lost, even in the absence of explicit prompts by leaders. An interesting phenomenon occurs as members announce their weight losses during celebration. With occasional exceptions, reported losses tend to increase as the leader moves around the room, handing out stickers for achievements. For a number of reasons, it is unlikely that members exaggerate their weight loss. First, typical losses range from about one pound to four or five pounds, and there are fairly clear, and relatively low, limits on how large a loss is considered reasonable. Second, since receptionists measure and record members' weights, and are almost always present during meetings, they present a validity check on members' reports. Although it is highly unlikely that a receptionist would contradict a member's reported weight loss, simply knowing that there is someone in the room who knows what you really lost may make you hesitant to distort the truth, even slightly. Third, members report their weight losses in highly precise ways, to two-tenths of a pound. I never heard a member say, "I lost about a pound," but I heard many say, "I lost eight-tenths."

If members do not purposely distort their losses, why do these generally increase with each loss reported? The most reasonable explanation is selective reporting. For the most part, reporting your weight loss is optional. Leaders typically begin celebration by asking the members of the group as a whole to share their accomplishments. Individual members decide whether and how to respond. The first weight loss reported is critical. If the loss is one to two pounds, it's followed by fairly similar losses, which slowly increase as more members report. If, however, the first loss reported is relatively large, such as five pounds or more, which is not all that unusual for new members, other members hesitate to report smaller losses. When they do, such as when a leader specifically asks them how they did, they are often embarrassed, and may explicitly state that their loss pales in comparison with the other losses reported. Selective reporting not only promotes a degree of competitiveness between members, but reinforces unrealistic weight loss goals. As members hesitate to report small losses, but freely announce large ones, particularly newer members can easily see losses of three to five pounds per week as not only possible but typical.

Leaders and members equate productivity and weight loss in another way. Leaders regularly single out individuals who have achieved large total weight losses. At one meeting Cheryl, who usually downplayed weight loss, called the group's attention to Sandy and Corinne. She labeled them "real success stories," and when prompted, both reported total weight losses of close to thirty pounds. On another occasion, Debbie directly addressed me during the meeting, much to my chagrin. She asked, "Rough week?" I said I had lost half a pound but it was rough going. It had been a stressful week, we ate out a lot, and I stopped recording everything I ate. Simultaneously diverting attention away from my frustrations and highlighting my productivity, Debbie asked me to share my overall success with the group. When I said I had lost fifty-nine pounds, members responded predictably with a lot of "oohs" and "ahs."

When individuals are singled out for large total losses, multiple messages are communicated. Individuals receive positive reinforcement for their achievements. At the same time, they are positive role models for other members. They are proof that the program does indeed work for members who are persistent in their efforts. Rewarding large total losses reinforces the belief that the successful member is the one who works hard, and the hard worker is the one who is most productive. Ironically, a good producer is a good reducer.

Laziness

If the successful weight-loser is the one who works hard, then by extension, the unsuccessful dieter must not be working hard enough. Considerable research documents the prejudice directed at overweight people, which may begin as early as nursery school (Goodman et al. 1963). In addition to facing considerable educational and employment discrimination (Rothblum 1994), fat people are confronted with the prejudicial attitudes of professionals, including nutritionists (Maiman et al. 1979), physicians (Maddox and Liederman 1969), and mental health professionals (Agell and Rothblum 1991; Young and Powell 1985). Within the model of weight loss as work, the prejudice takes a particular bent because it is commonly assumed that people voluntarily control their weight. Fat people are blamed for their condition. In this line of reasoning, if eating too much and exercising too little directly cause weight gain, the fat person doesn't work hard enough. The fat person is lazy.

The view of fat people as lazy persists despite considerable evidence that weight has more to do with physiological set points than with what one consumes (Rothblum 1994). Research continues to find that anywhere from 90 to 98 percent of weight-losers gain back the lost weight within five years; the longer the follow-up period, the more weight they have regained (Bennett 1986; Brownell and Jeffery 1987; Burgard and Lyons 1994; Garner and Wooley 1991; Rothblum 1994). But still, fat people are held responsible for their body weight, and this attitude extends to other areas of the beauty culture. Balsamo (1996:66) argues: "One of the consequences of the commodification and, correspondingly, the normalization of cosmetic surgery is that electing *not* to have cosmetic surgery is sometimes interpreted as a failure to deploy all available resources to maintain a youthful, and therefore socially acceptable and attractive, body appearance."

Actively participating in the feminine beauty culture requires not only time but a good deal of specialized knowledge and skill, as women learn how to care for skin, make-up, and hair, not to mention body weight (Bartky 1988). By extension, women who do not actively participate are assumed to not care about themselves, or to be too lazy to invest the necessary time and energy. Yet the logic is problematic. First, this enterprise is costly. Participation requires investing considerable resources in cosmetics, hair-care products, various tools of the trade, including hair dryers and curling irons, not to mention the services of a broad range of beauty experts, such as manicurists, hair stylists, trainers, and electrolysists. Many women simply do not have the necessary economic resources. Second, the assumption of laziness ignores culture's role and leaves little room for resistance. Women are left with little choice; those who do not participate in the beauty culture are not actively resisting it, they're lazy. Finally, and most important, the entire beauty project is a set-up. Since the goal is an unattainable cultural ideal, women are doomed to fail no matter how hard they work or how many resources they invest (Bartky 1988).

The Nature of the Work

In addition to highlighting the characteristics of good workers, the concept of work has implications for how the work of weight loss itself is understood. Most significant in the weight loss group are the program's structure and precision, the presumed rewards, and the nature of supervision.

Structure

At the same time that dieters see themselves as hard workers, they see dieting as a particular kind of work. Conceptualizing weight loss as work assumes that the process is highly structured and provides a large degree of control over members' behavior. Many members see the program's structure as an asset, as when Lisa complained that she wanted to count and write everything down. On another occasion when Debbie asked new members what brought them to the group, Connie said, "I pretty much know how to eat. I gravitate toward good foods, like fruits and veggies. But I need the structure."

Connie repeated the word "structure" several times as she explained why she was there. Structure is beneficial precisely because it imposes control over a process that has seemingly spun out of control. Rules are not simply restrictive and limiting, but provide a sense of security in the face of uncertainty. Following rules entails some loss of freedom and autonomy, but also brings at least some degree of predictability, which is one reason individuals submit to rules, even in the apparent absence of overt pressures or sanctions (Bartky 1988).

The time spent in orienting new members to the plan reflects the emphasis placed on structure. Members must know and understand the rules if they are going to do their work. Although the basic plan has been modified several times since I was introduced to it, new members are still taught the rules and introduced to the plan's structure as soon as they join. Several aspects are noteworthy. First, the plan's structure builds on the notion, widely shared by nutritional scientists, that foods can be rationally and coherently categorized into groups that differ from one another in important ways, but all of which are necessary, in the proper proportions, for a balanced diet (Lupton 1996). Second, the focus on portion sizes, total portions allowed in a day, grams of fat and fiber, and point values emphasizes the exact, quantitative measurement of food. Third, early versions of the plan were flexible only in the sense that predetermined portions of particular types of foods could be substituted for one another. For example, one-half banana, a small apple, and a cup of grapes are each equivalent to one fruit selection, and so could be substituted. However, an apple and a cup of yogurt could not be exchanged, even though each is one portion, since they are in different food categories. Finally, despite my initial confidence, the plan was somewhat complex and did in fact require some time to learn and practice it.

Even though members see the program's structure as an asset and frequently seek it out, they sometimes feel overly restricted. Structure can become a source of frustration. Weight-losers, like other workers, benefit in some ways from structure, but at the same time, there is a downside. Predictability, security, and control may be gained, but often at the expense of flexibility and freedom. At the extreme, structure becomes rigidity.

Members found two aspects of the plan especially restrictive. In each case the organization addressed members' complaints, but not without unintended and unforeseen consequences. First, members often complained about having to eat a certain number of specific foods every day and being unable to eat more of other foods. Many members had difficulty consuming two servings of milk daily, and some complained that they could eat more than two servings of fruit per day only if they used their bonus calories to cover them. The organization initially addressed the restrictions in food selections by recategorizing foods so that fruits and vegetables were combined into one group, as were milk and proteins. Next, members could count grams of fat and fiber rather than food selections. Subsequently food categories were done away with, and all foods received point values. Although members must eat five servings of fruits or vegetables and two servings of high-calcium dairy products daily, and still must count and keep track of what they eat, they are freed from having to limit themselves to eating a specified number of servings of specific kinds of food.

Second, members frequently found it hard to incorporate the plan into their daily lives. Dining out and special occasions posed significant problems, both because they often entailed eating high-fat, high-calorie foods and because weighing and measuring food was nearly impossible. Again the organization responded, and modified the plan so that members could save a portion of their weekly food selections and calories to be used on occasional indulgences, such as going out to eat, changing eating patterns on the weekend, or eating a particular food not regularly eaten, such as birthday cake. Although the organization promotes its plan as allowing members to eat whatever foods they like, in practice members find this very difficult to do and still lose weight. Changes in the program were designed to provide members with greater freedom in this regard, but clearly did so within the framework of weight loss as work. Saving selections for later indulgences fits well with the United States cultural veneration of the thrifty worker who spends only what is necessary and puts away the rest for a rainy day. Conversely, workers who squander or overspend what they have made will frequently find themselves in a deficit when a need arises.

Few of the changes have lasted. Economic competition from other weight loss programs and diet plans necessitates continual innovation. But more important, several of the changes were problematic, precisely because they undermined the structure built into the program. By allowing members to save up for indulgences, the group loosened its control and incorporated more flexibility for members. The change was even more dramatic when the fat and fiber counting plan was instituted. Both changes reduced the program's rigidity, and the fat and fiber plan was easier and more straightforward than keeping track of selections. Yet the changes generated problems almost immediately, largely related to calorie control. The idea of exchanging banked selections for indulgences was slippery, at best. Exactly how many calories and selections, of what sort, are equivalent to a piece of birthday cake, a banana split, or barbecued spare ribs and a pitcher of beer? Members were perplexed, and tended to underestimate how many selections had to be saved for their indulgences. The fat and fiber plan was even more problematic. While the standard program limits calories by establishing standard portion sizes and limiting the number of servings that can be consumed daily, the fat and fiber plan contained no such controls, with predictable results. To the extent that the organization has tried to provide greater freedom and flexibility, structure is subsequently decreased and members do not lose as much weight, and they do not lose it as quickly. In some ways, the new point system also decreases the program's rigidity and gives members more freedom, but at the same time it maintains calorie control. There is a potential, however, for flexibility to come at the expense of nutritional variety, which was explicitly built into the basic selection plan.

Members as well as the organization itself are ambivalent about the plan's structure. Individuals who want to lose weight come to the group looking for help to gain control over a process that has seemingly spun out of control, and they assume that a highly structured program will provide that control. At the same time, control brings with it the ever-present danger of rigidity. The organization, sensitive to members' complaints and dissatisfactions, loosens its control, but sometimes at the expense of productivity. It is in these continual struggles over structure and control that we most clearly see the concept of weight loss as work.

Precision: Weighing Every Ounce, Counting Every Bite

Given the program's structure, it is not surprising that following the plan requires a high degree of precision, which rests on measurability and the need to translate behavior into clearly quantifiable units. The measurement of body weight is the first place members witness the high degree of precision. Receptionists take great care in readying the scales for weigh-in, and the organization periodically sends people in to calibrate the scales. The care and attention given to the scales is in part due to the fact that members' weights are measured and recorded minutely. When I first joined the group, body weight was measured to the quarter-pound. Subsequently, measurements became even more precise when the group acquired electronic scales that measure weight to the two-tenths pound. Weight and weight losses are never rounded, either up or down. This is as true for members as it is for the organization. During celebration members report their weekly losses exactly, often to two-tenths of a pound. On the one hand, the precision may benefit members who might be encouraged by losing weight, even a small amount, compared with the prospect of not losing any or even gaining weight. On the other hand, the ability to measure weight this precisely is largely an illusion. The scales are not that reliable. Members frequently observe differences between the scales, and whenever the scales are calibrated, receptionists make a point of cautioning members that this may affect their weight compared with the previous week. Curiously, the effects are highly inconsistent; some members see greater than expected losses, while others see less than expected losses. Probably more important, body weight fluctuates not only from day to day but over the course of a single day and probably over two-tenths of a pound. On top of this, even slight variations in clothing from week to week may affect body weight. And yet despite leaders' and members' awareness of these variations, they continue to speak of weight and weight losses in highly precise and exact language.

The precision in body weight measurements affects members' behaviors as well as their language. Members choose their clothing for weigh-in carefully. Many members wear exactly the same thing, week after week, to minimize artificial variations in body weight. Members wear minimal clothing; t-shirts and either shorts or leggings are the standard uniform. In the dead of winter members arrive in sweat clothes, only to strip them off to reveal shorts and t-shirt before stepping on the scale. And it is the rare member who wears her shoes while getting weighed. A stack of paper towels is kept on the counter by the scale so members don't step on the scales with bare feet. But the strip-down goes even further. As they approach the scales, members remove belts, watches, jewelry, and any excess piece of apparel or accessory that might tip the scale. I was not immune. One evening, as I prepared for a meeting, I held a different t-shirt in each hand, trying to determine if one weighed less than the other. On the surface, the behavior is comic, if not ludicrous. But in the context of the group, members are responding reasonably to the emphasis on precision.

Following the group's weight loss plan also requires an extremely high degree of precision. The translation of foods into selections and exact portions is highly precise. Oddly enough, there is the pretense of less precision, since calories are not explicitly counted, which is a frequent source of confusion for members. To persons used to thinking of weight loss almost entirely in terms of calorie restriction, the idea of food selections is strange and confusing. The issue of portion control compounds the problem. One night's topic was "But I Eat Like a Bird." Debbie had a big plastic cereal bowl, a very large orange, and a large potato. Taking the role of a frustrated member, Debbie said, "I just don't get why I can't lose weight. I eat like a bird! Today, for breakfast, I had a bowl of cereal and one orange. And for lunch I had a baked potato. What am I doing wrong?" Debbie looked to the group for an answer, and Wendy said, "How much cereal does that bowl hold? And that orange is huge!" Debbie reported that the bowl held three cups of cereal, the potato weighed ten ounces, and the orange weighed nine ounces. Translated into selections, the cereal represented three bread servings, the potato, two bread servings, and the orange, two fruit servings. In this case one sort of precision is replaced by another. Although it is true that members don't count calories, they must measure portion sizes precisely.

The necessity of measuring and weighing foods causes tension and dissatisfaction. Members' notions of what constitutes a portion size frequently differ substantially from the organization's specified serving sizes. New members are commonly surprised, if not shocked, by how small a three-ounce chicken breast is, or how little pasta is in one cup. Standing in line behind a new member, I overheard her complain, "Last night I made a three-ounce burger, and it didn't even cover half the bun!" Re-educating oneself on appropriate portion sizes rests on the willingness and ability to carefully weigh and measure foods. One evening, near the end of the meeting, Peggy raised her hand and mused, "Even if I ever get to my goal, I don't know how I'll be able to stay there. I eat nothing but [the organization's] frozen meals at lunch and dinner. I don't know how to eat regular food anymore. You have to count everything, and it seems like a lot of work." Wendy responded, "It's not that bad. I have a lot of stuff memorized now. After a while you just kind of do it naturally, without even thinking about it." Wendy's response echoed Lisa' observation, that you have to measure everything until you "get a feel for how much an ounce is." Lisa and Wendy recognize that most people do not accurately judge portion sizes. However, they also imply that one can develop a feel for portion sizes and, at some point, can estimate them. Measuring and weighing food are not habits most people engage in on a regular basis. As such, members are most likely to be conscious of what they are doing in the beginning, as they change old habits and develop new ones. Initially weighing and measuring are more likely to feel like work, but will presumably become easier with time and practice. But Wendy's observation that "you just kind of do it naturally" is disturbing. While Peggy is aware that these are not "natural" ways of eating, Wendy suggests that members who buy into the program and adhere to the guidelines are successful to the extent that otherwise abnormal ways of relating to food come to be seen as entirely natural.

Weighing and measuring food are inconvenient for members. One evening while I was waiting in line to be weighed, Nancy was in line with her friend Anne. Nancy got a recipe book from the merchandise area. They were looking at the book and Anne said, "One of the things I hate about these recipes is that they don't tell you how much a serving is, so you have to divide it all up before you eat it." Frequently recipes specify how many servings the recipe makes, and note how many selections the serving counts for, but do not specify the quantity of an actual portion. If the recipe is for an easily divisible food, such as chicken breasts or sandwiches, it's not problematic. But in the case of casseroles or soup, the only solution, as noted by Anne, is to actually divide the food into the specified number of plates or bowls. It is even more frustrating when members eat out. Notoriously large restaurant portions, the impossibility of weighing and measuring food, and the difficulty of even knowing the ingredients of a particular menu item greatly undermine members' efforts to achieve precision. The organization has tried to accommodate members by converting portion sizes to more volume measures than weight. Presumably, pouring or spooning a food into a measuring cup is easier than weighing it on a scale, in part because most people own measuring spoons and cups. One of the more popular products available for sale by the organization is a set of serving spoons that are designed to hold exactly one-half or one cup of food, such as vegetables, potatoes, or soup. Leaders and receptionists frequently show the spoons to members and note that not only do they make it easier to measure food, they make it possible to measure food without anyone else at the table knowing what you're doing. The organization also provides members with hints and guidelines for estimating portion size. For example, a three-ounce chicken breast is approximately the size of the palm of your hand, and a one-ounce cube of cheese is roughly the size of the top of your thumb. Thus the organization continues to emphasize precisely measuring portion sizes, while recognizing that this is not always practical. One of the most popular pieces of merchandise available for purchase is a small booklet that lists the point values of a wide variety of foods at popular fast food restaurants.

If measuring and weighing food are important to achieve precision, even more so is scrupulous record keeping. Measuring and controlling portion size are insufficient if you don't control how many total portions you eat. Keeping meticulous records—recording everything you eat and checking off the number of selections and optional calories consumed—is the major strategy for controlling portion size and number. Each week members get a small pamphlet for recording everything they eat during the week. When Debbie asked the group what you find out by keeping scrupulous records of what you eat, Claudia said, "You can see what you're not getting enough of. I have trouble getting in my milks." Wendy said, "You can see where you're cheating." In both instances, they imply that carefully recording what you eat minimizes imprecision, which can result from eating too few or too many servings. A fairly frequent meeting topic is the necessity of recording absolutely everything you eat, including "bites and nibbles." Given the difficulty at times of estimating portion sizes, then translating them into the appropriate number of selections, my guess is that the intention is to discourage members from eating bites and nibbles. Still, I once watched in amazement as a member took a roll of breath mints from her purse, read the nutritional label on the package, and then recorded them in her food tracker.

The Payoff: Earning Your Keep

Hard workers who are committed, persistent, and productive expect to be paid for their efforts. But in the world of the weight loss group, where you pay to join, the payoff is much more abstract and ambiguous than a paycheck. Concrete rewards are minimal—stickers for weekly weight losses, exercising, and other small achievements; ribbons and gold stars for total losses in increments of five pounds; and a small gold lapel pin for reaching goal. Occasionally organizational promotions operate as a system of work bonuses. Members who attend a specified number of consecutive meetings can receive free products, such as a water bottle or a cookbook. In all cases, the monetary value of the items is small. The concrete rewards, however, are emblematic of the psychic rewards that the organization assumes motivate members to keep working. Psychic rewards take many forms, such as recognition from other people of one's efforts and success. Betty, whom we met earlier, was stuck within about five pounds of her goal weight range. Betty was visibly pleased and proud as she reported during celebration that just that morning she had unexpectedly run into a friend whom she had not seen in a while, who recognized that Betty had lost weight. The very point of celebration is to provide these psychic rewards. The value of a sticker that proclaims "I did it!" pales in comparison with the applause and recognition that accompany reported weight losses.

The most important psychical reward is the personal satisfaction that presumably comes from achieving a goal, analogous to the satisfaction that the good worker experiences from a job well done. But in the case of weight loss, the situation is more complicated. While a worker can often assume that a particular job or task will be completed, the weight-loser is not so sure. Betty is a case in point. At one meeting, Betty said, "This was my week to lose. I gained last week." She was four pounds away from her goal and wasn't sure she would ever get there. A couple of months later, as I arrived at a meeting, I saw Betty going in. After greeting me and asking me if I had made my goal yet, she sighed despondently and said, "I'll never make goal. I'm so tired of coming to meetings, but if I don't, I know what will happen." But the situation is further complicated. Even if a specific weight loss goal can be reached, in a sense the work never ends. Once members reach goal weight, they still face the task of maintaining their new weight. In a very real way, a weight-loser's work is literally never done. Even the satisfaction of meeting one's goal may be relatively short-lived.

Good workers also expect to be rewarded with promotions that bring greater material rewards. Promotion in a weight loss group is highly ambiguous, although it is not entirely unknown. A few, highly successful weight-losers may become employees of the organization, as either receptionists or leaders. Members who achieve particularly large losses are most likely to be targeted as potential employees, but these individuals appear to be tracked into positions as either leaders or receptionists on the basis of personality. While big losers are good role models and good organization representatives, leaders need a more outgoing personality. Wendy is a prime example. Ultimately losing almost one hundred pounds, Wendy is a highly successful weight-loser by organizational standards. She rarely missed meetings and was highly popular among both leaders and members. Actively participating in meeting discussions and activities, Wendy was, in fact, very outgoing. She frequently welcomed new members, initiated conversations with others before the meeting, and was open and engaging during group discussions. None of this was lost on Debbie, who urged Wendy to think about becoming a meeting leader as she approached her goal. About the time Wendy reached her goal she began training to become a meeting leader, and a month later, when Wendy was no longer attending weekly meetings, Debbie made a point of telling the group that Wendy had indeed become a leader and was leading a couple of meetings each week.

There is another, more subtle and ambiguous way that members experience promotion through their own ranks. Every meeting is characterized by a multidimensional status hierarchy among members. In his research on the small group movement in the United States, Wuthnow (1994) found that even Bible study groups often have a sort of spiritual pecking order, and that in general anything that a group values can be the basis of a hierarchy. In the weight loss group, one dimension of the hierarchy is regularity and persistence in meeting attendance. Members who attend regularly over some length of time are at the top of the hierarchy. Members who either attend very regularly for a limited amount of time until they reach their goal, or who make an effort to attend meetings fairly consistently over a longer period of time, fall in the middle. And members who attend irregularly, attend for a very short time and then drop out, or who show up to be weighed but leave before the meeting are at the bottom. Another dimension involves members' commitment to the program and willingness to actively participate in meetings. Members who grasp how the program works, are committed to following it, and who willingly talk about their experiences in front of the group are thought to have a high degree of expertise and insider knowledge, and are frequently called upon to share their expertise. While these bases of stratification are important, they interact with the third and most important dimension, the ability to lose weight. Adhering to the program and actively participating are important, but they mean little if you're not losing weight. The amount of weight lost clearly contributes to prestige and placement on the hierarchy. But ultimately the members who are most admired and who enjoy the most prestige are those who make demonstrable and steady progress toward their goal, no matter what the goal may be. Even members who attend regularly and talk frequently during meetings are viewed with a high degree of skepticism by other members, and are placed lower in the status hierarchy, if they don't consistently lose weight. Apparently, most members believe the program will work for anyone who works hard. Although Betty is well liked, and Debbie sometimes commends her for attending weekly, she is never held up as a success story or a role model. Rather than gaining sympathy, members who do not lose weight are assumed to be slacking off, not following the program, or not working hard enough. Thus they should not expect to reap the rewards.

Workers also expect vacations as part of their benefits. Time off from the job, and freedom from having to work, are positive rewards built into jobs. Vacations play a prominent role in the minds of weight-losers as well, but their meaning is much more ambiguous, and members' feelings about them are much more ambivalent. Literal vacations, such as trips or cruises, pose considerable problems for people trying to lose weight. Vacations are times to take a break from your normal routine, to do things you might not normally do, or conversely, to not do things you might otherwise feel compelled to do. Members expect eating habits, both how much is eaten and what is eaten, to change during vacations. As a result many members routinely expect to gain weight on vacation. When Jack said he was going to spend a holiday weekend on his boat with his wife and two friends, he referred to any attempt to prevent weight gain as a "lost cause." Six months after I joined the program, I spent five days in Florida. I gained one pound and noted in my fieldnotes that it was "not as bad as I thought it might be."

Vacations and holidays affect meeting attendance. Just as workers take off for a holiday, so do group members. Leaders recognize this and frequently offer and accept vacations and holidays as legitimate excuses for missing meetings. One evening a married couple, Suzanne and Joe, were at the meeting. They had come during the summer, stopped, and were now back. When Debbie asked them why they stopped coming, they had little to say. Debbie said, "The holidays?" and Joe responded, "That sounds good," and everyone laughed. At one of the first meetings I attended, seven members were present. Cheryl noted that there were a few more people at the meeting than there had been the last few weeks. She said that summer attendance always goes down, since people go on vacation and switch meeting times to accommodate changes in their schedules. Nowhere is this clearer than in the case of Estelle, a continuing member in her late sixties or early seventies. She joined with two friends, both of whom eventually reached their goal weights. Estelle experienced much more difficulty on the program, due in no small part to her lifestyle and vacations. Retired, and fairly recently remarried to a successful, retired businessman, Estelle traveled extensively. She frequently attended meetings for two or three weeks, then left for vacation, which could last anywhere from one to four weeks or more, depending on where she was going and the time of the year. Estelle's weight fluctuated accordingly. While she was home and attending meetings, she lost weight, but then subsequently gained several pounds while on vacation. Estelle repeated this pattern consistently and continually.

Members often discuss the difficulties posed by vacations, particularly in the spring and summer as they anticipate going on vacation and having to deal with the aftermath. Leaders remind members that they can attend meetings even on vacation. If they take their membership booklet with them and pay the cost of the meeting they attend, their membership will be honored. The regional newsletter lists all locations, days, and times for meetings in the area, and members traveling out of the region are urged to call an 800 number to get the locations and times of meetings in other locales. Only twice that I know of did members actually take advantage of this option. Members rarely attend meetings on vacation, in part due to the inconvenience but also due to the psychological association of vacations with relaxing and being free from your regular routine. Oddly enough, it is not unusual for members to lose weight while on vacation, only to gain it back after returning, or to gain some weight while vacationing, and then gain even more once they come back. On one occasion, Darla had just come back from vacationing in Hawaii. She had maintained her weight while on vacation, but had gained almost two pounds since coming home. Sandy referred to this as "vacation blues," and Cheryl concurred, saying, "It's often hard to get refocused after a vacation." If your activity level increases while vacationing, maintaining or even losing weight is not impossible. Furthermore, members may be particularly conscious of and sensitive to their eating patterns while vacationing, given the almost excessive attention paid to the eating risks involved. However, vacations have a psychological component as well. Even if a member is focused on staying on the program during vacation, it may be difficult to keep this up for any length of time.

Members also take figurative vacations by not following the program completely, working half-heartedly, or doing just enough work to get by. When Richard asked members what they would tell someone who had gone off the program after several good days, he implied that in some sense it is not possible to go off the program. Given the ranges of selections allowed, and the additional personal choices and optional calories, Richard suggested that occasional deviation from a strict interpretation of the plan could be tolerated over the long run. The point, however, was not clear to members. They operated on the assumption that these deviations do constitute going off the program, even if temporarily, and thus represent a vacation from the work of weight loss. A similar pattern was described by a lifetime member. Since she only weighed in once a month, Joan said, "I play games with five pounds," implying that she can gain about five pounds over the course of two or three weeks, but then lose it in the week or two before she has to weigh in. Joan has the skill of vacationing down to a fine art.

Bosses: Keeping Them on Track

If group members see themselves as workers, engaged in the work of following the program and losing weight, are group leaders the bosses for whom they work? In some sense, yes. Leaders occupy a different status than do members, and are more closely aligned to the organization. When leaders introduce themselves at the beginning of each meeting by stating how much total weight they have lost and how long they have kept it off, they highlight their status as successful, lifetime members. Also, since the meeting room is set up like a traditional classroom, leaders most frequently stand in the space at the front of the room. Even Richard and Linda, who move around the room, gravitate toward the front. Although the room is large enough, and the chairs easily movable, leaders never rearrange the chairs into a circle and actually sit with members, even at meetings with very low attendance. With the exception of Richard, leaders also emphasize their differences from members through their clothing, with professional business suits being the uniform of choice. Since most members wear as little clothing as possible, or at least wear very light clothing for weigh-in, leaders stand out from the rest of those at the meeting.

In some ways, leaders act like bosses. Leaders play a supervisory role: they call meetings to order, inform members of the discussion topic, and must communicate to members whatever information the organization determines to be important. Members know that leaders can request to see their weekly food trackers, especially if it appears that they are losing weight too rapidly. In actuality, leaders rarely ask to see a member's tracker, even though it is not uncommon for members to lose more than the prescribed one to two pounds per week. Conversely, members are more likely to request that leaders look at their trackers, frequently at the urging of receptionists, and usually because they are dissatisfied that they are not losing enough weight or are not losing it rapidly enough.

While the organization officially and formally gives leaders a supervisory capacity, and while leaders consciously or unconsciously use a number of strategies to differentiate themselves from members, leaders are limited in their roles as bosses. Bosses can keep workers on task and evaluate their performance only to the extent that workers' job descriptions are clear and their responsibilities are well defined and easily evaluated. But in the case of weight loss, goals are highly individual, frequently ambiguous even to members, and may very well change over time, sometimes repeatedly. The major role of leaders is not to evaluate, or even to supervise members' progress, but to support and motivate them as they move toward their personal goals. Leaders' roles as bosses are circumscribed since they are primarily socioemotional leaders, rather than instrumental, that is, task-oriented leaders. In fact, leaders' emphasis on providing socioemotional support may interfere with and impede their ability to be good instrumental leaders. Since the exchange of socioemotional support can lead to feelings of closeness and even friendship between members and leaders, it is sometimes hard for leaders to keep the group on task, particularly if it entails correcting or chastising members. This may be one reason why Debbie tolerates Joyce's frequent comparisons of herself with, and criticisms of, Peggy. Even though Joyce clearly violates group norms, Debbie usually ignores the comments or steers the discussion in a different direction.

Leaders' lack of real power exacerbates their reluctance to play the role of boss. Leaders have few sanctions, positive or negative, to either reward members for a job well done or to punish them for less than satisfactory work. Most important, unlike actual work supervisors, group leaders cannot actually observe the real work of weight loss. All leaders see is the output, that is, the number of pounds lost, and then only if members come to the meeting and volunteer the information. Leaders depend on highly self-motivated workers, that is, workers who are their own bosses. Members must keep track of and evaluate their own performance and progress, using the food trackers to meticulously document their work habits and the scale to receive immediate feedback. In a significant sense, the most successful weight-loser is the one who is self-employed.

Speaking of Work

The concept of work, like that of self-help, meshes well with a culture that venerates the self-made individual and a strong work ethic as a central virtue. Weight-losers who commit themselves to working toward a goal, and are persistent and disciplined in their efforts, expect to be amply rewarded. Indeed, if there is a central notion that animates the perspective of weight loss as work, it is that of discipline. Speaking of weight loss as work is significant in at least two ways. First, the human body figures prominently in the work metaphor, as it is the raw material upon which weight-losers work. In this sense, dieting is akin to cosmetic surgery and bodybuilding.

Second, like other types of work, weight loss is subject to increasingly strong and pervasive trends toward rationalization.

Objectifying the Body

As group members see themselves as workers, engaged in the work of weight loss, their primary tool is dieting. This tool is directed at and used upon the body. Members aim their efforts and energy at producing a body that conforms to a societal ideal of acceptable body size and shape. In contrast to traditional forms of fashion that attended to predominantly external appearances and what was put on the body (Seid 1994), now the body itself is manipulated and worked upon. As members speak of weight loss as work, they simultaneously objectify their bodies. The body becomes separated from the self and transformed into a lump of matter that can literally be worked into the desired shape, given enough persistence, energy, and hard work. Both men and women can see their bodies as objects, but there are important gender differences in how these processes play out. Compared with men, women are more conscious of and less satisfied with particular body parts, such as their hips and thighs (Jackson, Sullivan, and Hymes 1987). Bartky (1988) points out that "spot-reducing" seems to be a peculiarly female enterprise. Indeed, women are taught to objectify themselves from an early age, given the great significance placed on women's physical appearance as an indicator of not only their health but their overall worth (Spitzack 1990).

Nowhere are these gender dynamics in body objectification more dramatic than in the arena of cosmetic surgery. Cosmetic surgery is a five-billion-dollar-a-year industry, and while men's rates are increasing, women account for the majority of cosmetic surgery patients in every racial category (Hesse-Biber 1996; Kaw 1998). In 1998, over one million cosmetic surgery procedures were performed in the United States, of which 91 percent were performed on women (American Society of Plastic Surgeons 1998). Liposuction was the most common procedure among both men and women, but women accounted for 88 percent of the procedures. In addition, women accounted for 97 percent of buttock lifts, 91 percent of thigh lifts, 95 percent of tummy tucks, and 98 percent of upper arm lifts (American Society of Plastic Surgeons 1998). Of the twenty-four types of cosmetic surgery tracked by the American Society of Plastic Surgeons, with the exception of breast reduction in men, all were more common among women than men.

Cosmetic surgery, like dieting, is in the majority of cases an elective procedure, undertaken not to correct physiological deficiencies or to prevent real health threats, but to improve one's outward appearance (Adams 1997; Spitzack 1990). In the case of cosmetic surgery, "[surgeons] examine their patients as a technician diagnosing ways to improve a mechanical object" (Kaw 1998:176), and increasingly women are socialized into accepting surgically invasive procedures as a legitimate way to enhance their appearance (Morgan 1991). Women's acceptance of cosmetic surgery, as well as their continual participation in dieting and weight loss efforts, rests on the ability to transform the body into little more than a material object.

Bodybuilders similarly attempt to literally mold the body into a particular shape, one with a very high degree of muscular definition (Ewen 1988; Fisher 1997; Heywood 1997; Moore 1997; Schulze 1997). Weights are the tools used to achieve this body, and the process requires tremendous discipline and effort, that is, hard work. Discussing female bodybuilding, Moore (1997:78) comments: "Built bodies are literally built. The female bodybuilder's goal is to create a body, or, in common metaphor, to sculpt a body. Bodybuilders frequently view their bodies as living works of art, and they set out to achieve the perfect form by chiseling their quads or rounding their calves." Bodybuilding shares several important characteristics with dieting. Both enterprises rest on the presumed plasticity of the body, the notion that the human body can be molded and constructed into a desired shape (Heywood 1997; Schulze 1997). Like weight-losers particularly concerned with spot-reducing, bodybuilders similarly fragment their bodies into separate and distinct parts in their emphasis on muscle definition. And like the dieter who sees no end in sight, the bodybuilder is never quite satisfied with the results (Fisher 1997).

Weight loss, cosmetic surgery, and bodybuilding dramatically illustrate the objectification of the body. In all three cases, rather than being naturally beautiful, the body is conceptualized as a lump of matter that actually interferes with, obscures, or hides not only the person's attractiveness but also who the person really is. In the arena of weight loss, before-and-after testimonials, complete with dramatic photographic evidence of the physical transformation of the weight-loser, often convey this message. But these testimonials are particularly significant since they frequently suggest that personal transformation accompanies the physical change. One of the professional female bodybuilders interviewed by Fisher (1997:151) is quoted as saying, "[Bodybuilding] taught me a lot about myself and it helped me like myself better. It also makes me proud, most of the time, to remember that I have accomplished something. . . . like there was something I was working toward and I was able to do it and have success from it and recognition." Much like the cosmetic surgeon who promises to discover the beautiful person hidden inside the defective body, weight-losers testify to finding their "real selves" hidden inside the fat body. After losing nearly one hundred pounds over the course of two years, Hope told the group, "It took a long time, but I'm here. I made it. You know, I didn't really like the person I was before. Before I lost all the weight. But I'm a different person now. I'm not the same person I was. I like who I am now."

Measuring Up

If weight loss is work, and dieting is the tool used upon the objectified body, how do we know when our work is done, or even if we're doing a good job in the meantime? The concept of weight loss as work rests on the assumption that the good body can be defined and recognized and, most important, that it can be reliably and quantitatively measured. Although there are numerous ways to measure the good body, including mirrors, the fit of your clothes, photographs, comparisons with other women, or getting attention from men (Hesse-Biber 1996), for many women the ultimate measure of success is the number on the scale. The assumption is attractive in its simplicity, and meshes well with a highly rationalized culture, enamored of quantification and calculability. The argument goes like this: first, weight can be precisely and reliably measured. Second, there is an ideal body weight range that can be clearly and specifically defined for everyone. Third, there is a quantifiably demonstrable relationship between body weight and various measures of health, which themselves can be reliably and quantitatively measured.

Despite its simplicity and appeal, the argument fails on every count. The ability to precisely measure weight seems self-evident. You step on a scale and see a number that presumably represents your actual body weight. In reality, scales vary considerably in their precision, and body weight itself fluctuates, even over relatively short amounts of time. Furthermore, it is problematic to assume that there is an ideal weight range that fits everyone. The ideal ranges themselves have been revised, sometimes up and sometimes down, as new research and medical knowledge call into question the old ranges. Finally, it is highly problematic to continue to equate thinness with health. Evidence from medical research is inconsistent, hotly debated, and suggests that enhanced health may actually be associated with moderate over-weight (Cogan 1999). Moreover, equating thinness and health ignores cultural influences on both body weight and physical wellbeing.

Belief in the measurability of the good body is less a function of reality and more a function of the cultural belief that anything can be reliably and precisely reduced to and reflected by quantitative measures. Ritzer (1996, 1999) argues that increasing rationalization, a major component of which is calculability or quantification, is a historical, worldwide trend, most strongly evidenced in the United States. In the realms of fast food and other means of consumption examined by Ritzer, such as shopping malls, catalogs, and superstores, calculabil-ity is expressed as an emphasis on quantity and the reduction of ser-vice to numbers. Although it takes a slightly different form, calculability pervades the language and practice of weight loss. The emphasis on large quantities is apparent when members report how much weight they have lost in a week and when leaders highlight how much total weight particular members have lost. But calculability is most evident in the organization's attempt to reduce all aspects of weight loss to numerical representations. Weight is measured and reported in incre-ments of two-tenths of a pound; food is reduced to a point value based on calorie, fat, and fiber content; and exercise is represented by the num-ber of calories burned or number of food points earned. Weight-losers are not alone in this regard. In her study of professional female body-builders, Fisher (1997:139) found that "monitoring caloric intake, caloric burn, sleep per night, and the number of repetitions performed during a weight-training exercise was described by professional body-builders as a necessity, because their livelihood depended upon accu-rate monitoring of their bodies." One of the bodybuilders interviewed by Fisher (1997:145) suggested that bodybuilders can be distinguished from nonbodybuilders by "the degree of intensity, the amount of time that we put into looking the way we do, which means that our lifestyle is more bodybuilding-oriented than a person that comes in [the gym] three times a week to train, like a hobby. That person does not prob-ably weigh and measure everything that they put in their mouth." Although it may be true that the average person doesn't weigh and mea-sure everything he or she eats, the average weight-loser probably does.

Related to the rationalization and calculability of the weight loss process is the standardization of the human body. Weight loss, body-building, and cosmetic surgery all rest on the assumption that there is an ideal standardized body to which people are expected to conform. The notion of ideal weight ranges implies that there is a relatively narrow ideal to which everyone can legitimately aspire. For bodybuilders, the ideal body is that which in its muscular definition resembles the detail and precision of an anatomy chart (Ewen 1988). Even more insidious is the similarly quantified, ideal face used by cosmetic surgeons, that "symbolizes a desire for standardized ideals of Caucasian beauty" (Balsamo 1996:62). With the advent of technological imaging devices, cosmetic surgeons can immediately transform, via a computer screen, anyone's face to reflect the standardized ideals. The next step is to surgically mold the face into an approximation of the ideal. In all three cases, the good worker is the one who accepts the legitimacy of the end goal, and who evidences the discipline required to reach it. The logic becomes even more strongly moralistic when combined with religious prescriptions.

5 | "The Body Is a Temple"

At a meeting in the spring, shortly before Easter, Debbie had written on the blackboard, "Goals for the Holidays. Do I Want to: Lose Weight, Maintain, or Gain Weight?" Debbie was wearing a little apron and holding a silver serving tray. She walked over to Claudia, and said, "Here, wouldn't you like another hors d'oeuvre? I know how much you enjoy them. Have another!" Claudia shook her head, and said, "No." Debbie moved on to Jennifer and said, "I made this special dessert just for you because I know how much you like it." Jennifer promptly replied, "No, thanks." Then Debbie approached Estelle and said, "I noticed how much you enjoyed the dinner I made, so I wrapped up the leftovers for you to take home, so you can have them later." Estelle enthusiastically responded, "OK!" and everyone laughed.

The discussion that evening focused on difficult situations, commonly encountered during the holidays. Debbie referred to "red-light foods," those that are difficult to eat in small amounts. Several people mentioned chocolate, and Connie complained, "Everywhere you go, people have out dishes filled with brightly colored chocolates." Carolyn agreed, and said, "I won't have it in my house, but the trouble comes when someone else has it." Debbie asked for possible strategies to handle this situation. Connie suggested, "You could take something else with you that you could eat, so you won't be as tempted." Debbie said, "At work they know I love chocolate, so every day they set out one piece of candy on my desk, and that's all I eat." More than one member seemed incredulous at the idea that Debbie could know the chocolate was there and still eat just one piece.

Several people said that their red lights occur in social situations. Audrey said cocktails exacerbated the problem because they increased her appetite. Jayne said, "At work we used to go out for beer and to get something to eat probably at least three times a week. When I started [the program] I had to just stop going. It was easier for me that way." Jill said, "Going out socially is really hard. The worst part is that I feel like I'm depriving myself. And I really resent that I can't eat what everyone else is eating." In response to Jill, one member suggested taking a small serving of a food like potato chips, and then moving completely away from the food table, and another proposed rotating alcohol with nonalcoholic beverages. Jill didn't seem all that comforted or encouraged by the suggestions.

The concepts of self-help and work ultimately rationalize weight loss. In the weight loss-as-work model, the emotional trappings that surround weight loss are removed, revealing the concrete steps you have to take to achieve your goal. In the weight loss-as-self-help model, the potential exists to recognize and confront the emotional aspects of weight loss, since providing emotional support is the focus. And yet the ultimate purpose of the support provided is to help people get down to the real work, that is, to do what they have to do to lose weight. The self-help and work frameworks are clearly operating in the discussion of red-light foods. Intertwined, however, is another language, in which emotions play a larger role, although they are frequently seen as dangerous and in need of control. It is the metaphor of weight loss as religion.

Religious references, some more direct than others, occur frequently as group members discuss the challenges of losing weight. Temptation, sacrifice, and guilt are common themes. Though rarely mentioned explicitly, notions of sin lie close to the surface as food and eating are dichotomized into good and bad. Because temptation is omnipresent, the threat of falling from grace is constant. But at the same time, no matter how pervasive religious language is, dieting is not a religion. Consequently the religious model is not complete. The group and its members choose those elements of the concept that not only make sense, but are also compatible with the concepts of self-help and work. As a result group members emphasize those elements of the religious metaphor that mesh most easily with notions of discipline and self-control, and tend to downplay the more emotional, irrational, and transcendent elements of religion.

The discussion of red-light foods illustrates how the religious perspective operates. The very terminology "red-light foods" has interesting connotations. At this meeting, and at another meeting before Christmas, when the same topic is discussed, Debbie uses the term in the sense of a red traffic light. When the light flashes red, it communicates a clear warning to stop. Thus with red-light foods, you should stop before even beginning to eat them. Similarly, red lights warn of danger, and so red-light foods pose a threat to those who eat them; in this case, the danger involves eating too much. But the red light connotes not just physical danger but the danger of immorality. The infamous "red-light district" is associated with temptation, deviance, and sinfulness. Similarly, the dangers evoked by red-light foods are less a matter of simply overeating, and speak more to an apparent fall from grace, that is, giving in to temptation that leads one down the path of sinfulness. When Debbie solicits concrete examples of red-light foods, members name chocolate and alcohol as well as social situations where these red-light foods are most easily available, and the temptation greatest.

If the discussion of red-light foods is filled with references, some subtler than others, to danger, fear, temptation, and troubling emotions, the discussion of responses to tempting foods and situations is anything but emotional. One clear strategy is to remove the temptation, either by refusing to have the foods in the house or by avoiding situations where they are commonly found. A second strategy is to take the situation into your own hands and volunteer to bring an alternative, a healthy food or snack. A variation on this theme is to fortify yourself to better resist temptation. Members are told to eat something else, such as salad, before the situation, so that presumably they will be less hungry when faced with problematic foods. An additional strategy is to indulge in the red-light food, but only in clearly and strictly rationed amounts, for example, one piece of chocolate per day, or one alcoholic beverage to every one nonalcoholic beverage consumed.

Despite variations in the strategies and in individuals' preferences for some over others, all are highly practical and rational responses to complicated, emotion-filled situations. When Estelle enthusiastically gives in to temptation during Debbie's simulation, the incident provides comic relief. But nowhere during the entire discussion does anyone mention that many red-light foods are highly pleasurable and that the experience of eating them can be viewed as such. Rather, they are transformed into dangerous substances that somehow have to be restricted, resisted, or avoided. Jill feels that she cannot eat the same foods, nor eat in the same ways, that other people can eat. But her feelings of deprivation and resentment are totally ignored. Even more distressing is the matter-of-fact way that Jayne says she has simply stopped going out with co-workers after work. No one questions the reasonableness of giving up clearly satisfying and enjoyable social relations and companionship for the sake of losing weight. Rather, the implication is that Jayne got her priorities straight and chose the right path. The major elements of a weight loss concept that draws heavily, often explicitly, on the language and symbolism of religion are embodied in this discussion.

To begin the examination of how the religious metaphor operates, the first section of this chapter considers conversion. Although the majority of group members do not undergo a conversion experience, they do frequently change their perspectives, sometimes radically, regarding food, eating, and weight loss. Next, the chapter considers the four areas where the religious model is strongest. First, temptation is a frequent topic of discussion. Second, if the dieter's primary goal is to resist temptation, it is not surprising that references to sacrifice and deprivation are common. Third, since humans are not perfect, giving in to temptation is inevitable. Consequently, guilt, confession, and forgiveness are important dynamics underlying much of what occurs in the group's discussion and celebration. Fourth, sin may be inevitable, but from the group's point of view, there is no need to leave it unchecked. Surveillance emerges as a critical tool for keeping members in line. The next section examines several elements of the religious perspective that seemingly hold the potential to capture the more irrational, emotional aspects of weight loss. But their potential is tempered as the group emphasizes those elements that most easily mesh with its overriding rational approach to losing weight. First, as members try to explain unexpected weight gains, they combine strong beliefs in the fundamental mystery and unpredictability of the human body with seemingly scientific explanations of human physiology. Second, to the extent that dieters see weight gain and loss as uncontrollable, they at times resort to magic and superstition as ways to relieve anxiety and regain some measure of control. Third, we consider the very limited ways that taboos operate in the group. The chapter ends with a discussion of the major implications of the religion concept. With its emphasis on good and evil, it introduces a significant degree of morality into the weight loss process. As it is used in the group, the metaphor also captures the tension between the potential for ritual and community building, and the ultimate isolation and individualization of the weight-loser. Finally, the emotional aspects of weight loss are diminished as the religious concept interacts with and is affected by larger societal trends of rationalization, commercialism, and the spread of a scientific perspective.

Seeing the Light: Conversion

For some individuals, religious commitment results from a conversion experience. It may take a variety of forms and vary substantially from person to person, but usually results in a conscious commitment to a new way of seeing things. Commitment to a new diet or a new way of eating can be conceptualized similarly, and for some individuals, the result can be a rather sudden and dramatic turnaround. For one member in particular, religious conversion was more than a metaphor for her conversion to the weight loss program; her dieting conversion coincided with her actual religious conversion. Three weeks after joining the group, I noticed an extremely large woman, whom I didn't recognize from previous meetings. Several regulars greeted her as "Lois." She was talking to Amy and at some point in the conversation, Lois said, "The Lord has really helped me. . . . You know the body is a temple. I really believe that."

Later in the meeting, Richard asked Lois to share her story with the group. Lois said she weighed over four hundred pounds when she started the program, and had to stay attached to an oxygen tank at all times. She said, "I couldn't get in or out of my house without help, because I couldn't do stairs. The landlord wouldn't let us put up a permanent ramp, because he said he didn't want people to think he had a bunch of handicapped people living in the house." When Lois's family rigged up something with concrete blocks, neighborhood kids took them and broke them. But another group member, Jean, had gotten some bricks, and they were able to put something up so Lois could get out of the house to walk. After a short while Lois discovered that she could do without the oxygen. Lois said, "I went back to my doctor and told him I'm cured. I don't need the oxygen anymore. He didn't believe me, so he tested my blood gasses and he was amazed to find out that I didn't need the oxygen anymore." Richard asked her to stand up and do what she had done for him earlier. Lois stood up and pulled on the sides of her dress to show that it was hanging loose, and said, "I lost over eighty pounds so far. When I started, this dress was skintight, and I couldn't bend over to pull it down. Somebody had to pull it down for me." Lois attributed her success to the support she received from Richard and his wife, Eileen, an organization receptionist. When Lois first met Richard, she said, "I thought he was a phony."

Referring to Richard's before-weight-loss picture, she continued, "I couldn't believe he was the same person in the picture. The person in that picture obviously enjoyed food!" Lois also said she hadn't believed in God, but about the same time she started going to meetings, she "found the Lord," which she also attributed to Richard and Eileen. Throughout Lois's story members applauded, often interjected "that's terrific!" or "great!" and otherwise showed their approval and amazement at her story. It was all very inspiring.

Lois sees the religious and dieting changes in her life as inextricably intertwined. First, at the beginning of her story, Lois is close to being "lost," both spiritually and physically. Having to carry oxygen with her underlined the grave threat that her weight posed to her health and well-being. In addition, the great lengths taken to rig up a ramp system highlight Lois's extreme social isolation owing to her inability to leave her house. But by the end of the story, Lois has been "saved." Second, Lois constructs her ability to shed the oxygen tank as a rather miraculous cure. She does not draw a direct connection between exercise and enhanced health. In her tone of voice and the context of the story, Lois implies that dispensing with the oxygen is one concrete sign of the dramatic transformation she has experienced. In recounting her physician's skepticism at her pronouncement that she was cured, Lois poses a conflict between her faith on the one hand and the rationality of medical science on the other. In Lois's mind faith is the clear victor. Finally, Lois explicitly connects her religion and her weight loss when she attributes both her religious and her dieting conversions to the influence of the evangelizers, Richard and Eileen.

Lois's story is not typical, on either religious or dieting grounds. A majority of people, even those highly committed to a particular religion or religious belief system, do not experience conversion. Most people are born into, and subsequently grow into, a religion. Even when an individual changes religions, in many if not most cases it is a conscious choice in the context of a relatively rational decision-making process, rather than a dramatic conversion experience. Similarly, in the United States women are raised from a very early age to see dieting and attention to weight loss as a normal and acceptable way of living. Even those individuals who experience a dramatic turnaround with respect to dieting and weight loss rarely connect the changes with a religious conversion. Nonetheless, strong religious overtones color the conceptualization and discussion of weight loss, with significant implications for the ways that individuals visualize and understand the causes and consequences of being overweight.

Good versus Evil:
The Religious Metaphor

The ever-present struggle between good and evil, or between the sacred and the profane (Spitzak 1990), animates the religious concept of weight loss. The religious model is easily recognized in popular culture. A single individual is literally split into a good person, represented by an angel, complete with white gown and halo, and a bad person, represented by the devil, bedecked in horns and tail. With these characters perched on opposite shoulders of the person caught in the middle, the battle lines are drawn. All that is left is to wait to see which side emerges victorious. In the context of weight loss, the battle between good and evil is similarly played out.

One week the informational topic was "being your own best friend," which Richard said meant taking care of yourself and your needs. He put in a videotape which he said would introduce us to "Gail, who is just arriving home from a long day's work and is getting ready to sit down to her favorite pastime—dinner!" As the video begins, Gail arrives home from work. Her place set for dinner, Gail is just sitting down to eat when the phone rings. She answers, and apparently it's someone from the office who needs Gail's help with a computer problem. She begins to talk him through the problem and at the same time begins to nibble on a cake that's sitting on the table. At the end of the phone conversation, the person tells Gail she can enjoy her dinner now and, looking down, she realizes that she has eaten nearly the entire cake. At this point, a member exclaimed, "Oh my gosh, she ate the whole thing!" Amy turned to me and said quietly, "I've done that before." When Gail gets off the phone, she's very upset, chides herself for really blowing it, and obviously feels very guilty.

At this point in the video, another Gail appears, who represents the negative voice inside her. The negative Gail points out that since Gail ate almost the whole cake, she might as well go ahead and finish it. The positive Gail now makes an appearance, and tells her that she doesn't have to eat it; she can throw the rest out. Gail struggles with the two voices for a while, but eventually, realizing that the positive voice is the real Gail, she banishes the negative Gail. The video ends by displaying the slogan, "Be your own best friend." As Richard stopped the video, one member commented, "I liked that," and another said, "That was really good!" Richard asked if there was anything in the video people could identify with, but then immediately switched to the question of what Gail might have done differently. Members suggested that Gail didn't have to answer the phone, or she could turn on the answering machine. Jean said, "She could've told the person on the phone she'd call him back after she was done eating." But Richard was getting at something else, as he asked, "Why did Gail have the cake there to begin with?" Lori said Gail lived alone, and Richard asked, "How do you know she lives alone?" Melissa said, "Even if there's someone else in the house they don't need to be eating it either." But Richard was making another point, having to do with self-control. He said, "My weakness is potato chips, but I don't struggle with potato chips, except when I'm walking down the street on vacation in Nashville. I never eat potato chips anymore, except I plan on it when I know I'm going to a wedding, because I haven't been to a wedding yet where they've handed out bags of raw celery."

The videotape and ensuing discussion are remarkable for several reasons. Consonant with the metaphor of the battle between good and evil, the character in the video is split into two separate, warring selves. Particularly significant is the meaning of good and bad. The bad self gives in to temptation and loses control. The good self not only maintains sufficient self-control to withstand temptation, but feels the appropriate guilt and remorse when self-control is lost. Ultimately the solution to the ongoing battle is to remove the temptation.

As the battle between good and evil is played out, the message of the video, "be your own best friend," is subtly stretched and twisted to fit the religious metaphor. Taking care of yourself and your own needs is a positive message, and one that can have a particularly powerful effect on women, who are frequently socialized to put others' needs before their own. But in the context of weight loss, taking care of yourself is intertwined with exerting self-control, so attending to your own needs becomes subtly equated with self-deprivation. Saying no is a powerful technique of self-assertion and self-preservation. But in this case, to what, or to whom, are you saying no? Members viewing the videotape immediately pick up on and respond to the stress that Gail is feeling as a result of other people's demands on her time and energy. Members' strategies for dealing with the situation directly address the source of stress, particularly by telling others no, either by not answering the phone at all or by agreeing to help, but on one's own terms, that is, after dinner. But in keeping with the religious framework so pronounced in the video, Richard redirects and refocuses members' attention to why the tempting food is there to begin with. Consequently, the villains are not demanding people and the stress they cause, but tempting food, which leads to losing self-control. Saying no means refusing food, and "being your own best friend" means protecting yourself from temptation, rather than from exploitation by others. In this five-minute video and the related discussion, we see the most central elements of the religious metaphor: temptation, sacrifice, guilt, and surveillance.

Temptation

In a world where good and evil do constant battle, temptation is everywhere, so it is no surprise that resisting temptation is a frequent topic of group discussions, particularly around holidays. When Debbie dons her apron and pretends to tempt members with food at an imagined social event, members readily identify with the situation. And for the most part, they play their roles well, one after the other saying no, maintaining self-control, and withstanding temptation—until Estelle, coaxed to take home leftovers, enthusiastically accepts the offer, much to the amusement of other members. The incident provides comic relief and clearly hits a responsive chord, but what does it mean? What is its message?

On one level, being bad is equated with giving in to sensual pleasure, in this case, the sensual pleasure of food. To resist temptation you must deny yourself that pleasure. But it goes deeper. Much as the battle between good and evil is drawn in stark, black-and-white contrasts, so are the choices that weight-losers face. You give into temptation, or you don't. You maintain control, or you lose it entirely. The simple choice that members face when tempted by imaginary food is to entirely abstain, or completely give in and overindulge. Any possibility of a middle ground is lost, which is particularly striking given that the organization preaches moderation.

The apparent contradiction becomes clearer when compared with similar vices with which people struggle. From a religious perspective, alcohol and sexuality have posed the gravest threats, and despite their differences, both have been dealt with in quite similar ways, either through abstinence or through moderation. With respect to alcohol, conservative, fundamentalist religions often severely restrict, if not ban altogether, alcohol consumption. Sexuality is more complicated, given the need to reproduce. Religious groups solve the problem by either restricting the expectation of abstinence to a select group of people, such as clergy, or more commonly by restricting and delimiting the circumstances under which sexual behavior is acceptable. Less conservative religious groups usually advocate reasonable moderation, and expect individuals to know their personal weaknesses, that is, those things that are likely to be most tempting and most likely to lead them down the path of evil.

Like sex, food poses particular difficulties in the battle against evil. Fasting is in some ways analogous to abstinence from alcohol and sexuality, and several authors have explored the interrelationships between fasting, religion, gender, and eating disorders (Bell 1985; Brumberg 1988; Bynum 1987). Ultimately, however, people cannot do without food for any length of time. For the average person, moderation is the more reasonable approach, and so the message is that eating per se doesn't cause problems, but overindulging, that is, losing control, does. But in the scenario above, abstinence is preached, though only with regard to certain, specific foods. Food is divided into good foods and bad foods. Bad food leads to the sins of overindulgence and loss of self-control (Hesse-Biber 1996). For group members, red-light foods pose the greatest danger. Supposedly, red-light foods vary from one person to another, and the key is to know your weaknesses. In reality, there is a short list of common red-light foods. Chocolate leads the list, followed closely by alcohol and high-fat, salty foods like potato chips. The potential sinfulness of red-light foods extends to the situations in which they are often eaten, including parties, weddings, and holiday celebrations.

The Road to Righteousness:
Sacrifice and Deprivation

The dieter who withstands temptation is willing and able to deprive herself of desirable foods. The association of dieting with deprivation is pervasive. According to popular understanding, if overeating causes weight gain, then food restriction causes weight loss. In the name of losing weight, you deprive yourself of pleasurable foods and experiences, but the sacrifice pays off, as pounds are lost. New members occasionally express surprise if they follow the program and aren't hungry, which was particularly common when the organization instituted the fat and fiber plan. One week, Debbie asked new members how they liked the plan, and the consensus was that not only was it easy, but more important, they weren't hungry. Lou said, "I was really full. I couldn't believe how much I ate, but I still lost seven and a half pounds [in one week]. A diet's not supposed to feel like this." By implication, a diet is *supposed* to feel like hunger.

The organization's message on deprivation is complex and ambiguous. On the one hand, people hoping to lose weight clearly have to give up something, if not by eating significantly less food, at least by eating different foods than they have previously eaten. On the other hand, deprivation is unpleasant and hard to maintain over any significant length of time, especially in the absence of concrete rewards.

Lauren, who lost one and a half pounds during her first week on the plan, was disappointed with the loss. She complained, "I basically ate rice and peas all week; I didn't have time for anything else." The prospect of eating nothing but rice and peas is not appealing under any circumstances, but particularly when the payoffs don't outweigh the sacrifice. Yo-yo dieting and rapid turnover in weight loss groups are the predictable results. The organization responds with a rather odd message: you don't have to deprive yourself to lose weight; no foods are off-limits. When Richard suggests that it's not possible to go off the program, or when Cheryl solicits last supper stories from members to demonstrate how fast food can be incorporated into the weight loss program, the organization's official line is clear: there's nothing you can't eat. The line is repeated often and, in many ways, represents what Spitzack (1990) calls "antidiets," plans for losing weight that are supposedly not diets.

Not having to deprive yourself sounds good in theory, but reality is more complex. It is true that you can eat fast food on the program, but it is highly unlikely that you can eat the same items in the same quantities that you ate before joining and still lose weight. The women who share their fast food success stories clearly made changes, if not sacrifices. They either ate some foods instead of others, ate less, or ate in different ways, habits that are widely shared. One evening during celebration, Judy reported that she lost four pounds while vacationing in Florida. When Debbie asked what she had done to lose it, Judy replied, "We walked. My daughter and I watched each other. We never really splurged, except one night we went out for greasy hamburgers, but we took our napkins and blotted off the grease." In this case, Judy took multiple steps to prevent weight gain while on vacation, including altering her food by trying to remove the grease.

Altering food or substituting a "better" food for the one that's desired is a commonplace response to the need to sacrifice, one that simultaneously minimizes the sense of deprivation. At the beginning of one meeting, Debbie had on an apron and she greeted the group by saying, "Hi, I'm from Gertie's Home Cooking Restaurant. We have fried chicken and everything homemade from scratch." Debbie asked the group how we would feel about being somewhere like that. Betty laughed and said, "I'd love every bite of it. I love that food! But really, I'd rather not be there if I had a choice." This led to a discussion of common substitutions that can be made to make food healthier. Debbie asked for substitutions for foods she had listed on the flip chart: sour cream, sausage, light cream, butter, sugar, and cooking oil. Members suggested yogurt, low-fat or nonfat products, or using less than was called for in a particular recipe. Debbie asked, "How do you think your families would react? Would they be able to tell?" Everyone indicated they wouldn't, but the suggestion that ground turkey could be substituted for sausage or ground beef provoked Connie to say, "No way! No turkey for me." Betty said, "A dietician told me that unless you go to the butcher, pick out a boneless breast, remove all the skin and ask them to grind it, it has as much fat as ground beef." Debbie had a recipe for lasagna on the flip chart, and we went through and offered healthier substitutions for the ingredients. She then told us to take out our trackers, write down a food we would be cooking that week, and suggest substitutions we could make. She gave us a couple of minutes and then asked someone to share. Betty said she was making a rump roast for friends who were moving. She was going to cook it ahead, and then refrigerate it, so she could skim the fat off before using the broth for gravy.

In this context, the organization's position that there's nothing you can't eat takes on a new meaning. When faced with the prospect of traditional home cooking, Betty's first response is that she would love it, but on second thought, she suggests that the best choice is to choose not to be at the restaurant in the first place, thus avoiding temptation. The subsequent group discussion reinforces this as a wise choice. To the extent that substitutions can be made, members themselves will make them as they cook. Presumably, Gertie won't be substituting evaporated skim milk for the heavy cream in her gravy. Betty can choose to eat traditional home cooking if she wants, but it is best if she eats it at home, rather than in a restaurant, and only after she has consciously altered it in any of a number of ways to make it a better choice.

With respect to sacrifice and deprivation, members differ from the organization in their use of the religious concept. Traditionally, sacrifice plays a central role in religion. In the Judeo-Christian tradition, the Bible is filled with stories of extraordinary sacrifice, including that of Abraham, who is willing to sacrifice his son, and of Jesus, who sacrifices his life. On a more mundane level, followers are often expected to sacrifice certain activities in the name of religion. Tithing, whereby church members pledge a certain percentage of their income to the church, at times requires a considerable sacrifice. In many cases, religion involves sacrificing certain pleasurable activities, including food consumption. At times the sacrifice is restricted to specific time periods, as when Catholics were previously prohibited from eating meat on Fridays, or when Christians "give up" something for Lent. At other times, the proscription involves food that is not to be consumed at all, whether it be alcohol, beef, pork, or some other food. Given the strong cultural association between dieting and deprivation, it is not surprising that group members see sacrifice as a central component of their weight loss efforts. This is most obvious when members first join, as they readily generate long lists of foods they assume they will have to give up. But even longtime members speak frequently of depriving themselves of foods they previously enjoyed. For members, the association between diets and deprivation is hard to shake. In contrast to members' views, sacrifice is one component of the religious perspective that the organization actively attempts to downplay. Faced with mounting evidence that diets don't work, the organization wholeheartedly tries to distance itself from diets by employing a discourse of healthy eating and a focus on lifestyle modification. The organization's explicit message is that weight loss does not require deprivation. Yet members do not entirely internalize the message.

Giving In to Temptation:
Guilt and Forgiveness

Given the discomfort of deprivation and almost endless temptation, there is plenty of guilt to go around. This is one area where there is some tension between the concepts of self-help and religion. In her study of contemporary self-help books, Simonds (1992) argues that self-acceptance and self-love are common themes. Guilt is viewed as not only unnecessary but detrimental to one's physical and psychological well-being. As it is used in the weight loss group, the self-help model downplays past transgressions and negative emotions, and instead highlights positive steps that members can take toward healthier and more satisfying ways of living. But it is clear that many members experience guilt on a regular basis.

Members' concerns with cheating and guilt are especially striking since the organization insists that no foods are forbidden. What does it mean to cheat, if nothing is off-limits? One obvious response is that the organization's position is a marketing ploy, and as such is not true. But a more meaningful response is that the organization's statement is not entirely accurate, but largely due to omission, rather than commission. A more accurate rendition would read, "No foods are forbidden, as long as you limit yourself to the appropriate portion size and quantity, and as long as you write everything down, so that if necessary, you can compensate for overindulgences." What this statement gains in accuracy, it clearly loses in attractiveness. The reality is an ambiguous mix of being able to eat whatever you want, as long as you alter it to fit the program. From the organization's perspective, cheating doesn't necessarily mean eating forbidden foods. Cheating involves not playing completely by the rules.

Members largely share this view of cheating, although it is somewhat more complex. When Peggy finally lost two pounds after several unsuccessful weeks on the program, Debbie asked her what she had done differently. Peggy admitted that she had finally used her tracker to record everything she ate. Sheepishly, she said, "I'm embarrassed to admit it now, but this is the first time I've done it. . . . I could really see what I was eating and how I had been cheating before." Similarly, one evening when Debbie asked the group why tracking what you eat is beneficial, a member replied, "You can see where you're cheating." The prospect of getting caught cheating by others, and the resultant guilt, also came up in conversations. It is not coincidental that when the meeting topic was food secrets, the issue of hiding food from other people was a prominent theme. Linda began the discussion by telling members that she regularly snuck donuts from the break room at work so that co-workers would not see her eating them. When Linda asked members why they thought she acted that way, one member suggested that Linda probably felt "guilty or ashamed." Linda went on to ask the group, "Have you ever been eating with someone who knew you were in the weight loss group, and you were eating something, and they said, 'Are you sure you're allowed to eat that?' And that would make you feel guilty or unsure, like maybe you really weren't supposed to be eating it?" Later in the discussion of food secrets, Linda said that for a while she let her daughter help her by writing what Linda ate in her food tracker. The problem was that Linda would purposely not tell her daughter everything she ate, with the predictable result that Linda ate more food than she should have eaten.

In these instances cheating takes on a double meaning. First, like the organization, members see cheating as breaking the rules. Members are expected to track what they eat, so members who don't track are breaking the rules, that is, they are cheating. But second, despite the organization's best efforts to convince members that there are no forbidden foods, in many members' minds cheating means eating foods that they shouldn't have eaten. Hiding food, either literally or figuratively, by not tracking everything you eat, is problematic precisely because it implies you are eating foods that you shouldn't be eating. This point is even clearer in the video on "being your own best friend." After eating nearly an entire cake, Gail felt guilty, not because she failed to record it in her tracker, or even, in this case, because she ate more of it than she should have. By the time the group discussion ends, the consensus is that Gail shouldn't have eaten any cake at all. Her downfall, and her guilt, comes from having the cake there in the first place.

Guilt is a particularly useful tool in weight loss, precisely because it can be induced before the fact as a way to prevent future transgressions. At a meeting during the summer, the discussion centered on positive thinking and planning ahead. At some point Joe said he and Suzanne were going on a cruise in September and, "I know I'm going to go crazy. I'll be out of control." His tone of voice was matter-of-fact and implied little concern. Ruth said he didn't have to lose control, but Joe said, "Yeah, I know that's what's going to happen." Several people tried to convince Joe he didn't have to lose control, and Jodi asked, "But how will you feel afterward?" Despite members' efforts, Joe was convinced that losing control was inevitable, and Ruth turned the conversation to another matter. Joe's initial statement was future oriented. He identified a transgression that had not yet taken place, and he left no doubt about the likelihood of transgressing. Joe expressed no concern about the upcoming vacation, nor did he request practical strategies or group support for dealing with the anticipated temptation. Particularly striking is that Joe offered no excuses or justifications for the sin he was about to commit, and equated his transgression with a loss of control. On hearing of Joe's impending downfall, group members tried to persuade Joe that sinning was not inevitable. Most notably, they tried to call forth the guilt that would be experienced afterward. But the group's attempts were to no avail. What Joe saw as a realistic assessment of the situation, other members saw as a self-defeating attitude that could be changed, thus preventing the bad behavior and the guilty feelings that were certain to follow.

Food is the central issue in weight loss, and tends to provoke the most anxiety and potential guilt, but it is not the only problem. There are any number of rules that can be broken, so guilt can be induced in a wide variety of areas. One such problem area is not bothering to learn the rules in the first place. One evening as I was leaving the meeting, I stopped at the front desk to buy the new food guides. As I was writing a check, Ruth noticed two returning lifetime members who were leaving. She stopped them and said, "Aren't you staying for the initiation?" When they said no, Ruth said, "Don't you think you should?" They looked uncomfortable, and one mumbled to the other, "Should we stay?" Ruth said the program "has really changed a lot." They said OK, and went back to sit down.

Although the organization formulates the rules and tries to social- ize members into accepting them, it is not entirely successful. Ultimately the organization depends on members' cooperation. This is particularly evident in the case of exercise. The organization's official position is clear: successful weight loss requires both reformed eating habits and regular exercise. Members receive a number of written materials with suggestions and guidelines for incorporating exercise into weight loss efforts, and the weekly journals for recording food intake also contain space for recording exercise. Members are supposed to exercise for at least twenty minutes per day, and leaders encourage members to increase their activity levels. Leaders often suggest easy ways to become more physically active and reward those who do with stick- ers. It is highly apparent from group discussions, however, that a good number of members, if not the majority, do not exercise regularly. At the same time, members feel little guilt for not meeting the organiza- tional expectation. I never witnessed a member confessing a failure to exercise. Just the opposite. Members saw exercise as an extra for which they deserved special recognition. The matter-of-fact way in which mem- bers casually discussed their lack of exercise suggests that most simply did not share the organization's view of exercise as a requirement. Consequently, if you don't exercise, there's no need to feel guilty. Members resist the organization's efforts to formalize the expectation of regular exercise, and as a result it is virtually impossible to induce any significant degree of guilt for not exercising.

Confession

When members do see the error of their ways and feel guilty after transgressions, meetings provide a forum for public con- fession. As members admit to the group the various ways they have cheated or broken rules, the meeting becomes a public confessional, with other members as witnesses. Leaders are particularly significant as they make their own confessions, solicit confessions from members, and model appropriate responses for members. Linda was an effective role model, as she regularly began discussions with stories of her own mistakes. Indeed, Linda frequently repeated her story about sneaking donuts from her co-workers. Similarly, Debbie often told her own story about eating nearly an entire cake at a family celebration.

As leaders make their own confessions, they promote similar sharing by members. The first time I heard Linda confess about the donuts, the discussion topic was "eating secrets," a personal and po- tentially embarrassing topic, particularly for people who do not know one another very well. Linda broke the ice, provided specific examples of the kinds of secrets she had in mind, and created a more comfortable and less threatening atmosphere in which members could confess their transgressions. At other times, leaders directly prompt confessions, as when Linda asked the group, "Has there ever been a time when you didn't do very well, or pay attention to what you ate all week, and then the day before coming to the meeting, not eat or drink anything?" Linda's question provoked laughter and heads nodding throughout the room, so apparently the practice is fairly common. In this case Linda explicitly identifies a specific transgression, and then allows members to confess as a group, rather than put an individual member on the spot. As previous weight-losers and current lifetime members of the group, leaders are especially well suited for modeling confession. Not coincidentally, leaders' confessions frequently take on the tone of evangelical preachers who publicly admit the error of their ways and then suggest that they have seen the light.

Confession fulfills a number of functions. First, new members are socialized into the group and its procedures as they listen to members confess. Second, public confession bonds the group together, as members reassert their commitment to group norms and thereby highlight and strengthen the moral boundaries surrounding the group (Durkheim 1912). In Joe's case, public confession has little impact on the sinner. Although there is hope that he may redeem himself in the future, at this point Joe is lost. At the same time, other group members are reinforced in their beliefs that there are good and bad ways of eating. In addition, public confession is a useful and relatively easy way to relieve stress for individual members. Traditionally, it is through confession that sinners receive forgiveness. By confessing their sins to others, whether it is to a priest, the church, or the larger community, sinners publicly admit the error of their ways, and in return they receive absolution. Confession plays an important role in self-help. Simonds (1992) suggests that self-help authors often preface their books with their own confessions. By demonstrating that they, too, had a problem, recognized and admitted it, and were able to solve it, authors attempt to establish rapport with readers. Furthermore, according to Simonds (1992:153), "Self-help authors offer readers a sort of secularized confessional, where reading itself is the act by which they may achieve absolution." Similarly, members of the weight loss group do not literally receive forgiveness for their sins. But nonetheless, a sort of forgiveness is experienced as members admit their transgressions to the group and simultaneously reaffirm their commitment to follow the rules in the future. When the meeting topic was food secrets, members were encouraged to confront and deal with their secrets, first by talking to themselves about what they were doing, and then by telling someone else. In addition, public confession is a useful and relatively easy way to relieve stress for individual members.

Confession is clearly useful both for individual members and for the group as a whole. But at the same time, the effects are more insidious. Spitzack (1990:3–4) argues: "Body reduction/health discourses encourage examination, and guarantee a permanently 'in progress' actualization of women's freedom through confession. Healthy women are those who confess a multitude of misguided actions, deviant sensibilities, transgressive moral propensities, all in the name of salvation, the successful accomplishment of an afterlife." In this view, the good dieter not only accepts the group's teachings but continually examines herself for and finds faults. Confessing your sins provides relief from guilt, but it is temporary at best.

Keeping Them in Line: Surveillance

In the face of nearly endless temptation, guilt is not the only technique used to keep members on the right track. The effectiveness of guilt inducement rests on another technique, continual surveillance. To the extent that members feel they are being watched, they may be less likely to break the rules. Much as the community and church participate in this process in the area of religion, the group plays a significant role when it comes to weight loss. At times members are passive spectators, only subtly and indirectly participating in surveillance. During celebration, about a month after I joined, Richard got out his stickers and ribbons and asked, "Does anyone get a ten-pound ribbon? Has anyone lost their first ten pounds?" As Richard was handing out ribbons, Amy turned to me and said, "You'll get that next week!" I immediately felt some pressure, knowing that someone else knew how close I was to losing ten pounds.

At other times members play more direct and active roles in surveillance. When I arrived one evening, Debbie was talking to Doris, an older woman who had recently met her goal weight, about Doris's friend Estelle, who attended sporadically. Doris asked if there was something Debbie could say to Estelle to help keep her on track, and Debbie said she appreciated Doris's concern for her friend. Several months later, Debbie was weighing Meg, who usually came with her mother. Debbie asked how Meg's mother was doing, and Meg said, "She's good. She's going to try it on her own for a while. But I'll still come. We keep an eye on each other. We still help each other." Later that same evening, when Debbie asked Judy how she lost weight on vacation, among other things, Judy said that she and her daughter "watched each other." And on numerous occasions Joyce spoke openly, freely, and critically about her friend Peggy and the problems she had sticking to the program.

Two aspects of these disparate incidents stand out. First, in every case, a member talks to the leader or the group about an individual who is not present. Where a transgression or mistake is involved, the member brings it to the attention of the community, not the sinner. There is little direct effect on the erring member, but the message to the group is clear: your behavior is being watched and might be discussed, even in your absence. Second, all the incidents involve either friends or family members who joined and currently attend together. Although the group in general is highly discreet, members who know each other apparently feel freer not only to watch each other but to make their observations public, and share them with the leader or the group.

Group surveillance is important, even if unintentional, but its effectiveness is limited in a number of ways. First, the most common transgressions occur in private. Eating foods you shouldn't, eating more than you should, hiding food, and not accurately recording everything you eat are private behaviors, usually not visible, especially to other group members. The likelihood of getting away with rule breaking is therefore high. Furthermore, members frequently see one another only at meetings, although this is a matter of degree. (Since meetings draw from the immediate neighborhoods, members often realize that they know each other from different contexts. And it is possible to run into other members accidentally. Early one morning, a few months after I joined the group, I was out walking for exercise. As I crossed the street in front of a neighborhood elementary school, the crossing guard on duty looked at me, and then exclaimed, "Hey, I saw you at [the weight loss meeting] the other night!" On other occasions I ran into members at restaurants or the grocery store, and notably, I was immediately self-conscious about what I was eating or what I had in my grocery cart.) The effectiveness of group surveillance is also limited because meeting attendance, while highly encouraged, is still optional. Group members who do not regularly attend meetings are not subjected to group surveillance. Even among very regular attendees, sharing personal information, whether it is accomplishments, mistakes, challenges, or just general experiences, is largely voluntary, although some leaders, especially Ruth and Richard, at times called on specific members to share information. Leaders attempt to create a comfortable atmosphere, and individual members are never pressured into sharing information that they do not want to share. In some ways, members can choose to what extent they are subject to group surveillance, although it is nearly impossible to avoid it completely.

Fortunately for the organization, people outside the group do a good deal of surveillance work. Significantly, when Linda and Debbie confessed their transgressions, they involved attempts to avoid or subvert surveillance, most notably by hiding food or not eating in front of others. Members, too, frequently admit hiding food or trying to eat when no one else is around. At the very least, members feel as if their behavior is under public scrutiny, and several incidents suggest that this is not a figment of their imaginations. When Linda confessed that she hid donuts from her co-workers, she noted that since her colleagues knew she was a leader for a weight loss group, she felt self-conscious about eating donuts in front of them. She went on to ask members whether other people had ever made them self-conscious about what they were eating. This was an experience widely shared by members. Before a meeting, I overheard Lucy and Eve comparing their progress. When Eve found out that Lucy had lost seven pounds, she said, referring to Lucy's boyfriend, "You know Roger will tell you to slow down." Lucy replied, "Yeah, maybe I won't tell him." At another meeting Jodi and her friend Jackie were talking before the meeting started. While on vacation in Florida, Jodi had gained one and three-quarter pounds, then had stayed the same, then had gained three pounds in the past week. Frustrated, Jodi said, "I'm happy right here, where I am." Because Jodi was within her goal range, she had told her boyfriend, Kurt, that she could set a different goal than the one she had started with. Jodi went on to say, "He said I'd never be happy if I didn't meet my goal, and I said, yes, I'd meet it, but it would just be a different goal, but he said, 'I know you. You won't be happy until you weigh 135 pounds.' " Jodi continued to tell Jackie that Kurt gave her a hard time whenever she gained weight during a week, and finally Jodi said, "I'm just not going to tell him how much I gained this time." None of these members saw others' interest in their eating habits or weight loss progress as supportive. In fact, all saw it as interference, and as negative in its effects.

Aware that their eating habits are viewed and scrutinized by others, members become particularly conscious of their own behavior and do a good deal of self-surveillance. Given the limitations of group surveillance and the potentially negative fall-out from surveillance by friends and family members, the organization relies heavily on members to monitor themselves. As most religious groups and parents come to find out, controlling members' behavior through external means is highly inefficient, not to mention difficult. Consequently religious groups and parents spend considerable time and energy instilling individual consciences in converts and children. If individuals watch themselves, the organization doesn't have to. Meticulously recording everything you eat takes on considerable importance in this regard. Despite telling new members that leaders can request to see their food records, the organization emphasizes that keeping track of what you eat is primarily for your own benefit. With repeated references to the food record's importance in preventing and uncovering cheating, the food record is one strategy for carefully monitoring your own behavior. In effect, guilt can be self-induced, freeing the organization and leaders to provide mutual support and reinforcement.

The Emotion of Religion: Magic and Taboo

Religious metaphors are readily apparent in weight loss language that emphasizes temptation, sacrifice, deprivation, guilt, and surveillance. In the weight loss group, the religious concept is related to the work concept, much in the way that Weber (1904–1905) argued that notions of work in a capitalist society are highly related to the spread of Protestantism. A good Christian is a good worker, that is, one who is conscientious, methodical, and self-disciplined. Similarly, good dieters are highly motivated, methodical in following the rules, and willing to monitor and discipline themselves. But a religious framework can animate the language of weight loss in deeper, more ambivalently emotional ways. In its most elementary forms, religion rests on deeply embedded elements of magic, taboo, and ritual. These elements most directly address the continually troubling mysteries of life, and give to religion its excitement and emotionality. In the case of weight loss, the situation is somewhat more complex.

Explaining the Inexplicable

In large part religion functions to explain the inexplicable, to provide some understanding of the great mystery of life, and does so primarily by appealing to the transcendent mystery and power of God. People trying to lose weight also seek to explain the inexplicable. Weight gain is no mystery when members eat considerably more than they think they should, indulge in high-calorie foods, or otherwise act in ways that can be expected to result in additional pounds.

But at other times, weight gain is unexpected. Members do what they are supposed to do, eat what they are supposed to eat, but nevertheless do not lose weight or, even worse, gain weight. In these situations members desperately look for reasonable explanations for the unexpected gain, as when Joe asks, in a bewildered tone of voice, "What does it mean when you think you've had a really good week, and then you get here and it wasn't that great?"

Common responses to this query usually involve the body—first, its tendency to retain water, and second, the inconsistencies of body metabolism. Water retention is by far the most common explanation used for unexpected weight gain, but water retention itself is seen as having multiple causes. During my first week on the program I lost about five pounds. After following the program for a second week, I was sorely disappointed when I lost only one pound. Feeling I had worked hard all week, I hoped to lose two or three more pounds. In some ways, the first week's rapid loss set me up for disappointment. Rationally, I didn't expect to lose that much every week, but I still thought two or three pounds a week was reasonable. Searching for possible explanations for the low loss, I wondered if I had eaten something I shouldn't have, possibly the cheese omelet I had for breakfast on Sunday. But I had charted it, probably generously, and even if I hadn't, it fell well within the week's optional calories. Then I noted the date, and wondered whether it could be water retention related to the menstrual cycle. Even though it was probably a little early, I assured myself that it was close enough to be the probable cause.

Besides the menstrual cycle, high sodium intake is often blamed for water retention and consequent weight gain. One evening when I got back to the scales, Joyce and her daughter Carrie were at the scale with Peggy, who was about to get weighed. As Peggy stepped on the scale, she said, "Now, let's all cross our fingers." She had gained a pound. Carrie said, "That's OK, Peggy," but Peggy said, "How could I do that? I did exactly the same thing I did last week. But you know, I drank a diet pop this morning, and you always say not to drink pop when you're getting weighed." Joyce agreed. Later, when Debbie asked members what they had to share, Peggy and Joyce both said they gained a pound. Joyce said she had apparently just slipped that week and eaten a lot of things she hadn't been eating, but Peggy was puzzled since she had done exactly what she had the week before. Debbie asked the group why they thought this happened, "Why could you have a week where you follow the program, but the scale doesn't show it?" Wendy said, "I found that when I hit those weeks, if I just made sure

I did exactly the same thing the next week, I'd come in and be doubly happy," implying that the next week she lost even more than expected, so the trick was just to keep doing it. Peggy said she drank a diet pop that day and wondered if that had anything to do with it. Joyce said, "Pop is high in sodium," and Debbie explained that sodium leads to water retention. She asked the group for suggestions for limiting sodium intake, and Wendy's friend Emily said, "I'm on a no-sodium diet, and anything you buy in a can has a lot of salt. You should buy as much as possible fresh, and never add table salt to your food."

The explanations for water retention go even further. When Joe plaintively asked for explanations for a lower than expected loss, Ruth said, "This week everyone got hit hard by the weather." Joe replied, "Oh, you can blame the weather now?" and everyone laughed. Ruth said, "When it's hot and humid you retain water. Lots of people complained about their rings being tight." As amusing as some of the explanations are, members take them quite seriously, as do leaders. To some extent, the explanations are accurate. Sodium intake, the menstrual cycle, and the weather all affect water retention, which in turn affects weight. At the same time, in at least some instances, water retention is not likely the sole or even the major explanation of lower than expected weight loss or unexpected weight gain. The explanations are useful not because they are necessarily *true,* but because they ultimately *make sense,* and thus help to make a seemingly irrational situation understandable. Believing that a can of diet soda can result in a one-pound weight gain is far more reassuring than feeling that your efforts have had no payoff whatsoever.

A second category of explanations for lower than expected weight losses involves the inconsistencies and mysteries of body metabolism. Some of these explanations involve the tendency of the body metabolism to slow down in response to deprivation. The first week after Rose joined with her twelve-year-old son, Justin, he lost five pounds, but Rose gained weight. In explanation, she said, "I always gain weight the first week of a diet. My body just shuts down." On another occasion Heidi lost four pounds in just two days, and she told Donna, a receptionist, that she had been sick. Donna said, "You have to be careful when you're sick. Starving yourself can backfire." Heidi responded, "I've been eating, just not as much, because I didn't feel well." Similarly, one week when I gained half a pound after several weeks of losing very little, Donna suggested I have Debbie look at my food tracker, since "sometimes it's not eating enough."

Other explanations related to body metabolism rest on the assumed periodicity or cyclical nature of weight loss. One week I lost a quarter pound, following a loss of four pounds the previous week. When I expressed disappointment over the small loss, Donna said, "With the kind of loss you had last week, it's not unusual to have a smaller one the next week. Anyway, it's headed in the right direction." Donna's response was typical. On numerous occasions receptionists helped members justify small losses by suggesting that the metabolism slows in response to a large loss. This explanation is helpful as long as the overall trend is downward. It is less useful when very small losses continue for weeks, or when losses are regularly followed by weight gain. In this case, leaders and members resort to the notion of plateaus, to suggest that in response to long-term weight loss, body metabolism slows considerably, and despite members' best efforts, further weight loss is extremely difficult, sometimes for weeks. In the case of plateaus, leaders urge members to continue their efforts, since weight loss will presumably resume at some point. But in some cases, particularly as members approach their recommended goal weight range, further weight loss is unlikely, due to the body's physiological set point. When the set point is above the goal weight, members can be highly frustrated. One evening before the meeting began, Betty told me, "I'm never going to reach my goal. I just keep moving up and down around the same weight, and it's not really going anywhere." But rather than rethink her goal, Betty seemed baffled about why she couldn't lose more weight.

Body metabolism does play a role in weight loss. But as in the case of the explanations involving water retention, the accuracy of the explanations is unimportant. The body and its workings are mysterious and pose various difficulties and anxieties for the dieter, who is trying to control not only what she eats but her body's response to what is eaten. The explanations help relieve anxiety by imposing some logic on a seemingly illogical process. At first glance these explanations of unexpected weight gain appear to be anything but religious. Body physiology seems to fall squarely in the realm of science rather than religion. To some extent this is true. I never heard a member blame her weight gain on God's will. At the same time, the scientific basis of the explanations should not be overstated. When members blame weight gain on water retention or metabolism, they are not seeking scientifically verifiable causes. Rather, they are trying to make some sense out of a perplexing situation. In members' discussions, the body is not reduced to sheer physiological matter that behaves in scientifically predictable ways. In contrast, the body is unpredictable and ultimately inexplicable. The explanations work for members not because they are true but because they are comforting. The explanations, however, are not entirely successful. Even when members know there may be a good reason why they are not losing weight, they are likely to feel frustrated and anxious. As is true of some elementary religions, a common result is reliance on magic and superstition.

Magic and Superstition

The commercial weight loss industry commonly touts magical potions and procedures that supposedly lead to large and rapid weight loss with little or no effort by the weight-loser. Pills, diet drinks, herbs, and body wraps promise to melt away pounds and inches, and commercial diets promote certain foods or combinations of foods as able to speed up metabolism and melt away fat. In contrast, with its emphasis on lifestyle modification, the organization steers members away from believing in quick fixes, and constantly reminds them that weight loss requires commitment and hard work. During group discussions, leaders and members often recount their personal experiences with fad diets and gimmicks and frequently make fun of apparently magical approaches to weight loss.

Nonetheless, members are not immune to believing in magic, which is subtly evident as members discuss the importance of drinking water. When I joined the group, the organization urged members to drink eight eight-ounce glasses of water daily, and eight boxes were included on the food tracker so members could record their water consumption. The organization's recommendation is not unusual or unfounded, given the numerous benefits of drinking water. However, as members informally interact with one another, especially before and after meetings, water takes on magical qualities. At my first meeting, Lisa, a returning member, advised me, "Be sure to drink your water. It fills you up and you really do lose weight faster. You can count decaffeinated pop as part of your water." A few weeks later, Lois was talking to a couple of newer members about drinking water. Lois said, "I've had three quarts already today. I'm working on my fourth." She had a large water bottle with her, and she drank from it periodically throughout the meeting. Barb, who was sitting with Lois, joked, "I get my daily exercise walking back and forth to the bathroom all night." Lois said emphatically, "It really washes it all out of you." Like Lois, other members also brought their water to meetings, and the organization sold a large variety of water bottles to support their habit.

When members directly link drinking water with losing more weight and losing it more quickly, the magical aspects of water are most apparent. When Lois suggests that water "washes it all out of you," it is not entirely clear what it is that's being washed out. But Lois evokes not only the imagery of fat melting away but also the imagery of the cleansing and purification associated with the rite of baptism. As is true of much magic, members informally share the magical qualities of water with one another as part of the group's folklore. Officially, members can count milk, juice, and decaffeinated soft drinks, tea, and coffee toward half the daily water requirement. Occasionally leaders remind members of this, and members who closely read the written materials may be aware of it. But often members learn it from one another, as I learned it from Lisa. Most commonly, if a member complains about the difficulty of drinking eight glasses of water, another member is likely to point out that other beverages can be substituted for half the water.

The dependence on superstition and magical rituals to facilitate weight loss is also evident as members weigh in. At any given meeting, at least one and usually several members cross their fingers as they step on the scale. Crossing your fingers for luck is routinely done by many people, most of whom hope for a little luck, but few of whom actually believe in magic. At the same time, weigh-in is fraught with anxiety, heightened by many members' perceptions that the process is not entirely rational and predictable. If following the program always resulted in weight loss, there would be little need for magic. In an intriguing study, Gmelch (1995) found that magic among baseball players is most associated with pitching and hitting, activities with the greatest degree of uncertainty, whereas it is rarely associated with fielding, where players have considerably more control over the outcome. Similarly, reliance on magic is fairly common among players of games of chance, such as bingo, craps, or roulette (Burger 1991; Henslin 1967; King 1990; Oldman 1974). Members of the weight loss group rely on magic due to the uncertainty and apparent illogic inherent in losing weight.

Many members strongly prefer one scale over another. Not long after I joined, I was standing near the front of the line, waiting to get weighed. Pat came up from the front and stood over to the side, next to the first cubicle. When the woman in the cubicle was finished, Pat went in, and I realized she was in the cubicle earlier, but forgot to stop at the front desk to pick up her membership folder. About that time, the woman behind me said, "Which scale are you going to?" Confused, I hesitated a minute. Pointing to the first cubicle, she asked, "Are you going to that one?" Thinking that perhaps she saw Pat come up the side and thought that there were two lines, I said, "Whichever one opens up first." But she said, "It's just that some people like one scale more than the other." She pointed to the second cubicle and stated, "I'm going to that one."

In some ways, scale preferences are similar to other strategies for manipulating weigh-in, such as removing jewelry, shoes, and as many articles of clothing as possible, limiting sodium intake, fasting the day of weigh-in, and preferring to weigh in on certain days of the week or at certain times of the day. All aim at maximizing the amount of weight lost in a week, and all introduce some degree of rationality into a process that frequently feels unpredictable and uncontrollable. Most significantly, while all these strategies have some factual basis, their ultimate effects are likely to be minimal. In the case of scales, it is conceivable that scales differ in their precision and accuracy. But several things highlight the magical aspects of scale preferences. First, members do not seek the most accurate scale. Rather, they want the one that yields the lowest weight, regardless of its accuracy. Second, different members prefer different scales. Finally, the attachment that members feel to a particular scale is quite strong and is rarely broken, even when the results are less than hoped for in the short term.

Taboos

Given the uncertainty of weight loss, in addition to magic and superstition, weight-losers might be expected to rely on various taboos. Taboos were common among the baseball players examined by Gmelch (1995); they routinely avoided engaging in certain activities, wearing particular articles of clothing, or eating specific foods on game days or even during the entire season. Since the organization promotes the explicit message that no foods are off-limits, taboos surrounding specific foods, or the ways in which they are eaten, are virtually nonexistent. Near the end of a meeting, Corinne once asked if it mattered when she ate various foods, since she liked to eat somewhat more in the evenings. Cheryl said, "There used to be various beliefs about eating certain foods only at certain times of the day, but none of them have been proven, so it doesn't matter as long as you eat the right amount of each food sometime during the day." Occasionally, much to the amusement of everyone present, a member or leader would come across old organizational materials, sometimes from as many as thirty years ago, and share with the group various taboos, restrictions, or requirements. At one time, potatoes could only be eaten early in the day, and liver had to be eaten once a week. Although members found the stories funny, leaders used them to emphasize how much the program had changed and especially how much more freedom members now had to eat what they wanted. Taboos are associated with "the old days," and are presumably no longer necessary as we have become more enlightened.

At the same time, another taboo, unrelated to food, operates in the group and significantly affects group interaction. Regardless of whether you are overweight or not, most people in the United States feel uncomfortable sharing their body weight with others. Body weight is part of what Goffman (1971:38–39) calls the informational preserve, "the set of facts about himself [sic] to which an individual expects to control access while in the presence of others." Those few instances when individuals are forced to publicly announce their weight, such as when renewing a driver's license, are fraught with anxiety and embarrassment. When the information being preserved is potentially stigmatizing, individuals may use a number of techniques of information control in order to hide, obscure, or selectively reveal the stigmatizing condition (Goffman 1963). Since obesity is a clearly visible stigma, the obese person is already discredited. At the same time, obese persons can conceal their exact weight, or at least control to whom and under what circumstances the information is revealed. Nonetheless, this can be very difficult, if not impossible. In weight loss groups, body weight is the central concern. In discussing the tendency of stigmatized persons to form groups of sympathetic others, Goffman (1963) implies that within such groups information control is not an issue, since joining the group is an admission that you possess certain stigma. But this is not necessarily true in weight loss groups. Members may be publicly acknowledging that they are overweight, but this does not imply that they must openly divulge their weight. Indeed, weight loss groups may find it advantageous to allow members to conceal their weight, at least to some extent.

In the group, it is very difficult to avoid talking about how much people weigh for two reasons. First, since the focus is on weight loss, recording body weight is necessary to gauge progress. Although other indicators of progress, such as percentage of body weight that is fat, or body measurements taken in inches, might be feasible and even more accurate, body weight is an obvious and easily measured indicator. Second, lifestyle modification is an ambiguous and open-ended goal. Even members who accept that lifestyle change is the key to weight loss almost always have a finite and easily definable goal when they join. Some members want to lose a certain number of pounds, but most aspire to reach a specific weight.

At two particular points, balancing the group's need to focus on weight with members' desires to protect their privacy is especially problematic. First, and most obviously, is weigh-in. Second, since the group uses positive reinforcement to bolster weight loss attempts, celebration is another instance when members are expected to focus on, and talk about, their weight. In the first case, the organization privatizes and ritualizes weigh-in to relieve members' anxieties. In the second case, leaders and members employ a number of linguistic strategies to talk openly about weight without actually divulging body weight. It is at these times that the taboo against revealing one's weight is most precarious.

Scale Hazards. The few minutes prior to the meeting's official start, when members are weighed, are by far the most anxiety provoking in the meeting. At this point, another person actually observes and records members' weights. The organization attempts to relieve some of the tension inherent in the situation by privatizing weigh-in to the extent possible. When I first joined, the scales were located at the very back of the meeting room, in three side-by-side cubicles, open in front, and separated only by thin, portable walls. Small windows were cut in the walls, so receptionists in adjoining cubicles could pass materials and tools, such as stamp pads, back and forth, and could easily talk to each other during weigh-in. The physical arrangement of the scales also contributed to the semblance of privacy. Unlike those in most physicians' offices or gyms, the scales were manipulated so that the part of the scale that showed body weight was turned backward. The numbers on the scale were hidden not only from people waiting in line but also from the person getting weighed. The only person who could directly observe the numbers was the receptionist. The numbers were further obscured by a paper sign hung on each scale that read "No Bare Feet on the Scale."

The privacy of weigh-in was to a considerable extent an illusion, but nonetheless an important one. When I arrived at a meeting during the summer, an earlier storm had knocked out the electricity. Donna and Ruth had brought one scale to the front room, immediately to the left of the entrance, where there was more natural light. Three people were already waiting in line, and Ruth said she would bring up another scale. She dragged it from the cubicle in back, pulled it into the room, and said, "I'll set it away from the front window, so people looking in can't see." Donna said, "They can't see in anyway. The glass is tinted." When Michelle asked if that really mattered to people, Ruth said it did to some. As I got to the front of the line, the electricity came back on. Donna said she would go back to the scales in the cubicles, and Ruth could weigh in the front room until she had to start the meeting. Donna took the scale Ruth had brought up front, dragged it to the back, and indicated that some people could go back there to get weighed, though no one did. I stayed up front, but the room felt much less private than the cubicles, and I felt more exposed.

Even though the cubicles provided only minimal privacy, some privacy was better than none. About a year later, the group moved into new quarters in the same shopping center. The new location was smaller, and the space was arranged very differently. Instead of a suite of small rooms located around a medium-size meeting room, the new locale had one large room. Members entered at the back of the meeting room, where there was a counter with a scale at each end. Approximately three to four feet of space separated the counter from the last row of chairs. Consequently weigh-in was considerably less private. Not only were the scales no longer separated from one another by walls, albeit thin ones, but they were in much closer proximity both to people waiting in line and to those who had been weighed and had taken their seats.

When even the semblance of privacy was eliminated, the ritualization of weigh-in became especially critical. Weigh-in is highly structured and predictable, regardless of who is doing the weighing. After a member steps on the scale, the receptionist reads the scale and directly records the weight in the member's record. Although receptionists frequently say such things as "down another one this week," or "good job—you lost two pounds," I never observed a receptionist tell a member his or her actual weight. Rather, receptionists routinely write the weight in the record book, and then point to the weight with their pen. In order to find out their body weight, members have to read it in their books.

That the ritual is strongly adhered to is most obvious when it is violated. One time Donna weighed Peggy, wrote the information in her book, and told her how it had changed since the last time she had been weighed. Peggy looked at what Donna wrote, and said loudly enough for everyone in line to hear, "That's what I weigh? 154?" When Peggy violated the taboo against revealing one's weight, several people in line looked away and acted as if they hadn't heard, even though Peggy didn't seem to care. Donna was also uncomfortable. She said, "That's your weight," and pointed to it with a pen, without saying it out loud, and then said, "And this is your progress so far." Peggy frowned, seemed somewhat confused, and said, "Oh, OK," and went to sit down. So ingrained was the ritual that I never asked a receptionist what I actually weighed. Rather, after sitting down, I checked my weight in my record book. The combination of ritualizing weigh-in and providing at least a bare minimum of privacy allowed members to get publicly weighed but retain some control over personal information. The organization obtained the necessary information to track members' progress, but allowed members some degree of personal privacy.

Speaking of weight. Members also focus on how much they weigh during celebration, and here too the taboo against revealing your weight is clear. Theoretically, you could mark your progress by stating your current weight, compared either with your starting weight, or with your goal weight. Not once, however, did a member make a statement of this sort, even though the same information could often be inferred. Richard often reminded members that when he joined the group, he weighed about four hundred pounds, and had subsequently lost over two hundred pounds. Linda often introduced herself by saying that at various times she weighed over two hundred pounds, but now weighs nearly one hundred pounds less. Similarly, Lois readily tells other members that she started the program weighing over four hundred pounds, and to date has lost eighty pounds. Several points are noteworthy. First, everyone refers to what he or she previously weighed, rather than current weights. Second, all three divulge weights that are dramatically remote from their current weight and that consequently may be less threatening. Third, they avoid stating their exact starting weight, by qualifying it with "over" or "about." Finally, in each case the dramatic nature of their weight loss is heightened precisely by contrasting their very large starting weights with their current weight.

Leaders and members typically don't state how much they weigh, but instead speak in a language of weight *loss*. This was so pervasive that I usually didn't know what I weighed, but would calculate it by subtracting my weight loss, known to the one-quarter pound, from my starting weight. Members frequently spoke the language to each other. Indeed, premeeting conversations often revolved around comparisons of weight loss. As members sat down they asked each other how they had done that week, and even strangers seemed comfortable sharing their weight losses. Leaders also spoke the language of weight loss, particularly during celebration when members were recognized and rewarded for losing pounds.

Leaders and members also avoided talking about what they weighed, or even what they hoped to weigh, by speaking of goal weight *ranges*. The strategy was subtle and sometimes hard to see. In some ways it makes practical sense that people of the same height can fall within a weight range of twenty pounds or more. Organizational employees saw even these ranges as somewhat flexible and of varying viability for specific individuals. When my weight was still fifteen pounds over the recommended range, Debbie approached me before a meeting and asked, "Well, you're within your range, aren't you?" When I said I had at least fifteen more pounds to lose, she said, "Really? You don't look it. You carry it well! I have a friend who's like that. She's a couple of inches shorter than me, but weighs more—she's really solid." She asked if I had seen the new weight ranges that took age into account and said, "You need to tell us what's comfortable with you. The ranges are guidelines, but you'll know it when you get there." At that point Wendy sat down and Debbie went to talk to her. Wendy had set her goal at 114, giving her three pounds to go. Since Wendy is probably three inches taller than I am, when she said her goal was 114 pounds, I immediately looked at her and wondered whether I should try to go that low.

Several points about speaking in weight ranges emerge from this incident. First, ranges are based on both age and height. Not long after this conversation, Debbie asked if I was sure I was using the right height. When I said I had estimated and had never been officially measured, she suggested I get measured after the meeting. If I was taller than I thought I was, my goal weight would move into a higher range. Second, leaders frequently urge members to consider their subjective feelings as well as the weight on the scale to determine their goals. However, in this instance my subjective feelings were in part based on a comparison between myself and another member. As a result, I wondered if I should set my goal almost ten pounds lower than I had originally planned. Third, despite the relatively large and flexible ranges, members always set a specific weight as their goal. Indeed the organization expects members to set a specific goal, and allows them to become lifetime members only when the goal is met and only if the goal falls within the recommended ranges. Clearly individual members and the organization conceive of goals as reaching a specific weight. At the same time, couching the weight within a wide range makes the goal appear more flexible, and allows members to speak of their goals in less specific language, once again avoiding the mention of a specific weight.

Overall, the group is relatively free of taboos. With respect to food taboos, some foods are problematic, such as chocolate, alcohol, or potato chips, because they have little nutritional value and, most important, make overindulgence easy. And indeed some members choose to abstain rather than regulate their intake. But even so, no one suggests that these foods are taboo. The one taboo that group members do share is the cultural taboo against revealing their own or someone else's body weight. Steps are therefore taken to allow members to be weighed, and to talk openly and freely about weight loss, while being simultaneously protected from the unnecessary and potentially embarrassing revelation of their weight.

Speaking of Religion

As members and leaders talk about losing weight, they draw heavily on religious language and imagery. Good and evil, temptation, sin, guilt, and confession animate members' speech as they try to make sense of complex and ambivalent emotions surrounding food, the body, and weight loss. Other observers have noted the connection between religion, gender, eating, and weight issues, most notably as they relate to fasting and anorexia nervosa (Bell 1985; Brumberg 1988; Bynum 1987). But the religious metaphor also underlies nondisordered eating. Seid (1994:4) argues:

> We have elevated the pursuit of a lean, fat-free body into a new religion. It has a creed: "I eat right, watch my weight, and exercise." Indeed, anorexia nervosa could be called the paradigm of our age, for our creed encourages us all to adopt the behavior and attitudes of the anorexic. The difference is one of degree, not of kind. Like any religion worthy of the name, ours also has its damnation. Failure to follow the creed—and the corporeal stigmata of that failure, fatness and flabbiness—produce a hell on earth. The fat and flabby are damned to failure, regardless of professional and personal successes. Our religion also has its rewards, its salvation. In following the creed, one is guaranteed beauty, energy, health, and a long successful life. Followers are even promised self-transformation: The "thin person within," waiting to burst through the fat, is somehow a more exciting, sexy, competent, successful self. Virtue can be quantified by the numbers on the scale, the lean-to-fat ratio, clothing size, and body measurements. And, in a curious inversion of capitalist values, less is always better.

Similarly, Hesse-Biber (1996) characterizes the contemporary obsession with thinness as a cult, complete with rigid rules, rituals, gurus, and conversion stories.

The concept of weight loss as religion, as used by group members, is significant for three major reasons. First, the concept captures the high degree of moralizing that characterizes our thinking about food, eating, obesity, and weight loss. The division of the world into the sacred and the profane deeply colors dieters' everyday experiences and infuses their speech with notions of right and wrong, good and evil. Concomitantly, guilt is one of the most common states of the weight-loser. Second, ritual and community are at the heart of most religions. Ritual and community are also relevant in the weight loss group, although they operate somewhat differently than in traditional churches, and ultimately dieters are individualized and isolated. Third, the religious framework can potentially call forth the more positive, emotional elements of religion and spirituality. However, this potential is effectively neutralized as weight loss is increasingly rationalized.

Morality

Durkheim (1912) argues that the division of the world into the sacred and the profane is at the very core of religion. Furthermore, "the Judeo-Christian ideology—unlike that of many other societies—is both dualistic and absolutist" (Counihan 1998a:108). There is no middle ground between good and evil. Morality is understood in black-and-white terms, as an absolute dichotomy between right and wrong, sin and salvation. Western societies add to this dichotomy a dualism between the mind, representing all that is rational and good, and the body, associated with irrationality and evil (Counihan 1998a). As a result, control over the body by the mind is a central moral imperative.

In the United States, particularly in women's experiences, food intake is a central arena in which these moral ideologies are played out (Counihan 1998a; Germov and Williams 1999). Counihan (1998a:109) argues: "Sexual control may have become relatively unimportant, but limitation of eating in the midst of affluence, constant availability of food, and relentless promotion of consumption through advertising is both difficult and highly revered." In this scenario, the mind-body dualism is complicated. In general, the body represents the profane, but this is not equally true of all bodies. On the one hand, the fat body, associated with self-indulgence, giving in to temptations of sensual pleasure, and losing self-control, most clearly represents the profane (Hesse-Biber 1996; Spitzack 1990). On the other hand, the thin body is the outward sign that the mind has won its battle with the body. The thin body is redeemed as it represents restraint, control, and resisting temptation.

This absolutist, dualistic morality extends to food, which is simplistically divided into good and bad (Burgard and Lyons 1994; Hesse-Biber 1996). Again, there is little middle ground. Food that is healthy, that is, nutritionally sound, is acceptable, while food that leads to overindulgence and weight gain is forbidden. In the language of group members, "red-light foods" signal temptation, danger, and sinfulness. The absolutist nature of the ideology explains the tension between moderation and deprivation that characterizes members' discussions of foods such as chocolate and alcohol. In theory, the organization preaches moderation, but the message tends to fall on deaf ears. Members find it hard to believe, if not ludicrous, that high-fat, sweet, or salty foods, such as chocolate, ice cream, or potato chips, can be eaten in moderation. Rather, in typical dualistic fashion, these and similar foods are bad. They are best avoided.

One of the pitfalls of moralistic dualism, of course, is that sin is inevitable. While moderation is possible, absolute goodness is not. Guilt is the predictable outcome. As members use group time to confess their sins, they frequently express guilt due to overeating. But at least as common, if not more so, is guilt over eating foods that they shouldn't have eaten. In this context, exercise takes on particular meanings. Exercise can be seen as punishment for overeating (Burgard and Lyons 1994). Sin occurs as overindulgence or indulgence in bad foods, followed by guilt that literally can be worked off through the hard labor of exercise. Alternatively, exercise is the payment made for the right to sin. In a rather curious inversion of the sin-guilt-punishment-forgiveness cycle, members can use exercise to earn points for more food, or for foods not regularly eaten. In both cases, exercise is directly tied to indulgence, either as the punishment exacted for past indulgence or as the ticket to future indulgence. Rarely do members or leaders talk about the health benefits of exercise independent of weight loss, and it is virtually unheard of to suggest that exercise can be pleasurable in and of itself.

Ritual and Community

For Durkheim (1912), ritual, as a decidedly group phenomenon, is at the core of all religion, and it is in and through ritual that community is defined, constructed, and experienced. Ritual is also at the core of the weight loss group, most obviously in celebration, and it is here that some semblance of community is constructed and reinforced. As members share their frustrations and accomplishments, connections are made. Even as a critical observer, I found it impossible not to be touched by Corinne's pride in losing enough weight to be able to help her young daughter learn to ride a bike, or by Lois's isolation due to extreme obesity, and her newfound freedom as she shed her oxygen tank and was able to leave her house.

The weight loss group is a supportive community, in some ways similar to a self-help support group, but also similar to a church. Not coincidentally, as churches build fellowship and community through sharing food, food is also at the center of the weight loss group's fellowship. Actual food sharing is infrequent, although it occurs on occasion. A beverage table is set up for every meeting, and members commonly drink tea, both regular and decaffeinated coffee, or nonfat hot cocoa during the meeting. Occasionally members bring in food to share when they have tried a recipe for low-fat cookies or some other low-point dessert. And at times the organization gives away food products as door prizes for members in attendance. More commonly, food is figuratively shared, as members exchange recipes, suggestions for accommodating restaurants, and other tricks of the weight loss trade. But while food sharing does occur, it is food restriction that unites members of the weight loss group.

Certainly fasting is a significant religious ritual, practiced in many non-Western, tribal societies, but with a number of crucial differences:

> Many non-Western peoples practice fasting, but rarely with the totality or relentlessness of Western fasting women . . . feasts regularly interrupt periods of reduced consumption, as in the harvest festivals that follow the annual lean times among the Gonja of northern Ghana. . . .
>
> In tribal societies fasting is ordinarily collective and ritualized. A social group or the whole of a society will avoid certain foods; their fasting will follow traditional forms, be endowed with specific meanings, and be sanctioned by society . . . temporary and partial fasting is followed by a public feast and is imbued with significance through collective celebration. Both feasting and fasting—through the ability to control appetite, defer consumption, and share food—affirm humanity and sociability. By contrast, the Western fasting we are considering is solitary, sometimes secretive, and not publicly ritualized. (Counihan 1998:106)

Counihan is discussing extreme fasting, practiced by women with anorexia nervosa or women who, in part for religious reasons, starve themselves, sometimes to death. But the difference between prodigious women fasters and women who diet is in some ways a matter of degree, and their food restriction differs fundamentally from that practiced in non-Western, tribal societies.

Fasting in tribal societies is intricately connected to feasting. Food restrictions are followed by food indulgence. But no such connection exists for dieters. Although the weight-loser can save up for, or exercise in exchange for, an occasional indulgence, there is no explicit ritual connection between restriction and indulgence. Indeed, members are regularly admonished not to reward themselves for weight loss accomplishments with food. One leader told the group, "Food rewards are how we ended up here in the first place." Food restriction is routinely followed not by indulgence but by more restriction, as leaders continually remind members that they are learning a new way to eat. The ritual link between feasting and fasting is effectively broken.

Furthermore, fasting in tribal societies is often a group activity that fosters connection and bonding among community members. On the surface, this is paralleled in the weight loss group. Group members often share experiences of discrimination directed against overweight persons as well as the frustrations and accomplishments associated with weight loss, and these shared experiences promote bonds among them. But on a deeper level, dieting isolates individuals and diminishes the potential for community building. This isolating potential was clearly apparent when Jayne said she had stopped socializing with co-workers because losing weight was easier that way. And it is apparent when members bemoan the obstacles presented by family celebrations and holidays, and suggest it is easier to avoid them. Counihan (1998a:102) observes: "Self-denial of food and refusal to eat with others represent a severe rupture of connection . . . on the most general level food refusal universally signifies rupture of connection."

Emotion and Rationality

A religious perspective on weight loss has the potential to reflect and reinforce the deeply emotional aspects of dieting. Ritual, along with themes of the unknown, transcendence, and otherworldly rewards, give to religion its mystery and power. Theoretically, the same could happen as a religious metaphor is applied to weight loss. Indeed, this does occur to some extent as members seek to understand the apparently illogical process of losing weight, confess their transgressions before others, and sometimes resort to magic and superstition. But overall the potential for the framework of religion to reflect and reinforce dieting as an emotional experience is largely unrealized, for two reasons.

First, dieting is not literally a religion. Rather, a religious framework provides a language that captures some of the critical ways in which religious concepts and perspectives color the weight loss experience. When members speak emotionally about overindulgence and other slips along the dieting path, they clearly draw on religious understandings of temptation, sin, guilt, confession, and forgiveness to make sense of their experiences. But as a language, the metaphor of religion is both incomplete and flexible. As a result, leaders and members can adapt the analogy to weight loss by choosing those elements that are most useful and modifying them as necessary.

Second, it is well to remember that religion itself has changed as it has been affected by and interacts with other societal changes in the United States. For one thing, Ritzer (1996, 1999) argues that the trend toward increased rationalization continues to spread. Emphases on efficiency, calculability, predictability, and automation increasingly characterize a broad range of societal institutions and organizations, including the economy, politics, education, medicine and hospitals, and religion. In a related vein, more and more of our lives are subject to commercialism, and consumption has been elevated as a central value (Ritzer 1999). According to Ritzer (1999), our very consciousness has been transformed, as consumption is increasingly central to our thinking and choices. Furthermore, in continuing a long-term trend, science maintains its foothold as a superior and valued source of explanations for and perspectives on a wide range of phenomena (Wuthnow 1994).

Religion is not immune to these trends. According to Simonds (1992:50), the New Age movement and self-help more generally demonstrate the intermixing of and interaction between religion, commercialism, and science: "Recent self-help books are most often associated with the field of psychology and may seem, on the surface, to comprise a secular genre. But several of the readers I interviewed spoke about their spiritual "growth" and religious convictions. . . . Odd though it may seem, a belief in supreme powers outside the self (which forms the foundation of religious belief) has developed strong ties with a genre that offers guidance toward gaining supreme faith in the self, itself, and that is predicated upon the principles of psychology-made-simple." In the realm of self-help, science has not supplanted religion as a source of insight into human behavior and existence. Instead, religion has become more varied, and religion and science have been combined with and accommodated to each other in a variety of ways.

Even authors of overtly religious self-help books are said to frequently appeal to science to support their arguments (Simonds 1992).

More mainstream religion has also been affected by these societal trends. In his examination of new means of consumption, Ritzer (1999) argues that shopping malls, with the incorporation of nature, festivals, balanced and symmetrical architecture, community, and ceremonial meals, share much in common with religious cathedrals. But he goes on to argue that "we can bring this discussion full-circle by pointing out that although the cathedrals of consumption have a quasi-religious character, religion has begun to emulate those cathedrals" (Ritzer 1999:25–26). As one example, Ritzer offers "mega-churches" that often incorporate contemporary architecture, shops and restaurants, and multimedia presentations, emulating not only shopping malls but amusement parks. Consequently, "we are thinking about more and more places as settings to be consumed and as locales in which we can consume. For example, we are increasingly inclined to think about universities, hospitals, churches, and museums in this way. We see ourselves as consuming them and being able to consume things in them" (Ritzer 1999:188–189).

Rationalization, commercialism, and related trends affect religion in other ways as well. In the small groups examined by Wuthnow (1994), specifically in adult Sunday school classes and Bible study groups, the notion of a spiritual journey was becoming more rational and pragmatic. According to Wuthnow's respondents, spiritual growth not only requires hard work and discipline, but can be divided into concrete, predictable steps. This view is echoed in Simonds's (1992) examination of self-help books. Likewise, while not banished, God is clearly transformed in the face of science, rationalization, commercialism, and other secularizing forces. In effect, God is brought to earth, domesticated, and located solidly in the realm of interpersonal relations (Simonds 1992; Wuthnow 1994). Wuthnow (1994:239) argues:

> The advantage of this conception of God, as most group leaders we talked to see it, is that God becomes more relevant in individuals' daily lives. The disadvantages are less apparent, but are nevertheless worth considering. One is that God ceases to be a supreme being who is in all respects superior to humans. Rather than being the inscrutable deity of the Reformation, for example, God is now a buddy. God no longer represents such awe-inspiring qualities as being infinite, all-powerful, all-knowing, and perfectly righteous. God is now on the same level as yourself,

except perhaps a little warmer and friendlier. . . . The other danger of the present conception is that a God of daily relevance can also become a God of triviality.

As God becomes a buddy or companion, concerned as a friend might be in your everyday life, the power, mystery, and transcendence of God fade into the background.

What do these changes have to do with weight loss? In society at large, religion has not disappeared, despite strong secularizing trends. But religion has adapted to a new context. Churches, religious rituals, and ideas about spiritual growth and God have undergone fundamental changes. To be sure, the changes have had a greater impact in some areas and on some people than others. But there are few areas in which they have not been felt at all. Likewise, in the weight loss group, the religious metaphor is present, and it is meaningful. However, it is a religious metaphor that has accommodated and interacted with strong rationalizing pressures. As a result, the emotional, transcendent aspects of religion are downplayed and muted, although they never entirely disappear.

6 | "If I Had a Plan"

At a meeting in the spring, a few weeks before
Easter, the approaching holiday loomed large. On
this particular occasion, the focus was on overcoming obstacles posed
by holiday celebrations. Near the end of the meeting, after a long discussion of strategies for resisting holiday temptations, Debbie told
the group that the most important way to prepare was to go into holidays and other difficult situations with a well-thought-out plan. To
illustrate her point, she shared a story about a family Easter celebration that had taken place a few years before she joined the group. Debbie
told us that she baked a bunny cake, of which she was very proud,
and took it to the family Easter dinner. She went on to say, "Well, I knew
the cake was in the kitchen, and so after dinner, I volunteered to do the
dishes, and I said I didn't need any help. The whole time I was doing
the dishes, I would cut off just a thin slice of cake, one slice at a time.
By the time I was done, I ate most of the cake. On the way home, I was
in the car with my parents, and I felt really sick from eating all that cake.
I finally told my dad he needed to stop. I went into a restaurant, and
I got into the restroom, and I blacked out from all the sugar I had eaten."
To tie the story to the meeting theme, Debbie finished by saying, "If I
had gone to that family dinner with a plan for dealing with the bunny
cake, I wouldn't have eaten so much that it made me sick!"

Debbie's story is remarkable on a number of counts, not the least
of which is the way she tells it. The account is matter-of-fact, recounted
with little emotion, and emphasizes the need to deal rationally with

complex, emotional situations. Self-help, work, and religion are the most common concepts animating the language of members in the weight loss group. Not only do these metaphors capture the most common perspectives on weight loss in the United States, but the organization actively promotes these views of weight loss. Specific assumptions regarding the causes of overweight and obesity and specific approaches to losing weight are built into the structure and philosophy of the organization. Despite their differences, the concepts of self-help, work, and religion share important commonalities. Most important, individuals are held personally responsible both for being overweight and for losing weight. In the perspectives of self-help and work, weight loss is largely stripped of its emotional components, rationalized, and reduced to the relatively simple solutions of education and discipline. The metaphor of religion has the potential to tap into the more emotional aspects of weight loss, since at least theoretically it can draw on the rituals and transcendent imagery that animate religion in its most basic forms. But as seen in the previous chapter, the weight loss group downplays some elements of religion, and emphasizes temptation, sacrifice, guilt, and surveillance. Buttressed by strong trends toward increasing rationalization in the United States, the more emotional aspects of these experiences are minimized. The good dieter, like the good Protestant (Weber 1904–1905), is reasoned, methodical, and disciplined. Consequently, in the context of self-help, work, and religion, overweight people learn to make the right choices, resist temptation, and suitably modify their lifestyles.

The organization likely attracts members who share these views of weight loss. Many members come to the group already speaking these languages or at least familiar with them. Members who join with different perspectives on weight loss may drop out of the group or through group interaction and socialization, eventually come to share the metaphors and change their language accordingly. There is, however, an alternative view. Were members to join a group like Overeaters Anonymous, they would be exposed to a language and perspective that sees obsessive overeating as an addiction that cannot be cured, but can be treated by faithfully following the prescribed 12-Step program (Lester 1999; van Wormer 1994). The weight loss group described here is not a 12-Step group, and consequently it distances itself from an addiction model of weight gain and loss. Although glimpses of it appear, the addiction concept is most notable in its absence.

To see better how the group positions itself against the addiction model, we begin the chapter with a brief description of Overeaters

Anonymous, which serves as a useful contrast. We then examine three areas where the potential for an addiction framework seems to be high, but is never fully realized. First, as a physiological process closely associated with the unruly, unpredictable, irrational body, hunger is one area we might expect to incorporate the language of addiction. But ultimately the group strips hunger of its emotional content, reduces it to nothing more than a physiological urge, and effectively tames it. Second, issues of control are almost entirely conceptualized as matters of individual willpower. In this area the weight loss group stands in stark contrast to Overeaters Anonymous and an addiction model of overeating. Third, an addiction model is based on a clear dichotomy between normal and abnormal/disordered eating. Notions of normal and abnormal eating also operate in the weight loss group, but their meanings contrast markedly with those in 12-Step and other recovery programs. The chapter concludes with a discussion of the implications of an addiction model of weight loss. Current theory and practice regarding addiction tend to draw on both medical and spiritual perspectives. In many ways the weight loss organization attempts to distance itself from the addiction model, in both its medical and its spiritual manifestations, most notably in its emphasis on willpower as the key to weight loss. At the same time, the weight loss group is subject to some of the same trends and forces that contribute to contemporary views on addiction. Consequently the weight loss organization borrows some elements of an addiction model and adapts them to serve its purposes.

Overeaters Anonymous, Addiction, and Recovery

Overeaters Anonymous (OA) and similar recovery groups are based on a distinct philosophy of obesity and weight loss. Founded in 1960, OA now has approximately 8,500 meeting groups in over fifty countries (Overeaters Anonymous, Inc. 1996–1998a). Designed for anyone suffering from compulsive overeating, OA is based on the 12-Step Alcoholics Anonymous program, which OA modifies only by substituting "food" for "alcohol," and "compulsive overeaters" for "alcoholics" (Lester 1999; van Wormer 1994).

The philosophy and approach of Overeaters Anonymous incorporate a number of basic propositions. Most generally, OA assumes that compulsive overeating is undesirable and thus in need of change (Lester 1999). Second, OA states, "We believe that compulsive overeating is a progressive illness . . . one that, like alcoholism and some other illnesses, can be arrested" (Overeaters Anonymous, Inc. 1996–1998b), but since it is an emotional, spiritual, and physical disease, it cannot be cured (Lester 1999; van Wormer 1994). Third, the compulsive overeater must accept her or his powerlessness over the disease and instead submit to a higher power (Hesse-Biber 1996; Lester 1999; Overeaters Anonymous, Inc. 1996–1998c). A number of other concepts also operate in OA, including the belief that the addict can clearly be distinguished from the nonaddict; the commitment to the lifetime use of a self-label in recognition that compulsive overeating is incurable; and the understanding that recovery comes from addressing the internal emotional and spiritual illness, rather than by losing weight (Lester 1999; van Wormer 1994). Like Alcoholics Anonymous, OA focuses on abstinence, but unlike the alcoholic, who must abstain from alcohol, the overeater must abstain not from food but from overeating. OA states: "By admitting inability to control compulsive overeating in the past, and abandoning the idea that all one needs to be able to eat normally is a 'little willpower,' it becomes possible to abstain from overeating—one day at a time" (Overeaters Anonymous, Inc. 1996–1998a). To aid in recovery and continued abstinence, OA offers compulsive overeaters eight tools: a plan of eating, sponsorship, meetings, the telephone, writing, literature, anonymity, and service (Overeaters Anonymous, Inc. 1997).

Personal stories are central to Overeaters Anonymous's approach to recovery from overeating, and tend to follow a predictable, basic structure: "The most prominent themes include the period in life when compulsive eating began or became salient; use of food to soothe emotional pain; denial that the compulsive eating poses a problem; hitting a 'low point,' often characterized by some sort of 'craziness' (stealing, hiding in the bathroom and eating, vomiting several times a day, etc.); discovery that OA [Overeaters Anonymous] exists; first meeting (often followed by a period of vacillation or resistance to the program); acceptance of the program and a feeling of 'coming home'; and how life has been transformed since finding OA" (Lester 1999:147–148). None of these elements appears in Debbie's binge story about the bunny cake. She gives no justification for her actions, but implies that she simply wanted to eat the cake. And while bingeing to the point of blacking out might certainly qualify as the sort of "craziness" recognized by OA, Debbie does not represent it as such, nor does she see it as a turning point in her life. Most notably, the deep emotion that accompanies storytelling in OA (Lester 1999) is virtually nonexistent in Debbie's story. Rather, she emphasizes planning ahead as a rational strategy for coping with difficult eating situations.

Two general themes underlie the Overeaters Anonymous philosophy and approach. First, because OA explicitly defines overeating as a disease, it reflects and reinforces the increasing medicalization (Riessman 1983) of social problems, including obesity and weight loss. Second, because OA more specifically defines the illness of compulsive overeating as an addiction, it highlights the problematic nature of the human body, which continually threatens to run out of control. With its emphasis on losing and regaining control, the addiction approach overlaps to some degree with the religious approach. Indeed, in the case of OA, the addiction and religious models are conflated, as the only solution to the incurable disease of overeating is to hand oneself over entirely to a higher power. But while the religious perspective emphasizes the problematic nature of specific foods that are especially tempting, the addiction perspective locates the problem not in certain foods but in specific individuals' responses to particular foods.

The weight loss organization examined here targets people with weight problems presumably attributed to bad habits that can fairly easily be changed through education and lifestyle modification. The very philosophy and structure of the organization build on this assumption. This is not a 12-Step program designed for people with severely disordered eating problems. Groups such as Overeaters Anonymous and other 12-Step programs are more likely to attract members who feel that they have "hit bottom." In this context, expressions of desperation are likely to be more common, and a greater emphasis is likely to be placed on celebrating significant, personal milestones on the path to recovery. This is not meant to suggest that weight loss group members never feel desperation. A pervasive pathos characterizes group meetings. Members may not have hit bottom, but those who have tried and failed numerous times to lose weight commonly experience frustration and, on occasion, desperation. But whereas the Overeaters Anonymous member sees the solution in surrendering control to a higher power, the weight loss group member holds on to the belief that personal control is not only possible but necessary. Nowhere is this clearer than in the weight loss group's approach to hunger.

Hunger

Discussions of hunger are most notable in their scarcity. Leaders sometimes mention hunger, usually to distinguish the organization's approach from diets, which because they are based on deprivation, lead to hunger. Ultimately this is their downfall. In contrast, leaders argue that because under organization rules no foods are forbidden, and because the plan is based on lifestyle modification, not a short-term diet, deprivation and hunger are unnecessary. But despite leaders' best efforts, members struggle with hunger. I was most acutely aware of hunger during the first several days after I joined the group. My hunger, due to a rather dramatic decrease in the number of calories I consumed, was exacerbated by the seemingly inordinate amount of time spent planning meals, preparing foods, and weighing and measuring everything I ate. In addition, being fond of chocolate and other sweet foods, I experienced what I described in my journal as "severe sugar cravings." Consequently I was anxious, irritable, and spent a great deal of time counting the minutes until my next meal. All told, those were not pleasant days.

I was not alone in my experience of hunger. During one group discussion, Peggy said that she did OK early in the day, and she would have lunch, but then, "every day about 2:00 I'll be ravishing [sic] hungry!" Frustrated, Peggy asked what she could do. Debbie directed the question to the group, and Joyce said, "In the afternoon, I always have my special snack. I take my chocolate graham crackers, spread peanut butter on them, and I have that every single day." Debbie picked up on Joyce's suggestion and started talking about different kinds of snacks you can eat, and how high-fiber snacks are really filling. She compared a can of green beans, with relatively little fiber, to a can of sauerkraut, with more fiber, and suggested that the latter would be more filling. At this point, Peggy looked highly skeptical, and asked, "You mean you could actually sit down and eat a can of sauerkraut for a snack?" Then Jayne spoke up and said, "When I hit a hungry time, I just make myself exercise, and then I'm not hungry anymore." If Peggy's facial expression was any indication, she found this suggestion virtually unbelievable.

The group's response to Peggy's problem is noteworthy both for what it implies about the conceptualization of hunger and for what it suggests about the group's perspectives on food. Members see hunger as a physiological urge, experienced by the physical body. Emotions are assumed to be irrelevant. In reacting to Peggy's description of her feelings of being "ravishing hungry," no one takes note of the intensity of her language. Even the physiological aspects of Peggy's experience are downplayed. No one, including Debbie, asks her when or what she eats for lunch. Instead, Peggy's struggle is transformed into a routine discussion of suitable snacks, and when Debbie suggests that high-fiber foods like sauerkraut are particularly filling, the relationship between hunger and appetite is completely submerged. The separation of hunger and appetite is even more apparent when Jayne suggests that exercise can be substituted for food, implying that perhaps the hunger is not real. Indeed, leaders often suggest that members may think they are hungry, when they are actually eating for emotional reasons. Thus leaders urge members to think before they eat, to check in with their bodies as well as their emotions, and to take the time to determine whether they are responding to physiological urges or emotional urges. After this self-assessment, if the member concludes that she is not really hungry, the solution is to do something else, like exercise. If, on the other hand, the member concludes that she is indeed hungry in a physiological sense, the solution is to eat a healthy, filling snack.

Once hunger is defined as a purely physiological urge, food becomes important primarily as a means to assuage the hunger. Missing is any recognition that food can be pleasurable in and of itself. Furthermore, the fact that some foods may be more appetizing than others is completely downplayed. Unlike the alcoholic who can abstain from alcohol, the overeater cannot abstain from food. However, as is suggested by Overeaters Anonymous, the overeater can abstain from overeating. In the context of the weight loss group, overeating is prevented by choosing good foods, that is, those foods that fill you up, making it less likely that you will eat more than necessary. In this context Debbie's suggestion that sauerkraut is a good snack is somewhat understandable. But what Debbie doesn't acknowledge, despite Peggy's skepticism, is that for many people, sauerkraut is not an especially appetizing snack. Ultimately hunger and appetite seem to have little to do with each other.

Yet hunger and appetite are deeply and intricately connected in complex ways:

> Hunger is not often regarded as an emotion, as it is viewed more as a drive or instinct unmediated by social states. Yet, it would be difficult to argue that hunger is purely a biological phenomenon, given the web of cultural significations that surround and govern the ways and amounts and times that we eat. The physiological relationship between the body's recognition of the need for food and the emotional state is clearly complex. There are different kinds of hunger, related to the concept of appetite. An appetite is an emotionally flavoured hunger: the appetite experienced when a favourite food is being cooked and is almost ready to be served differs from that of the simple hunger felt when the stomach is empty and requires food. So too, lack of appetite is often an emotional response, an interaction between a feeling of anxiety, ner-

vousness, grief or even joy or elation (the emotion of being "in love" is often associated with a loss of appetite). In such an emotional state involving loss of appetite, hunger may still be experienced as a gnawing feeling, an awareness of an empty stomach, but the desire to eat is stifled; food may even appear nauseating. On the other hand, the experience of hunger, if strong enough, and if not satisfied, may inspire the emotions of anxiety, irritability or anger. An appetite, or desire, for a certain food may exist independently of a feeling for hunger, and hunger may exist without having much of an appetite. (Lupton 1996:33)

The complexity of the relationship between hunger and appetite, body and emotion, is entirely absent in the discussion of Peggy's "ravishing" hunger. Appetite is ignored altogether, hunger is reduced to a biological urge, and the appropriate response to hunger is a rational calculation of the most effective food or activity for assuaging it. Only in this context does it make sense to suggest that exercise is an appropriate substitute for food. At the same time, group members express a degree of ambivalence concerning the pleasures of food. On the one hand, some foods are clearly seen as more practical, better choices than others, precisely because they fill you up and consequently decrease the likelihood of overeating. On the other hand, the group pays much attention to making good foods, that is, nutritionally sound and filling foods, taste good: hence the time spent discussing suitable substitutions for high-fat ingredients, suggestions for filling snacks and easy meals, and the exchange of recipes. The sensual pleasure of food, some of which is relatively lacking in nutritional value, tends to be downplayed, if not entirely ignored. Consequently, comfort food is an oxymoron, if not an unhealthy or even dangerous way of viewing food. From this perspective, obtaining pleasure and comfort from food is highly problematic, and the ultimate value is placed on maintaining rational control over the body and its urges.

Keeping It under Control

If there is a single, overriding theme that characterizes the weight loss group's perspective on and approach to losing weight, it is the importance of getting and maintaining control over your eating. Only one week after I joined the group, and after speaking with me only briefly, Cheryl predicted I would do very well on the program, because I seemed "focused." Cheryl never explicitly mentions control, but being focused connotes discipline, concentration, and staying on track, that is, maintaining control. Discussions at meetings routinely concern keeping one's control, particularly in difficult situations. Preparing for and managing holidays are frequent discussion topics. At the meeting when Debbie role-played a tempting hostess at a holiday celebration, gaining weight was at least theoretically presented as a viable option for holiday eating. But in the ensuing discussion, not a single member admitted she intended to gain weight over the holidays, and very few said they simply intended to maintain their weight. Instead, all seemed intent on keeping their holiday eating under control, and subsequently continuing their weight loss through the holiday season.

Ruth, Debbie, and Richard routinely ended meetings by asking members what challenges they expected to confront in the coming week, and asking for suggestions for meeting the challenges. Members frequently mentioned upcoming vacations, business travel, and a wide variety of social events, including family reunions, weddings, birthday celebrations, picnics, sporting events, and parties. Along with holidays, these situations are significant to members precisely because they pose the threat of losing control, and hence demand constant vigilance. But, while special occasions present particular challenges to maintaining control, members generally see loss of control as a constant threat, and maintaining control as a never-ending challenge.

Given the extreme value placed on self-control, two relatively minor incidents stand out. The first involves Jack, who joined and attended with his wife, Nancy. As the Labor Day weekend approached, Jack told the group that he and Nancy were spending the weekend on their boat with friends. Convinced that he was going to lose control over his eating, Jack characterized the weekend as "a lost cause." The second incident, described earlier, involved Joe, who joined and attended with his wife, Suzanne. Ruth was leading a discussion on positive thinking and planning ahead. In stark contrast to the point and tenor of the discussion, Joe reported that he and Suzanne were going on a cruise, and he emphatically stated that he was quite certain that he would "go crazy" and "out of control."

Joe and Jack both explicitly focus on control, but interestingly, assume that in their cases, loss of control is not only expected but inevitable. In stark contrast to the majority of conversations pertaining to control, neither Joe nor Jack asks the group for suggestions for maintaining control, nor does either man express any interest whatsoever in the suggested strategies for planning for and coping with problematic situations like holidays or vacations. Indeed, in the case of Joe, both Ruth and group members try to, first, convince him that loss of control is not inevitable, and second, appeal to the presumed feelings of guilt and regret that he will experience after his overindulgence. Joe is not in any way swayed by the group's efforts, and Ruth, not entirely sure how to respond, moves the discussion to another topic.

When the incidents with Joe and Jack are considered in conjunction with the routine and pervasive attention given to self-control, two themes emerge. First is the grave necessity of exerting one's willpower over the always threatening, potentially unruly body. In the context of the weight loss group, the greatest failing is giving in or, ultimately, giving up. Losing weight is the concrete goal that members work toward, but from the group's perspective, small and slow weight losses are tolerated as long as you demonstrate your willingness to keep striving to control your eating. Willpower is the greatest virtue, and it is precisely Joe's and Jack's lack of willpower that provokes the greatest concern among other members. This is one area where the group obviously positions itself against an addiction model. The group's expectation of and emphasis on willpower clearly contrasts with the view of Overeaters Anonymous that sheer willpower is incapable of overcoming the compulsion to overeat (Lester 1999; van Wormer 1994). According to OA, overeating can be controlled only when the belief in willpower is abandoned, and one's problems with food are handed over to a higher power, explicitly stated in the first three steps of the 12-Step plan:

1. We admitted we were powerless over food—that our lives had become unmanageable.
2. Came to believe that a Power greater than ourselves could restore us to sanity.
3. Made a decision to turn our will and our lives over to the care of God as we understood Him. (Overeaters Anonymous, Inc. 1986–1998c)

Handing over control, even to a higher power, is highly unlikely to resonate with individuals for whom the greatest threat is losing control and the highest virtue is personal willpower.

The organization's concern with willpower reflects the traditional mind-body dualism so common in Western thought (Williams and Bendelow 1998). As will be recalled, in this way of thinking, the body represents all that is mistrusted. The body is instinct, physical urges, drives, and troublesome emotions that continually threaten to run amok. As physical matter, and a lower form of being, the body must be tamed and controlled. In contrast, the mind represents rationality, and the human being's ability to rise above and master the body, thus, it is the mind that exerts the requisite control over the unruly body. Flowing from the mind-body dualism, the group's concerns with hunger and willpower converge. On the most basic level, hunger, as a physiological urge, is clearly associated with the body, and it is the mind, via willpower, that tames the hunger and reasserts control over the body. But the situation is somewhat more complicated. When hungry, members are exhorted not to mistrust, tame, and control the body but, rather, to listen to it very closely. It is not the body per se that causes problems. Purely as a physiological state, hunger is a real experience. Emotions, not physiological urges, are problematic. First, emotions may confuse or at least distract the mind, and thereby interfere with its ability to accurately read the body's messages. Hence, when members experience what they think is hunger, they are directed to first determine whether or not they are *really* hungry, or whether they are experiencing emotions such as sadness, frustration, or anger. Furthermore, in their association with appetite, emotions can interfere with the mind's ability to rationally respond to the body's hunger in an appropriate fashion. Leaders therefore remind members that if in fact they are truly hungry some food choices are considerably better than others. In sum, willpower consists not so much in mastering or conquering the body, but in taming the emotions, so that the mind can first move into synchrony with what is actually occurring in the physical body and then respond to the body in a rational manner.

The second theme that emerges from group discussions about willpower and self-control is the gendered nature of concerns about control. It is not insignificant that throughout over two years of observations, the only two times that loss of control is seen as both inevitable and nonproblematic involve men. The vast majority of women in the group see the potential for losing control as inevitable, but they also firmly believe that with advance preparation and an iron will, maintaining control is entirely possible. Why, then, are Joe and Jack apparently immune? Why do they so readily concede loss of control, and, why do they express no regret about giving in? Given the very small number of men that join the group, it is impossible to draw strong conclusions, and it is hazardous indeed to make generalizations based on two incidents. At the same time, reading Joe's and Jack's responses against previous research and theorizing raises important issues concerning gender and control. Bodies are not all equally threatening. Deeply held beliefs about gender overlie and interact with the traditional mind-body dualism (Williams and Bendelow 1998). It is women's bodies that are most problematic. While men are associated with thought, logic, and rationality, women are associated with mysterious bodily urges, emotions, and irrationality. Add to this the fact that patriarchal power distributions preclude women from exercising effective power and self-determination in most areas of their lives, and it becomes understandable why dieting women see willingly giving up self-control as so threatening and problematic.

Normalizing Problem Eating/ Problematizing Normal Eating

The use of an addiction model for understanding issues of body weight and weight loss is most apparent in the literature on eating disorders, most notably, anorexia nervosa, bulimia, and compulsive overeating (Lester 1999; Spitzack 1990; van Wormer 1994). With respect to the last, Overeaters Anonymous holds as fundamental the belief that the compulsive overeater suffers from a physical addiction to overeating (Overeaters Anonymous 1996–1998a). In fact, speaking of eating disorders only makes sense if it is assumed that it is possible to identify normal eating.

The weight loss group also distinguishes between disordered and normal eating, but at best the distinction is fuzzy. Take, for example, the discussion of "eating secrets" that took place at one of my first meetings. Linda started the discussion by describing her own propensity to sneak donuts at work, rather than openly eat them in front of her co-workers. She went on to recount a story told by a member at a different meeting: "She was in my other group. She used to hide food all the time. Once, she hid some food in the laundry basket and then forgot she put it there. After a week or so it started to smell, and that's when her husband found it!" There was little response when Linda asked members to share their own secrets. She tried to prompt admissions, first by asking how many people didn't chart everything they ate, and later, by asking whether anyone failed to follow the plan all week, only to refrain from eating and drinking before coming to the meeting and getting weighed. In response to both questions, several members laughed and nodded their heads. Right before closing the meeting, Linda said she had a book of recipes for easy entertaining that she would give to someone for disclosing an eating secret. Lori immediately raised her hand and said, "I like to eat at night!" Linda seemed puzzled, and asked, "Well, what do you eat?" Lori paused for several seconds and responded, "Oh, potato chips, pretzels, Doritos." Linda asked, "All at once?" Lori answered, "No, not really." At this point, out of time and somewhat perplexed, Linda gave Lori the book and said, "OK, you win."

Presumably a discussion of eating secrets would be fertile ground for uncovering disordered eating. But an examination of the secrets revealed suggests otherwise. Members obviously see hiding food and eating secretly as problematic, both because they are out of the ordinary and because they imply that the eating itself is deviant. But when a member asked Linda why she found it necessary to hide her donuts from other people, she shrugged and replied, "It was just me being weird." Once hiding food and eating secretly are defined as individual quirks, their political and cultural contexts are ignored, and women's problematic and ambivalent experiences with food and eating go unrecognized and unexplored. Similarly, fasting is seen as a problem on one level, since it is closely associated with deprivation, but it is at least widely tolerated, if not actively encouraged, as a logical way to cope with and manipulate weigh-in. Not charting everything you eat is only a problem in the specific context of the weight loss group, and it is not at all clear why eating at night would be a problem, unless it were done secretly, or done to the extent of binging.

So, from the group's perspective, what is normal eating and what is not? The relative lack of evidence of highly disordered eating by members is not surprising. The organization's official policy is that individuals with eating disorders cannot join the group. Consequently, very few group discussions concern behaviors that are clearly recognizable as disordered. The one exception appears to be binge eating. On the surface, eating to extreme excess is seen as abnormal. When Gail, the character in a videotape, eats nearly an entire cake, and Debbie describes blacking out from a "sugar overdose," these are readily recognized as extreme and problematic behaviors. In a related vein, members frequently use very negative language to describe the feeling of fullness that accompanies eating large amounts of food. One day at the scales I overheard Dana tell the receptionist, "I knew I didn't do good this week. I felt like a big, fat balloon—all bloated and stuffed. You know, like you feel after Thanksgiving when you've eaten all that food." But while binge eating is seen as not entirely normal, there are problems with its very conceptualization. The differences between binge eating, compulsive overeating and occasionally overeating, are not at all clear. Furthermore, the emotional aspects of binge eating are not dealt with at all. When Debbie described her "sugar overdose," she did not mention what motivated her to consume a large quantity of cake, nor did she describe what she felt at the time. When members viewed the videotape concerning Gail's consumption of a whole cake, they tried to discuss Gail's stress and frustration. But Richard effectively ignored their attempts and turned the discussion to why Gail had the cake there to begin with. When bingeing or overeating is discussed, it is almost always in the context of identifying concrete, rational solutions for their prevention.

At the same time that binge eating is seen as at least disorderly, if not disordered, a wide range of potentially problematic behaviors are tolerated, if not encouraged. First, it is clear that a fairly large number of members fast prior to weigh-in to compensate for overeating and to manipulate scales. Members readily admit to skipping meals before getting weighed, even though several meetings do not begin until seven or seven-thirty in the evening, and hunger is a frequent topic of discussion before meetings begin, as members anticipate being able to eat after the meeting ends. Second, relatively large and rapid weight losses are common, even though the organization officially recommends a weight loss rate of one to two pounds per week. Large losses, ranging from five to over ten pounds are not unusual, especially during a member's first week on the plan. Not only are large losses tolerated, but they are admired and rewarded. While leaders encourage members to recognize all weight losses, no matter how small, members erupt spontaneously into "oohs," "ahs," and applause when losses over three pounds are announced. Rarely is concern expressed when a member loses a very large amount of weight in a single week. One day I was sitting next to Betty when Dawn announced that she had lost eleven pounds in her first week on the program. Betty frowned and whispered, "I don't think that's good." But Betty was apparently alone in her concern. No one, including the leader, seemed troubled by Dawn's rapid and large loss. Rather, it was greeted with applause and verbal encouragement to keep it up. Third, the organization not only accepts but expects nearly compulsive attention to food and eating. It is common for leaders and members alike to blame overeating on mindlessly eating, that is, not paying attention to what you are eating. Members are told to count and write down every single thing they eat, including licks from a cooking spoon and breath mints. At one meeting, the discussion topic was "counting bites and nibbles." The necessity of weighing and measuring portions increases the time and energy members must invest in preparing and attending to food.

While an addiction model of weight loss implies that it is useful to distinguish abnormal eating from normal eating, the very meanings of normal and abnormal are distorted in the weight loss group. Binge eating is conflated with overeating, and a whole range of odd if not disordered behaviors, such as fasting, rapid weight loss, and investing large amounts of time and energy in food and eating, come to define normal ways of eating and losing weight.

Speaking of Addiction

The observed weight loss group is not a 12-Step program, nor does it target individuals who clearly suffer from severely disordered eating. There is no explicit discussion of overeating as an addiction. Indeed, in many ways, the organization positions itself in contrast to an addiction model of weight gain and loss. Even among individuals and organizations that define compulsive overeating as an addiction, and addiction as a disease, there are different interpretations of what this means. First, the medical approach sees addiction as a disease in a traditional medical sense. That is, the condition is assumed to have a physiological basis, and medical practitioners are seen as the legitimate diagnosticians and purveyors of treatment (Riessman 1983). Second, the spiritual model of addiction is best reflected in the philosophy and approach of Overeaters Anonymous. Addiction is defined as a disease, but the emphasis, particularly for treatment, is placed on a higher power rather than on the medical establishment.

The two models overlap in some ways, but differ substantially on a number of points. First, although both models view addiction as a disease, the medical model focuses almost exclusively on the physical manifestations of the disease, while the spiritual model recognizes significant emotional and spiritual components. Second, the models differ in their views on the importance of willpower. In suggesting that the ill person must want to get better, the medical model recognizes some role for willpower, but the spiritual model argues that willpower is entirely insufficient, and may in fact interfere with treatment. Consequently the models differ on a third dimension, the presumed cure for the disease. From the medical perspective, the ill person must willingly cooperate with medical practitioners, who have full responsibility for delivering treatment. The spiritual perspective on curing is somewhat more complex. Addiction, whether it is to alcohol, gambling, or overeating, is a progressive disease and cannot be cured. It can, however, be arrested, but only if the addict surrenders his or her illness and treatment to a higher power. Fourth, the approaches differ in how much they emphasize emotions. Medical practitioners have recently paid more attention to the emotional and psychological components of physical illness, but emotions are most relevant as they affect the ill person's desire to get better. In contrast, from the spiritual perspective, emotions are at the very core of addiction. The medical and the spiritual models are similar, however, to the extent that they both individualize illness and define the cultural, political, and economic context of addiction as irrelevant.

Does the weight loss group take anything from these models of addiction and disease? Although the group does not define overeating as a disease, it certainly recognizes it as unhealthy. In contrast to both models, the weight loss group privileges willpower as the key to dealing with overeating. The weight loss group therefore places complete responsibility for treatment solely in the hands of the overeater, rather than in a higher power or medical practitioners. Additionally, in contrast to the spiritual model, but similar to the medical model, the weight loss group downplays emotions, although the group recognizes that emotions may interfere with the ability to exert willpower. What the weight loss group clearly shares with both models of addiction is the view that the cultural, political, and economic context of overeating is largely inconsequential.

In sum, the weight loss group shares little in common with the medical and spiritual perspectives on addiction. This position has several significant consequences. First, the one commonality between the group's perspective and the addiction perspective is the belief that weight is an individual issue, devoid of social, economic, or political relevance. Consequently the group individualizes and depoliticizes weight issues. An addiction model sees individuals as solely responsible for both the cause and the cure of the addiction: "Although they are free and, therefore, outside the market economy, twelve-step programs still fuel the medicalization of women's obsession with weight. They replace a focus on women's oppression and exploitation with the apolitical perspective of addiction, suggesting that therapy, rather than political action, will provide the 'cure.' Women in these programs are locked into depending on others" (Hesse-Biber 1996:117). The weight loss group is not a 12-Step group, and does not advocate therapy as a solution for overeating, but it does focus on the internal sources of overeating and argues that willpower is the key to control. The group pays virtually no attention to the billions of dollars spent on advertising highly processed, unhealthy "convenience" foods, the environmental and health hazards of a highly profitable fast food industry, or the narrow, nondiverse representations of women's bodies that proliferate in popular culture. Discussions of convenience foods and fast food do occur, but only as members share strategies for incorporating them into the program. And while members at times share stories of the prejudice and discrimination they have encountered due to their weight, the only solution advanced is losing weight to conform to societal standards.

Theoretically, a disease model of behavior can lessen the guilt and shame associated with conditions like alcoholism, attention deficit hyperactivity disorder, or depression. Persons diagnosed as ill may be less likely to be blamed for their conditions (Hesse-Biber 1996). This is not the case, however, for obesity. Despite accumulating evidence of a genetic component, popular opinion still holds that the major cause of obesity is overeating, a behavior freely chosen by and completely under the control of individuals. Like cigarette smokers who contract cancer, obese persons are assumed to have gotten what they asked for. Ultimately the group's perspective, like the addiction model, diverts attention away from the political, economic, and cultural context of overeating, weight gain, and weight loss, and holds individuals entirely accountable for both the causes of and the cures for their conditions.

The second consequence of the group's perspective relates to the human body and the effects of emotions on body weight. Were the group to model itself after 12-Step groups, emotions would receive significantly more attention. Overeaters Anonymous explicitly recognizes the centrality of emotions in the manifestation, experience, and treatment of compulsive overeating (Overeaters Anonymous, Inc. 1996–1998a). Lester (1999:146) states: "The physical recovery—losing weight—is not a focus of the program, although it usually occurs as a result. Recovering from the inside out is often a difficult notion for newcomers to accept. As one OA member noted, 'we are conditioned to seek "quick fixes" such as Jenny Craig, Slim Fast, and Weight Watchers, so the idea that one should focus on feelings rather than on weight often seems quite alien and frightening to newcomers.' " In contrast, to the extent that the weight loss group addresses emotions, they are seen as largely problematic and in need of control, a view that harks back to the traditional mind-body dualism. Emotions, dangerous and potentially out of control, are allied with the body, and must be rationally controlled by the mind (Williams and Bendelow 1998).

Nowhere is the contrast between the approaches of OA and the weight loss group clearer than in the concept of journaling. Writing is one of the eight tools of recovery employed by OA:

> In addition to writing our inventories and the list of people we have harmed, most of us have found that writing has been an indis-

pensable tool for working the Steps. Further, putting our thoughts and feelings down on paper, or describing a troubling incident, helps us to better understand our actions and reactions in a way that is often not revealed to us by simply thinking or talking about them. In the past, compulsive eating was our most common reaction to life. When we put our difficulties down on paper, it becomes easier to see situations more clearly and perhaps better discern any necessary action. (Overeaters Anonymous, Inc. 1997)

Similar to popular understandings of keeping a journal, writing in OA involves active self-reflection about one's experiences and emotional responses. The point of journaling in OA is to explore the complex feelings that surround food, overeating, weight gain, and weight loss. In stark contrast, when weight loss group members and leaders speak of "journaling," they are referring to keeping meticulous records of everything they eat. The weekly journal members receive is a small pamphlet with spaces for recording daily food consumption. Although there is a small amount of space to write questions for the leader, there is no space for self-reflection. Nor is it ever suggested that members might find it useful to keep a personal, reflective journal. Devoid of all emotion and reflection, the weight loss journal is reduced to a rational, quantitative record of food intake.

As emotions are downplayed, willpower and self-control are elevated in importance. The mind ultimately triumphs. And yet the situation is not quite this simple. Emotions are obviously apparent in the weight loss group, especially during discussions as members describe accomplishments, setbacks, and frustrations and openly express disappointment, anger, jealousy, resentment, despair, pride, and other feelings. In some ways the organization's goals conflict with members' needs. While the organization emphasizes rational strategizing, group members also seek emotional support from the group. Furthermore, the group does not unilaterally privilege mind over body. Since hunger is a real, physiological state, and because hunger must be satisfied, leaders counsel members to listen carefully to their bodies. Emotions are not inconsequential. Specifically, they may interfere with the ability to accurately read the body. Leaders repeatedly remind members to ask themselves whether they are truly hungry. Only if they are not distracted by emotional responses can members determine what the body is actually experiencing. The goal is not so much for the mind to conquer the body as it is to bring the mind and body into greater synchrony. The obvious downside to this formulation is that eating is solely a matter of physical nourishment, and the emotional aspects of food and appetite are banished.

The third and final implication of the group's perspective is that the borderline between normal, disorderly, and disordered eating is severely blurred. In general, the addiction model reinforces the distinction between normal and abnormal eating. But in the weight loss group, abnormal and normal eating take on specific and peculiar meanings. Because members define themselves as overweight and come to the group specifically to lose weight, abnormal eating is eating which leads to weight gain. Consequently overeating, indulging in high-fat, high-calorie, non-nutritious foods, eating to relieve boredom, sadness, frustration, or other emotions, and eating for sheer pleasure are problematic and disorderly, if not disordered. In contrast, normal eating is eating that is regimented, nonemotional, and carefully monitored and controlled. Somewhat similarly, to help individuals determine whether or not they are compulsive overeaters, Overeaters Anonymous (1996–1998b) offers a series of questions that includes the following: "Do you eat when you're not hungry?" "Do you give too much time and thought to food?" "Do you look forward with pleasure and anticipation to the time when you can eat alone?" "Do you crave to eat at a definite time, day or night, other than mealtime?" "Do you eat to escape from worries or trouble?"

Contrast this approach to the definition of normal eating advanced by the dietician and therapist Ellyn Satter (1987:69):

> Normal eating is being able to eat when you are hungry and continue eating until you are satisfied. . . . It is leaving some cookies on the plate because you know you can have some again tomorrow, or it is eating more now because they taste so wonderful when they are fresh. Normal eating is overeating at times: feeling stuffed and uncomfortable. It is also undereating at times and wishing you had more. Normal eating is trusting your body to make up for your mistakes in eating. Normal eating takes up some of your time and attention, but keeps its place as only one important area of your life. In short, normal eating is flexible. It varies in response to your emotions, your schedule, your hunger, and your proximity to food. (quoted in Burgard and Lyons 1994:220)

Several dimensions of this definition conflict with the weight loss group's definition of normal eating. First, appetite and emotion, rather than sabotaging weight loss efforts, are recognized as legitimate reasons for and components of eating. Second, rather than suggesting that the body should be controlled, or even listened to, Satter goes further to insist that the body be trusted, an alien notion indeed in most weight loss groups. Finally, flexible eating is a far cry from the rationalized, systematic, and controlled approach that the group advocates. In Satter's view eating behaviors that in the group would be seen as problematic, come to define normal eating.

7

"Be Your Own Best Friend"

Given the strong and pervasive criticism of the weight loss industry by feminist scholars and activists, the operation of a feminist perspective in the weight loss group seems unlikely. However, the feminist movement has affected women in the United States to varying degrees and in various ways, despite a concerted backlash, particularly in popular culture (Faludi 1991). Ironically, for its own economic survival, the weight loss organization must continue to attract women who to some extent have been sensitized to the negative consequences of a cultural obsession with physical appearance and thinness. This task is facilitated as feminism is subtly mainstreamed into popular culture, and made to appear compatible with such traditional values as self-determination, hard work, individualism, and consumerism (Douglas 1994; Macdonald 1995). Feminism is now more palatable to a general audience, but at the same time the potential for radical change is diluted.

Glimpses of a feminist concept of dieting and weight loss are apparent when weight changes are related to women's roles. Usually this is framed as an exercise in stress management. One evening Debbie had written on a sheet of newsprint, "stress defined: the nonspecific response of the body to change." She began by reading the definition and suggested that it is useful to distinguish between chronic and acute stress, and between sources of stress that are controllable and uncontrollable. When she asked for examples of things that cause stress, members listed job pressures, family problems, relationships with others, illnesses, and financial difficulties. Connie said, "Stressors aren't just bad things, like getting sick. Weddings or a child coming home from college are also stressful. They're good things, but they can be really stressful." Debbie went on to solicit suggestions for managing stress. Faye said, "You gotta set priorities," and similarly, Hope said, "Look at your schedule; see what you can get rid of." Nancy said, "Delegate— you don't have to do it all yourself." Betty suggested, "Get moving; it always helps to exercise and get rid of some of the tension." Jayne said, "Change your routine." Debbie listed the suggestions on the newsprint and asked for examples of how members had used these or other strategies. Connie replied, "Before my kids left for college, I cooked dinner every night. But with work schedules and school activities, lots of times they wouldn't even be there to eat it. But then they would get home later and they wanted help cooking something, or they wanted me to do something, or they would leave their messes all over the kitchen for me to clean up. Finally, something just clicked. I said, 'No, I'm done. They can do it themselves.' " After hesitating a moment, Connie continued, "It felt really *powerful!*" Debbie acknowledged the value of Connie's approach, but because we were running out of time, said she wanted to end the meeting by leading us through a stress-relief exercise. After telling us that we were going to "take a mental vacation," Debbie said, "put your feet flat on the floor, gently rest your hands in your lap, close your eyes, and picture your favorite place." Quietly, Debbie asked, "Where are you?" After pausing a minute, she said, "Who is with you?" and then after another pause, she asked, "What are you doing there?" Debbie said we should stay there for a while, and then she remained silent for two to three minutes. She ended the exercise by noting that visualization was an easy technique we could use whenever we felt stressed.

As the discussion of stress management unfolds, both the potential and the limits of a feminist approach to weight loss become apparent. There are several problems with the discussion. The suggested coping strategies are not evaluated for relative effectiveness or viability in different situations, nor are they evaluated for the degree to which they address the root causes of women's stress. Exercise and visualization may alleviate some physical manifestations of stress, but they do nothing to alleviate or minimize its sources. Nor do they reduce the likelihood of future stress. Prioritizing, delegating, reviewing and changing your schedule, and saying no to others may be more effective, but only if they reduce the inequitable demands placed on women's time, attention, and energy.

All the strategies are individual solutions to what is clearly defined as a personal problem. Members do imply that interpersonal relations and women's roles contribute to stress. But an explicit critique of gender roles or gender-based discrimination is conspicuously absent. Connie's attempt to assert herself and draw boundaries around her time and energy is a significant step. However, the gender-based household division of labor that holds women responsible for feeding and nurturing others goes unquestioned. The entire discussion only reinforces the view that stress is a personal problem, not a public issue, and should be addressed via individual coping strategies rather than institutional or societal change (Mills 1959).

Despite the limited, problematic conceptualization of stress in the group, there are nonetheless fleeting indications of a budding feminist consciousness. Some of the coping strategies, including prioritizing, delegating, and saying no, involve redrawing personal boundaries. Similarly, during the discussion of Gail, the video character who ate an entire cake due to job-related stress, members assert that Gail should have responded to her co-worker's request for help on her own terms. Most important, the possibility of a feminist metaphor is clear when Connie tentatively but explicitly states that saying no to others feels *powerful*. Granted, in neither discussion of stress is the potential for a feminist framework fully realized. Not coincidentally, the metaphor is more apparent in the speech of members than of leaders. Although Debbie recognizes the value of Connie's self-assertion, she does not encourage further development of this theme, but instead ends the meeting with a visualization exercise. Likewise, Richard steers the discussion of the video away from the ways in which Gail could have protected herself from exploitation by others and toward the ways that Gail could have avoided the tempting cake.

Despite considerable obstacles, a feminist approach of sorts occasionally surfaces during group discussions. In part this occurs because the organization appropriates pseudo-feminist themes in an attempt to continue to attract women to the group. The organization uses a language of women's liberation, but the language is co-opted as liberation is defined almost solely in terms of individualism and self-reliance. In contrast to the situation with the addiction model, the organization does not suppress or resist a feminist model of weight loss. Instead, it uses a selective, watered-down version of liberal feminism to promote itself.

At the same time, the organization does not unilaterally impose meanings on members. As individual women participate in conversations, they draw on personal perspectives and experiences to inform and interpret the discussion. As discussions unfold, meanings can be negotiated and renegotiated. Connie realizes the power of saying no in the context of her familial roles and relationships. When she states her observation, it can be assimilated, negotiated, responded to, or rejected by others. That is, once Connie raises the issue of empowerment, she expands the language available for understanding the complex relationship between gender roles, stress, and eating. This potential, however, should not be overstated. If fat is a feminist issue (Orbach 1979; Rothblum 1994), a commercial weight loss group seems an unlikely site for feminist discourse. And indeed, for a number of reasons, while the potential is certainly there, a truly feminist metaphor of weight loss is latent, at best.

To examine how a feminist conception of weight loss is co-opted and limited, the chapter begins with an examination of three pseudo-feminist themes that are frequently discussed in the group. First, taking care of yourself is a message that holds some feminist potential. During the early years of the most recent women's movement in the United States, especially in the women's health movement, self-care was presented as a personal alternative to the traditional medical system, one that could also be the springboard for larger societal change (Boston Women's Health Book Collective 1998). But in the language of the weight loss group, self-care is conflated with self-indulgence, if not self-absorption, and is robbed of its subversive potential. Second, the theme of self-acceptance poses a challenge to the group. Although the organization may benefit from boosting members' self-esteem, its economic viability rests on women's continuing dissatisfaction with their bodies. Third, it is difficult for the organization to completely avoid discussions of women's gender roles. Cultural notions of femininity include expectations of both what women do and what they look like. Dieting and being thin are norms embedded in women's roles. Furthermore, food preparation and consumption are activities closely tied to women's gender roles in families. But while the group recognizes these issues, they are predominantly defined as personal problems to be resolved through individual coping strategies.

After considering these pseudo-feminist themes, the chapter moves to a discussion of the possibility that the weight loss group can act as a sort of consciousness-raising group. The group brings together women from a variety of situations and encourages them to speak about their experiences with food, dieting, and weight loss. As women share their stories, it is possible that they might develop some awareness of the sociocultural forces at the root of their experiences. But at the same time, the group is limited in a number of ways from realizing its potential in this regard.

The chapter ends with a discussion of the tensions that result when the organization co-opts a feminist approach of weight loss. Although the organization must continue to appeal to women who have presumably been affected in some way by the women's movement, it is also a profit-making enterprise that depends on women's continued dissatisfaction with their bodies. The result is a pseudo-feminist language that holds some potential for resistance, but is highly unlikely to promote real social change.

Feminist Themes

When a feminist concept of weight loss emerges, it manifests itself in particular forms. There is little evidence of radical feminist thought or action. Rather, we see a variation of liberal feminism that meshes well with United States cultural values of individualism and self-determination. A feminist metaphor is most apparent in discussions of taking care of yourself, self-acceptance, and the effects of interpersonal relationships and gender roles on weight loss.

Taking Care of Yourself

Recently I saw a bumper sticker that read, "Feminism is the radical idea that women are people, too." As simplistic as the message is, it captures a fundamental tenet of feminism as it has played out in the United States. Traditionally, women have been responsible for placing the needs and desires of others above their own, both within the family and outside it. Self-denial and self-sacrifice have long been hallmarks of femininity in the United States. In this context, the notion that women's needs and desires matter is radical indeed. As the contemporary feminist movement emerged in the United States in the 1960s and 1970s, consciousness raising and assertiveness training became increasingly popular strategies, at least for individual change (Taylor and Whittier 1993). As women became increasingly aware of their exploitation at the hands of others, self-assertion and boundary maintenance emerged as significant individual strategies for self-protection. Many women began to see taking care of themselves as a virtue rather than as a sign of selfishness.

Themes of caring for yourself, and prioritizing and asserting your needs, appear frequently during weight loss group discussions. At times the organization explicitly promotes these ideas through meeting topics like "be your own best friend." Leaders also encourage members to take care of themselves and to give priority to their own needs. In particular, leaders suggest that members are more likely to meet their weight loss goals if they are trying to lose weight for themselves, rather than for others. Wendy illustrates the validity of this view when she admits that she was motivated to join the group by insecurity in her marriage, and her fear that her husband might leave her for a thinner woman. But in the course of group discussions and success at losing weight, Wendy redefines her goal, stating, "Now I want to get to my goal for me."

Rewarding yourself for successes and accomplishments is a tangible way in which a member is encouraged to practice self-care. One evening during the motivational segment of the meeting, Richard led a discussion of the importance of rewarding yourself in small, concrete ways. He began by sharing a story of what he said was his earliest memory of feeling that kind of "pride or reward." Richard said, "I was in the first grade and was taking home my first craft project. It was a gift for my mom. It was made out of two paper plates, and had a picture on it. I think it was supposed to be a cow. And it had strings at the top, so you could use it to hold coupons or mail, or something. Now, you can imagine what this thing looked like. I didn't color inside the lines, and somehow I had cut off the cow's head, and the strings weren't tied right, so by the time I got it home, it was looking pretty bedraggled. But what do you think my mom said when she saw it?" Jean enthusiastically responded, "It's beautiful!" Richard replied, "That's right. She said, 'Honey, it's beautiful!' and I felt ten feet tall! That's what this is all about, feeling that pat on the head."

Richard focuses on emotional rewards that members can give themselves, but that also play a central role in the group's dynamics. The exchange of emotional rewards and encouragement is at the very heart of celebration. The value of stickers and ribbons pales in comparison to the applause and vocal reinforcement received for losing weight. Although few leaders force members to tell the group how much weight they have lost, most actively encourage members to do so, as they recognize the value of receiving "that pat on the head." Indeed, leaders are quick to remind members that no loss is too small to be appreciated. When a member sheepishly reports that she "only lost two-tenths of a pound," she is emphatically told, "you now weigh two-tenths of a pound less than you did last week!" In addition to emotional rewards, leaders regularly encourage members to give themselves small material rewards for meeting specific goals, such as losing five pounds or breaking a zero. Leaders often ask members how they plan to reward themselves for meeting a particular goal. Almost always, members plan to buy themselves something, most commonly a piece of jewelry, perfume, nail polish, flowers, or some item of clothing. In show-and-tell fashion, members frequently bring their purchases to the meeting, to show to the leader and other members.

I recognized the effectiveness of the self-care message not long after joining the group. After three weeks on the program I had lost nine pounds. After my fourth meeting I went to the grocery store, and as I entered I walked through the floral department. On a whim, I stopped and looked at the cut bouquets, and thought it would be nice to buy myself flowers. After a few minutes, I decided it would be better to wait until the next week, when I would probably reach the ten-pound mark. But the meeting topic that night had been "be your own best friend," and as I left the floral department I mentally debated whether or not I should buy the flowers. On the one hand, it didn't seem worth the money, especially since I would probably meet my first goal the following week. On the other hand, it wasn't much money, I hardly ever did anything nice for myself just because I wanted to, and most important, I deserved a treat. Under most circumstances I would have delayed buying the flowers, but having just attended the meeting and being encouraged to be my own best friend, I went back and bought the flowers.

Looking back on it, I find the triviality of the incident and the time I spent debating whether or not to spend ten dollars on a bouquet of flowers embarrassing. At the same time, I am convinced that the incident is not idiosyncratic. Repeatedly during group discussions, members recounted similar experiences as they struggled with feeling that it was legitimate to take care of themselves. The struggle is especially acute for women who are overweight. In addition to being socialized to see nurturing others as more important than self-nurturing, many have felt further devalued as a result of the prejudice and discrimination directed at people who are overweight (Joanisse and Synnott 1999). In this context, even small steps toward self-nurturing should not be discounted.

Although self-care can be valuable, is it appropriate to suggest that it is a feminist message? Yes and no. Self-care is compatible with deeply embedded cultural values of independence, individualism, and self-reliance. But it is well to remember that until the feminist movement of the 1960s and 1970s, these values applied to men much more clearly than to women, who conversely were exhorted to put others' needs and desires above their own. One stream of early liberal feminism consequently focused on extending values of freedom and self-determination to women (Taylor and Whittier 1993).

Advertisers and other purveyors of popular culture soon recognized the market potential of women's liberation and began to incorporate aspects of feminist discourse into advertising slogans and other popular culture directed at women (Douglas 1994; Macdonald 1995). But as this occurred, potentially feminist themes were transformed into messages that served advertisers' and marketers' needs far more than they addressed women's real concerns. Self-identified feminist self-help authors urged women to invest less of themselves in others, and to become not only more self-reliant but more self-involved, in other words, more like men (Simonds 1992). Similarly, advertising campaigns of the 1970s and into the 1980s employed the rhetoric of individualism, pleasing yourself, and freedom to convince newly liberated women to indulge themselves by consuming everything from cosmetics to household appliances (Douglas 1994; Macdonald 1995). In the 1980s and 1990s, messages of independence and freedom were intertwined with discourses of health and fitness (Macdonald 1995). Today the diet and fitness industries offer an endless supply of diet programs, exercise videos, health club memberships, and exercise equipment, not to mention fashionable work-out clothes for women who must now demonstrate self-care through body-shaping regimen that are costly and at times painful (Macdonald 1995).

Feminist themes of a sort do emerge in popular culture, but there are obvious problems with their translation. First, the lines between self-care, self-indulgence, and self-absorption are fuzzy indeed. Second, to the extent that action is urged, it is clearly individual action. Simonds (1992:48) argues in the case of self-help, "Though self-help readers do feel a sense of commonality with other women through their reading, the genre fails them in that it encourages individually oriented and adaptive endeavors to achieve personal change." More specifically, and most obviously in advertising, the action that women are urged to undertake is shopping. According to advertisers, it is through consumption that women can most easily care for themselves.

There are similar problems when the weight loss group appropriates pseudo-feminist themes of self-reliance and self-determination in the guise of self-care. As techniques for individual self-assertion and life enhancement, taking care of and rewarding yourself are invaluable. It is less clear that they lead to self-empowerment, and their potential for structural change is virtually nonexistent.

Self-Acceptance

The organization fairly easily incorporates messages of self-care into its program. Self-acceptance poses a greater challenge in a group predicated on body dissatisfaction. This theme appears when Joyce tells other members that if you're going to be successful on the program, "You have to find what's right for you, what works for you." Joyce's position is somewhat odd, given that the program is relatively precise and rigid. But Joyce suggests that members must be consciously aware of and accepting of themselves—their preferences, personalities, and lifestyles—so that they can adapt the program to themselves, not vice versa.

Leaders also recognize the importance of self-acceptance in some ways, most notably when they talk to members about setting their ultimate weight loss goals. One evening, before the meeting began, Debbie asked me if I had set my goal yet. At that point I was still fifteen pounds above the upper limit for my age and height. After telling her that I had not yet chosen a goal, I said, "I don't know what's realistic. I haven't even been in range since before I had my first child." After chatting a few minutes, Debbie said, "You need to tell us what's comfortable for you. The ranges are guidelines, but you'll know it when you get there." At a meeting about a month later, during the group discussion I noted that I was currently going up and down about half a pound each week, and that the last ten pounds had been a real struggle. Debbie noted that I was very close to my goal, and suggested that I might want to reevaluate my goal range. Several weeks later I moved just below the upper limit of my weight range. When I told Debbie, she said, "Anywhere in that range is OK to stop. You need to consider how you feel about it; how easy or hard it's going to be to maintain it." There is some tension here. On the one hand, the organization provides goal weight ranges based on height and age. Members who want to achieve lifetime member status must set a personal goal that falls within the appropriate range. On the other hand, leaders encourage members to be sensitive to and take into account their personal feelings as they set their goals.

At other times, leaders promote messages of self-acceptance even more explicitly. One evening, Debbie asked those present if they ever gave themselves negative messages due to their weight. When she solicited examples of negative self-messages, people suggested, "I'll never be as thin as the woman in the magazine," "no one will ever ask me out if I don't lose weight," and "I couldn't possibly do that, as heavy as I am." In response to the last example, Debbie said, "This one is really common. Don't we do that a lot? Put off doing things we want to do until after we lose weight?" Debbie directed us to write down two negative messages we send to ourselves, and then divided us into pairs to rework the messages into more positive ones. I wrote, "Even with all the weight I've lost, I won't look as good in a bathing suit as the other mothers at the swimming pool." In reworking the message, my discussion partner, Kim, suggested, "You may not have perfect thighs, but for somebody else, it's something else that's not perfect. Maybe her arms are flabby, or she has a big stomach." After the exercise, Debbie uncovered the flip chart, where she had written, "What's important is who you are, not what you weigh." She closed by urging members, "Don't put off doing things until you lose weight. If there's something that you want to do because it will give you pleasure, you should do it now. Don't wait!"

Self-acceptance is the unequivocal message communicated throughout this discussion of negative self-messages. But simultaneously, some of the difficulties inherent in preaching this message in a weight loss group are evident. Despite the organization's overt message of self-acceptance, negative self-messages and particularly negative body-feelings are common. Members often use words like bloated, stuffed, heavy, flabby, and huge to describe their bodies. Dissatisfaction is directed not only at the overall size of the body but at the size and shape of specific body parts. One evening Debbie asked if anyone had tried any of the organization's exercise videos. No one had, but Wendy said that her husband had given her an aerobics tape for Christmas that she really liked, called "Chest and Abs of Steel." Laughing, Wendy looked down at her breasts and said, "I wondered if that was a hint, like, is there something wrong with them?" Wendy's comments provoked clear interest in the group, and several members wanted to know where they could purchase the tape. The presence of negative body-feelings is not at all surprising. Members come to the group specifically to change themselves, not to learn self-acceptance.

The discussion of positive messages and self-acceptance is problematic for another reason. Kim's solution to a negative self-message isn't a more positive self-message, but rather a positive comparison of one's self to others who are evaluated more negatively. Kim's strategy is not unusual. Analyzing interviews with overweight women, Cordell and Ronai (1999) argue that as a strategy of identity management, overweight women often construct continuums based on weight, neatness, and health. Positive identity management comes from knowing that one is not as heavy as, is neater than, or is healthier than others on the continuum. Sadly, when I joined the group, I took some small comfort in knowing that I was not as overweight as others present, an example of the continuum that Cordell and Ronai (1999:37) label "at least I'm not as fat as she is." Kim employs a variation on this theme when she suggests that in addition to body weight, individual body parts can also be placed on a continuum. Similarly, at another meeting, Connie explained that she joined the group seeking structure, noting, "I pretty much know how to eat. I gravitate toward good foods, like fruits and veggies." Connie also constructs a continuum, albeit subtle, this time based on health, when she implies that even though she is overweight, her eating habits are healthier than those of others. Although these strategies offer some small boost in self-image, they leave intact the negative valuation of being overweight and reinforce the tendency for competitiveness between women.

The most problematic aspect of the discussion of self-acceptance is the absence of any systematic critique of the cultural messages that perpetuate women's negative self-images. It is abundantly clear that overweight persons encounter pervasive prejudice and discrimination. The obese individuals interviewed by Joanisse and Synnott (1999) eloquently described experiences of criticism and maltreatment by parents, siblings, and other family members; humiliation at school; loneliness and isolation; negative experiences in romantic relationships; and discrimination and harassment by employers, medical professionals, and strangers. At times members share these sorts of experiences in the weight loss group, and occasionally members criticize popular media, particularly magazine advertising, for perpetuating negative body images and low self-esteem. But the potential for systematic, change-oriented criticism is undermined by the explicit purpose of the organization. Always, in the context of the weight loss group, the solution to prejudice and discrimination is individual change. Members come to the group not to change society but to change themselves to more closely conform to societal standards of beauty and thinness.

Ultimately the message of self-acceptance is transformed into a message of enhanced self-esteem. The latter results from self-modification, in this case, weight loss. This message is echoed in advertising that plays on women's discontentment with their bodies and appearance and, in a nod to feminist themes, encourages women to be happy with themselves, but presumably after they buy the product being promoted (Macdonald 1995). A 1970s advertisement for Max Factor cosmetics told women, "It's not what you wear; it's the way you wear it" (Macdonald 1995:88), but obviously you have to buy it before you can wear it. More recently, Nike has used the self-acceptance theme in ads targeted at women with messages that include "make your body the best it can be for one person. Yourself. Just do it"; "it's not the shape you are, it's the shape you're in that matters"; and "when was the last time you felt really comfortable with your body?" (Macdonald 1995:204–205). In one of the most egregious re-appropriations of the self-acceptance theme, Special K cereal uses role reversal to suggest the absurdity of women's body pre-occupations. After showing a parade of men bemoaning their body sizes and shapes, a voice-over asks women to consider why they obsess about their bodies. This after years of ads portraying stick-thin women who presumably got that way from eating Special K cereal.

Interpersonal Relations and Gender Roles

In some ways, a weight loss group is an ideal set-ting for thinking critically about women's gender roles. Issues of phys-ical attractiveness, health, stress, food and eating, cooking, and the division of household labor all relate to socially constructed gender roles, and all are frequent topics of group discussions. Women's rela-tionships with other people are obviously relevant to and have effects on losing weight. Preparing, cooking, and eating food are frequent top-ics of conversation. The vast majority of meeting attendees are women, and almost without exception, it is assumed that members are respon-sible for cooking in their households. Indeed, faithfully following the program is probably considerably more difficult if someone else is doing the cooking. In my own case, a subtle change in my division of labor with my husband accompanied my time in the program. Frankly, it was easier to follow the program when I had more control over meals. Even when my husband cooked, which he regularly did before I joined the group, I spent more time planning menus, suggesting recipes, and reminding him of the importance of exact measurements. A somewhat more traditional division of labor was not necessitated by the program, but it certainly made it easier to follow it. In other cases, group mem-bership increased the burdens placed on women to feed themselves and their families. Leaders often argue that food on the program is healthy, can taste good, and can easily be served to one's family. But in real-ity, members regularly recount having to cook two meals, one for themselves and one for other family members who refuse or see no need to change their eating habits.

The significance of interpersonal relationships is clear in other ways as well. When Debbie began a meeting by asking members to take a couple of minutes to tell the group about themselves and their accom-plishments, the responses were striking. Connie said, "Well, I've been married twenty-four years. I have three children, and the youngest one just left for college this year." Carolyn introduced herself by saying that she and her husband had just celebrated their twenty-fifth wedding anniversary. Next, Estelle said, "My biggest accomplishment was raising five kids; most of that time I was divorced, so I did it alone. Now, I'm married to the love of my life. We've been married four years." Laughing, she continued, "and my doctor told me that marriage at my age, after being single for twenty-five years, was a chance of zero!" Finally, Toni said, "I'm a single mom. I have a little boy, and a daughter, and I'm getting married in a couple of months." The uniformity of responses is striking. Toni, an African American woman, was in her late twenties or early thirties, both Connie and Carolyn were in their late forties, and Estelle was probably in her late sixties. But despite the differences among them, all four introduce themselves to the group by describing their marital status and the number of their children. If they at all address their accomplishments, they focus on familial accomplishments. Relationships with others are important to members not only in a general sense but also because at times other people, especially boyfriends and husbands, play more direct roles in the weight loss process. When Jodi complains that her boyfriend is pushing her to meet a goal that she is beginning to see as unrealistic, and when Eve suggests that Lucy's boyfriend will probably encourage her to lose weight more slowly, both acknowledge the direct involvement of significant others in their weight loss experience. Similarly, Wendy concedes the involvement of her husband when she says he bought her an exercise video as a gift.

On a regular basis, members recognize that they are not losing weight in isolation. Jodi and Lucy see their boyfriends' involvement as interference, and, as is clear from the discussion of "Chest and Abs of Steel," Wendy is at least ambivalent about her husband's involvement. In most instances, however, members see involvement by significant others as positive, and in the vast majority of cases they describe family members, friends, and co-workers as highly encouraging of their weight loss efforts. But despite frequent references to relationships with other people, discussions rarely address the potentially problematic aspects of interpersonal relations, especially as they relate to women's gender roles and their complex, ambivalent relations to food. Little is said of the demands placed on women to feed others while simultaneously depriving themselves of food in the pursuit of thinness. Nor are gender roles as a source of stress ever systematically critiqued. And even though members at times allude to experiences of prejudice and discrimination, the significant others who populate their conversations are overwhelmingly positive and supportive. As it is, the potential for a feminist critique of women's gender roles and interpersonal relationships lies dormant.

Consciousness Raising: Potentials and Limits

Tentative and embryonic as they are, glimpses of a feminist concept of weight loss are evident in discussions of taking care of yourself, self-acceptance, and relations with other people. I argue that a feminist consciousness of sorts can develop in a weight loss group. During the early years of the contemporary feminist movement in the United States, consciousness raising proved to be an efficacious strategy (Evans 1979; Freeman 1975; Taylor and Whittier 1993). Its power and potential rested on the simple fact that it is dangerous to bring women together in a group and let them talk to one another. As women joined together in small groups and shared their personal stories, they slowly came to recognize and critique the structural conditions at the root of their experiences.

Can similar processes unfold in a weight loss group? Maybe. The gender imbalance of the group is not inconsequential. The vast majority of members are women, and despite racial and social class homogeneity, members vary substantially in age and, most important, in body size and shape. Members differ in how overweight they are, how long they have been overweight, and in the severity of the negative consequences of being overweight that they have experienced. But sharing personal experiences is the cornerstone of meetings. What members share is the first-hand experience of negative attitudes toward people who are overweight, and a desire to do something about their condition. Herein lie both the potential and the limitation of consciousness raising. On the one hand, as members discuss their personal experiences of being overweight in a society that worships thinness, it is at least theoretically possible that members can be moved to a greater recognition of the structural conditions that underlie their shared experiences. On the other hand, the organization is not silent in these discussions, and its position is clear—the key to happiness is individual change, and specifically, the key is to lose weight. Consequently, the potential for consciousness raising is present, but is consistently limited by three aspects of the organization and its approach.

First, several characteristics of the meeting space and structure are significant. The physical room arrangement impedes the development of cohesion among members, and reinforces the privileged status of the group leader. Even at meetings where attendance is relatively low chairs are never arranged in a circle, but are always placed in rows that face the front of the room. The consequences for group discussions are obvious. Speaking to the backs of people's heads is never conducive to an ongoing conversation. At times, it is nearly impossible to hear what someone on the other side of the room has said. The lack of eye contact between members, and the ease with which someone sitting in the back of the room can remain virtually invisible, diffuse responsibility for maintaining group conversations and make it relatively easy for many members, if not most, to not participate at all. Consequently, conversations are almost always mediated through the leader. The leader asks a question, a member responds, the leader possibly reiterates the answer and solicits another response, and so on, back and forth between the leader and individual members. Additional factors further inhibit group cohesiveness. Group size varies, but it is not unusual to have as many as fifty or more members present at a meeting. Furthermore, turnover in membership is high, making it difficult for many members to get to know one another and feel comfortable enough to share personal experiences.

None of these obstacles is insurmountable. As most teachers of large classes know, it is possible to effectively facilitate discussions in large groups. At the very least, large groups can be divided into smaller ones. But the content and structure of meetings also limit group cohesiveness. Group members do not choose the subjects under discussion. The organization determines meeting topics and provides leaders with prepackaged discussion outlines. Some leaders do not rely heavily on the outlines, but even then, they retain considerable control over discussions. This situation contrasts sharply with the consciousness-raising group, or even a 12-Step recovery group, where discussion topics and formats are entirely generated by members. Most important, the organization strongly influences the overall tenor of meetings. Overwhelmingly, weight issues are individualized, and the vast majority of meeting time is spent identifying individual strategies for coping with problems and issues.

The second organizational characteristic that limits the potential for consciousness raising is the group's economic nature. The group is solidly situated in the multibillion dollar weight loss industry, and its primary purpose is to make money. The profit-making nature of the organization pervades meetings. Not only must members pay to join the group, but they are continually surrounded by merchandise available for purchase, and it is not unusual for leaders to incorporate product endorsements into the discussions. Profit making is not necessarily bad. And it is clear that group leaders and organizational employees often sincerely desire to provide beneficial support and service to individuals seeking help. But the central fact remains: this weight loss organization and others like it depend for their economic survival on continual self-dissatisfaction among a significant proportion of the population. For all the talk of self-acceptance and taking care of yourself, the organization has a clear stake in the continuing desire of individuals to change themselves to conform to societal standards.

The third and final limiting characteristic is more abstract. The very tone of the organization, its meetings, and the interaction that occurs are strongly colored by a powerful cultural narrative that holds considerable sway in the United States. The "before-and-after" story is one of the most common and popular stories we tell. The plot is simple: as the story begins, the protagonist is ill, isolated, lost, or somehow deficient. As the story unfolds, the protagonist faces a number of challenges and obstacles. Through hard work, determination, and willpower, the protagonist overcomes the challenges and emerges at the end of the story not only victorious, but a changed person. The before-and-after story is prominent in self-help literature (Simonds 1992), as well as in advertising that promises personal transformation through consumerism (Macdonald 1995; Ritzer 1999).

The power of this narrative is at the very heart of what the organization promises its members. Leaders prominently display their before-and-after photographs at the front of the meeting room and encourage members to do likewise. The monthly newsletter, distributed at no cost at meetings, is filled with before-and-after stories, always accompanied by pictures that provide dramatic and concrete evidence of physical transformation. But the organization promises even more. Newsletter stories unequivocally imply that personal transformation accompanies the physical changes, and group discussions often center on the potential to change from who or what you were before to who or what you can become after losing weight. Self-transformation is the pot of gold at the end of the rainbow.

The specific before-and-after story told in the weight loss group is based on several underlying assumptions. First, fat is bad. Second, fat obscures the person you really are. Third, anyone can lose weight if she really wants to, and she works hard enough. As in the traditional American success story, willpower and hard work lead to personal transformation. The story is simple, attractive, and comfortable, but it poses dilemmas that revolve around the question of what body weight really has to do with who you are. In other words, what is the relationship between body and self? The complexity of the issue is apparent during group discussions. Leah, at age seventeen, was one of the youngest regular attendees. One evening, she spoke appreciatively of her boyfriend, Erik, who "loved me even before I lost weight. He could see who I really was, and that was more important than how much I weighed. I mean, he's really supportive and all. He goes to work out with me all the time. It's just that it hasn't changed the way he feels about me." Leah went on to contrast Erik's reaction to that of other school peers: "There are kids at school who didn't pay any attention to me at all before, and now, it's like all of a sudden they want to be my friend." When Debbie asked how she felt about that Leah said, "I don't know. It's kind of weird. You know, it's like, I'm still me. I'm still the same person I was before. But I guess they didn't see that." Carolyn said, "Would you really want to be friends with kids that didn't like you because you were heavy?" Leah hesitantly said, "Well, yeah, that's true," but then Kathy said, "But I think we really do change when we lose weight. If you're really heavy and don't have much self-confidence and stuff, that affects who you are. But if you lose weight, and you feel good about yourself, I think you act differently, too. You're more outgoing or friendlier, because you feel more confident."

As members respond to Leah's observations, they talk through a number of responses to the question of whether or not you are the same person after you lose weight. Leah suggests that she is the same person she was before losing weight, but this was not obvious to her peers, whose views were dominated by her fat. In other words, excess weight is a barrier that makes it hard for other people to see the real person who resides inside. Similarly, members imply that fat can obscure our view of ourselves and diminish our self-confidence. But Kathy goes even further when she suggests that weight loss results in personal change. Her view is at times echoed by other members as they examine before-and-after photographs. On numerous occasions members have looked at a before picture and exclaimed, "It doesn't even look like her!" Clearly they are responding to sometimes dramatic physical changes that occur when individuals lose large amounts of weight. At the same time, their astonishment suggests that they are looking at a different person. But despite these reactions, most members adamantly contend that losing weight has little, if anything, to do with who you are. Holding to traditional dualisms, members see the body and the self as entirely distinct entities. Furthermore, as physical matter, the body can be modified, manipulated, and transformed by weight loss without having any impact on the true self.

The before-and-after narrative thus takes a specific form in the weight loss group. Physical transformation is believed to be possible for anyone who wants it badly enough and is willing to work for it. Personal transformation is more problematic. Despite strong and recurrent themes of personal change in the before-and-after stories promulgated by the organization, members hold tenaciously to the view that the physical body can be transformed with little impact on the real person within. In any case, the before-and-after narrative strongly impedes consciousness raising in the weight loss group. As long as members are convinced that individual transformation of any sort is possible and desirable, social transformation is unnecessary.

Speaking of Feminism

In the past several decades, advertisers have used images of the women's movement, and feminist themes, to promote a variety of consumer products (Douglas 1994; Macdonald 1995; Rothblum 1994). Women are told that cigarette smoking is both the symbol and the outcome of women's progress, and advertisers continually remind women that they have earned the right to indulge themselves in everything from chocolate to diamonds to new furniture. In her examination of popular culture directed at women from the 1960s to the 1990s, particularly popular music, television, and movies, Douglas (1994:12–13) argues: "We [women] love *and* hate the media, at exactly the same time, in no small part because the media, simultaneously, love *and* hate women. . . . The war that has been raging in the media is not a simplistic war against women but a complex struggle between feminism and antifeminism that has reflected, reinforced, and exaggerated our culture's ambivalence about women's roles for over thirty-five years." In contrast to Faludi's (1991) argument of a strong, concerted, unwavering backlash against feminism in the media, Douglas (1994) finds that popular media are a bundle of contradictions. According to Douglas, in girl group music of the 1960s that present women as simultaneously rebellious and self-defeating, TV genies with magical powers who are nonetheless kept in bottles, police officers who can overpower all sorts of bad guys without messing up their hair or running their pantyhose, and countless other examples, we see a continual struggle between feminism and antifeminism. Feminist themes are not absent in the media, but they are mediated, co-opted, and juxtaposed with clearly antifeminist themes.

The weight loss industry also incorporates some pseudo-, liberal feminist themes into its advertising. Weight loss is yet another way in which women can take care of themselves. Even more important, themes of control pervade organizational literature and advertising. But in the organization's version, empowerment is equated with self-control, which is then easily conflated with weight control. As women continue to struggle for real power in numerous social arenas, weight control remains the one area where they are not only allowed but expected to exert control. Ultimately the theme of empowerment is diluted. To the extent that themes of self-determination, self-control, and self-acceptance animate group members' language, the organization highly mediates the feminist perspective. Feminism is effectively co-opted.

Co-optation, however, has its dangers. As Bartky (1988:43) argues, "Domination (and the discipline it requires) are never imposed without some cost." In the first place, the effectiveness of consciousness raising attests to the power of talk. Women come to the group to talk about weight. As they do so, they draw on varying, sometimes conflicting understandings of dieting and weight loss. To be sure, the organization has a clear stake in controlling the languages and views that circulate. But control is never complete. Members bring various assumptions about and perspectives on weight loss with them when they join the group, and at times these conflict with the organization's perspective. Furthermore, if I am correct in arguing that the organization has co-opted some of the themes and language of feminism, then the organization makes it even easier for members to employ a feminist metaphor as they talk about dieting and weight loss. Focusing on advertising, Macdonald (1995:92) argues: "Co-opting even selective elements of feminist discourses might also be regarded as a gesture in their direction. 'Making the most of yourself' does begin to transform the passivity of narcissistic self-contemplation into the dream of active and dynamic self-fulfillment even as it reins that dream back into the feminine activity of 'going shopping.' " There is no doubt that the weight loss organization offers a version of feminism that is diluted, mediated, and limited in its potential for real empowerment. At the same time, the organization cannot fully determine how the language is used or what sense members make of it.

A weight loss group seems an unlikely site of resistance. On one level, women who join such a group have apparently submitted to cultural norms that hold thinness to be the ideal standard for their bodies. This view is reflected in the research literature. Honeycutt (1999:167) suggests that women who have joined and lost weight in commercial weight loss groups have bought into "hegemonic notions of attrac-tiveness." In her conceptualization, there is little room for resistance within the confines of a weight loss group. However, as limited as they are, fleeting glimpses of resistance appear. First, many members do not completely buy into the program, even if they accept that los-ing weight is possible and worthwhile. Despite the program's rigidity and seeming inflexibility, many members pick and choose those elements of the plan that work for them. Furthermore, many women join the group but eventually drop out. Certainly not all dropouts are actively resist-ing. For many, joining the group is only one attempt in a continuing effort to lose weight. Some dropouts will return, others will continue to try a variety of diet plans, and still others will join different groups. But for a few, dropping out may represent at least a small step in the direc-tion of questioning the viability and worth of the dieting enterprise.

Questioning and perhaps resisting the organization's stance on weight loss may be facilitated by the fact that the weight loss group simultaneously provides concrete evidence of both the successes and the failures of dieting. Among the women interviewed by Honeycutt (1999), those who successfully lost weight in a weight loss group con-tinually saw evidence that weight loss is possible. The group observed here also goes out of its way to provide ample evidence that it is pos-sible to lose weight if you work hard enough. Leaders are the most obvi-ous success stories, but during celebration members continually see individuals who are losing weight. The result is strong reinforcement for the belief that individuals can control their body weight. But what Honeycutt fails to appreciate is that the weight loss group also provides ample evidence of the failures of dieting. Some members fail to lose weight, drop out, and return, sometimes repeatedly. Groups usually include former lifetime members who had reached their goal weights, only to regain significant proportions, if not all, of it back. And many current members struggle continuously. The number of members who actually meet their goal is small. What sense do members make of this? For some, the evidence of success is enough to outweigh the evidence of failure. Others may decide that since other members are obviously losing weight, they are to blame for their own failure. If they were only more committed, or if they only worked harder, surely they too could be successful. But at least some members, faced with the continual struggles surrounding them, may begin to question the viability of diet-ing and weight loss.

Even if many women, particularly women in a weight loss group, do not actively resist pressures to conform to societal beauty standards, they are not cultural dupes, completely socialized into blind and unquestioning acceptance of societal dictates. Wooley (1994:23) convincingly argues that "ever since the triumph of patriarchy, men have controlled the means of representing women and their bodies." But as accurate as it is, this statement begs the question of what women make of these representations. Wooley's position on this question is clear as he goes on to state, "this monopoly has precluded the development of a collective subjectivity among women and made them accomplices to their own oppression." There is no doubt that cultural representations are powerful. Honeycutt (1999) found that even the women she interviewed who were members of a national fat activist organization shared certain antifat biases. Rather than advancing the position that fat can be beautiful, these women accept the view that thin is better, but argue that it is not their fault that they are fat. While we concede the power of cultural representations, we should avoid assuming that women are little more than passive receptors of the messages communicated. We can learn something here from cultural studies, where a view of the overwhelming, all-encompassing, indoctrinating power of the media has been countered by a perspective that views audiences as active and critical interpreters of media (Croteau and Hoynes 2000). This is not to suggest that cultural representations have no effect, nor does it imply that women are entirely free to interpret, respond to, or appropriate them in any way they see fit. Rather, women are active meaning-makers, but they do so within a particular historical and cultural context. And the current context provides women with a number of critical tools to use in responding to media, including feminist discourse. Douglas (1994:279) reflects:

> Thanks to the women's movement, my consciousness as a woman and as a mother was very different from my mother's. I was aware of our country's pathological schizophrenia about mothers and children: revere them in imagery, revile them in public policy. But this wasn't my own lonely observation; unlike my mother, I could read, hear, and see other women, in a variety of places, articulating these same criticisms. I also had the language, as well as the sense of obligation, to dissect the media's role in sustaining this hypocrisy. Although this new consciousness, like the old, is riddled with chasms, fault lines, and tensions about who I am as a woman and who I can and should be, it provides me with the armor and a few lances against a mass media that, after all these years, still doesn't get it.

Although it may be too much to assume that most, or even many, women who join a weight loss group have developed a similar feminist consciousness, certainly some have.

It is well to remember that although the narrow, ideal beauty standard that venerates thinness is strong and pervasive, competing representations are available. Among other things, increasingly visible and vocal size-acceptance and antidiet movements have recently emerged in the United States (Sobal 1999). Both movements rely on accumulating evidence that body weight is a function of genetics and dieting is doomed to fail. The size-acceptance movement actively advocates for the rights of obese individuals. Popular culture is also beginning to offer alternative representations. The greater visibility of plus-size models, more magazines targeted specifically to large women, and popular talk shows that present large individuals in a popular light all contribute to new and varying perspectives on body weight, and represent sites of burgeoning resistance (Cordell and Ronai 1999; Sobal 1999). Increasingly clothing manufacturers are responding to the demands of large women for attractive clothing in plus- and super-sizes (Sobal 1999).

It is also well to remember that the meaning-making surrounding weight and dieting is not yet completed among feminists. At the very least, feminists are ambivalent. For some, though presumably a minority, body weight is simply not a feminist issue (Rothblum 1994). Others, particularly liberal feminists, suggest that a concern for femininity and physical attractiveness is compatible with demands for women's liberation (Bartky 1988; Rothblum 1994). Still others argue that the crucial issue is the full and active participation of women in their own bodily reconstruction, whether it occurs through weight loss or cosmetic surgery (Adams 1997). The point is simple: the cultural meanings of body weight and dieting are contested, even among feminists.

8 | Speaking of Weight

Women speak in many different ways about weight and dieting. Words like temptation, willpower, discipline, sinfulness, control, and hard work reflect and reinforce certain ways of thinking about women's bodies. A weight loss group is a rich site for listening to women talk about losing weight. Women come to weight loss groups already holding assumptions and beliefs about how overweight they are, why they are overweight, and what they have to do to lose weight. As they speak about their challenges and accomplishments, varied meanings of weight loss become apparent. But as they speak, meanings are also negotiated. Women differ, sometimes dramatically, in how they view their bodies as well as in their experiences with and perspectives on dieting. At times their perspectives conflict, and in the process of group discussion the conflicts are confronted, negotiated, and sometimes resolved.

I have used five concepts of weight loss to represent patterns in the ways that women think and talk about losing weight. These five frameworks rest on different assumptions about the causes and cures of being overweight and incorporate different ways of speaking about weight loss. The *self-help concept* is reflected in discussions of lifestyle modification, nutritious eating, and the health benefits of losing weight. Making smart choices is the key to getting and keeping control over your body weight. The *concept of work* rests on a view of the body as a material object that can be molded into the desirable configuration with enough hard work and discipline. Reflecting broader societal trends toward the increased rationalization of both work and leisure, the metaphor of work calls attention to the high degree of precision and rigidity necessary to shape the body. The *concept of religion* is rich in references to temptation, sin, guilt, confession, ritual, and magic. Food is highly suspect, as its sensuous and dangerous nature presents numerous temptations for potential sinners. The *concept of addiction* also focuses on danger, but it is the body itself that poses the greatest challenges. Ruled by mysterious drives, appetites, and desires, the body is potentially always ready to run out of control. Finally, the *concept of feminism*, subtle, submerged, and clearly co-opted, is filled with references to self-care and promises liberation for the woman who takes control of her body and her life.

Organizations as well as individuals use various concepts of weight loss. Just as individual women speak about what it means to be overweight and to try to lose weight, so do organizations speak about these processes. At times organizations speak through individuals. The weight loss group depends on leaders and other organizational employees to communicate its perspective. But organizations additionally speak through their written materials—advertising, newsletters, educational information. Organizations also communicate nonverbally. The clothing and physical appearance of its employees as well as room décor all transmit messages about what the organization is and how it operates. The weight loss group is no different from other organizations in this regard. Most of the time, employees, written materials, and nonverbal messages work together to convey a relatively clear and consistent message. But at times they contradict one another, and leave room for conflict and negotiation.

Combining Concepts

The five concepts coexist in a single group in part because despite their differences, they share certain themes. Most obviously, all five rest on the clear and basic assumption that it is possible to lose weight. So fundamental is this belief that it is never questioned, even in the face of seemingly overwhelming evidence to the contrary. Although weight loss groups include individuals who are losing weight, they are also filled with people who have failed, sometimes repeatedly. Nonetheless leaders and members hold tenaciously to the belief that anyone can lose weight, if she only wants to badly enough. The five models also share the assumption that not only is losing weight possible; it is good for you. Weight loss is expected to bring with it numerous benefits, most significantly enhanced health and well-being.

Beliefs that weight loss is possible and beneficial are related to a central theme that runs throughout all five frameworks, although it takes a somewhat different shape in each. Control permeates discussions of losing weight. When the focus is on self-help, control takes the form of self-responsibility. From this perspective, successful weight-losers are those who recognize and accept responsibility for their health and well-being and consequently make the right choices. What weight-losers need is accurate information and support, which they presumably use to adopt an appropriate and healthy lifestyle. When weight loss is viewed as work, control emerges as discipline and willpower. "Keeping at it" in a precise and rigid way is the key to losing weight and maintaining the loss. Somewhat similarly, in the perspective of feminism, control is conceptualized as self-determination. The liberated woman *takes* control of her body and her life. Weight loss is a concrete way that women can demonstrate that they have taken charge.

Control is more problematic when views of weight loss are informed by the concepts of religion and addiction. In the former, control is threatened by temptation that comes from outside, particularly from foods that are sensual and dangerous. Traditionally religious groups have relied heavily on punishment as a deterrent to transgression and deviance. To be sure, people who fail to maintain a socially acceptable weight face a number of negative sanctions. But relying on external means of control is costly. In the realm of weight loss, if control is to operate at all, it must come from the conscience. Inducing guilt is the most effective way to keep people in line. Control is also problematic in the framework of addiction, but in this case, threats come from within. It is the body itself that is most dangerous. Addiction represents a body that has run amok. Driven by mysterious and suspect instincts, subject to invisible forces, and at continual risk of disease, the body at times appears beyond control. But all is not lost. Like the religious approach, the model of addiction seeks control from within. But it is not faith in a higher power or religious sensibilities manifested by a guilty conscience that maintain control. Rather, it is the mind—reason, logic, rationality—that overrules the body.

Surveillance is a second common theme. Women, especially dieting women, watch their bodies, watch their weight, and watch what they eat. And if they fail to do so, they can rest assured that others will watch for them. In the frameworks of self-help, work, and feminism, willingness and ability to watch one's self connote a sort of enlightened self-consciousness. Mindless eating results in bad habits and weight gain. Conversely, successful weight-losers think about what they are doing (at times compulsively), rationally weigh their options (and their food), and logically choose the appropriate action (for their own enhanced health and well-being). In the frameworks of religion and addiction, watching is more akin to vigilance. From this perspective, the weight-loser is continually threatened, both from within and from without. Surrounded by a boundless supply of fast food restaurants, high-fat convenience foods, and luscious indulgences, weight-losers confront temptation everywhere they turn. As if that's not enough, the body presents its own challenges, always ready to run wild given an opportunity. Letting your guard down is the greatest threat to losing weight.

The five concepts of weight loss are also similar in what goes unspoken. First, discussions of hunger are remarkably few. The weight loss organization downplays hunger. Hunger and diets go hand in hand, but what with nutritional deficiency and increased risks of a range of negative health outcomes, including gall bladder problems, high blood pressure, even death, diets have gotten bad press of late. What is a weight loss group to do? An obvious solution is to claim that the group's program is not a diet, but a healthy way to eat and live. To the extent that the group can distance itself from diets, it may be easier to attract new members, who are presumably well aware of diets' shortcomings. Deprivation is impossible to maintain for any length of time. Bingeing is the predictable outcome. In contrast, the group promises a new lifestyle that will enhance your health and well-being and, critically, will not leave you hungry. Talk of hunger poses a threat to the organization's image. The group therefore invests much time and energy in convincing members that they can follow the program and lose weight without feeling hungry.

At the same time, discussions of hunger do occur. Members get hungry. As they chat informally before meetings, mention of hunger is common. Very few eat immediately before getting weighed, and fasting the entire day is not uncommon. In general, new members frequently experience hunger, especially during their first week or two, as they adjust to eating smaller quantities of food. And despite the organization's best efforts to convince members that they can follow the program and feel satisfied, members at times admit to being hungry. Because hunger is viewed, by both members and leaders, almost exclusively as a physiological urge associated with the material body's drives and biological requirements, it figures most prominently in the concept of addiction. Hunger is problematic precisely because it threatens the weight-loser with loss of control. The solution ultimately is to use the mind's power to reassert control. The key, members are told, is to manage hunger rationally by determining whether they are really hungry and by logically choosing to eat food that is nutritionally sound and filling.

Second, there is virtually no discussion of the social construction of the concept of ideal weight. When members join the group they immediately receive material that includes ideal weight ranges, broken down by sex, height, and age. Individuals who want to achieve the status of lifetime members must choose a specific goal weight that falls within the ideal range. Several assumptions underlie and bolster members' and leaders' perspectives on the ideal weight ranges. The ranges are assumed to be facts that occur naturally, that is, it is natural for a woman of a specific age and height to fall within a given weight range. The ideal weight ranges are also assumed to lead directly to optimal health and well-being. Finally, supposedly all can reach their ideal weight range if they try hard enough. So taken for granted are these assumptions that members rarely question the viability of the ranges. On the few occasions that I heard members raise doubts about them some thought the ranges were too high, and others thought they were too low.

The conceptualization of ideal weight is problematic on a number of grounds. The ranges themselves are relatively recent, having been first constructed and used in the 1940s, and are based on questionable data and assumptions (McKinley 1999). The assumed direct relationship between body weight and optimal health continues to be hotly debated. And the very notion of ideal weight ranges is thoroughly saturated with cultural biases regarding the ideal body type, particularly for women. In other words, while ideal weight is a social construct, it is viewed as a naturally occurring fact in the context of the weight loss group.

Recognition of the actual material limits of the human body is the third element missing from group discussions. Genetic components of body weight are rarely mentioned. To the extent that members see their families of origin as relevant to their body weight or weight loss efforts, they are likely to focus almost exclusively on socialization. Members often complain that as children they learned poor eating habits; food was often used as a reward for good behavior in their families; and food played a central role in many of their family traditions and celebrations. Although members readily recognize that they have inherited a whole range of attitudes and habits that affect their weight, they rarely recognize that they may have also inherited a body type and a propensity toward a given body weight. These beliefs are reinforced by the fact that the ideal weight ranges do not incorporate any recognition of variation in body type, nor do they say anything about the percentage of body weight that is fat.

Furthermore, the idea of a "set point" to which individual bodies might naturally gravitate is rarely acknowledged, in part because the concept seems to counter the belief that body weight is completely under individual control. Consequently, when set points are discussed, it is generally assumed that they fall within or very near the ideal weight range. Metabolism is the one physiological process to which members and leaders do attend. The overriding view is that metabolism is potentially problematic. Members recognize individual variations in metabolism, and they often blame metabolism for plateaus in the weight loss process as well as for lower than expected losses in a given week. But discussions reflect the belief that metabolism can be infinitely manipulated. Much time is spent discussing how the body's metabolism can be increased. The two most common suggestions are to exercise and avoid deprivation.

Living with/in the Body

The absence of attention to critical discussions of hunger, the social construction of ideal weight, and the limits of the material body attest to the fact that women who are trying to lose weight are unwilling and/or unable to confront the actual materiality of the human body. Ultimately the material body presents challenges, not limits. This is not to suggest that group members do not talk about the body. They do, almost endlessly. Indeed, it is precisely concerns and feelings about the body that bring them to the weight loss group. To understand fully and more critically how dieting women interpret and experience their bodies, we must consider what they do say, in conjunction with what they leave out. We can begin by examining the similarities and differences between the five concepts of weight loss with respect to perspectives on the body.

The body is submerged in the concepts of self-help and feminism, whereas the self figures prominently in both. Self-help focuses on taking responsibility for your health and well-being, and similarly feminism focuses on the importance of self-determination. Within these two frameworks, the body is most significant for what it says about the self. Presumably the slim body unequivocally communicates several messages: "I take care of myself," "I live right," "I make smart choices," "I'm healthy," and "I'm in charge." In other words, from the perspectives of self-help and feminism, the body acts as a marker or sign for otherwise invisible or private attitudes and behaviors. We may not see what and how a particular woman eats, but we can presumably deduce it from looking at her body.

The body figures more prominently and centrally in the concepts of work, religion, and addiction, but in different ways. The body is most central in the concept of work, for here the body is the actual material object that is worked on. The body is plastic, moldable, and almost infinitely transformable with the right tools and techniques. Here weight loss merges with cosmetic surgery and bodybuilding. All three take the body as raw material that can be shaped and worked into the desired shape, and all three see body fat as dispensable—it can be shed, via liposuction or other surgical procedures, dieting, exercise, drugs, or extreme weight-lifting. Finally, all three evidence a kind of detachment from the material body, as if the individual can step outside of and away from the body to view and respond to it objectively. And there is always something else that can be improved—another pound that can be lost, another body part that can be toned, another wrinkle removed, another muscle defined.

From the perspectives of religion and addiction, the body is more problematic, though in different ways. In the concept of religion, the greatest challenges to weight loss are external. The body faces continual temptation from outside, most notably from sensuous, flavorful, high-fat food that leads to overindulgence. But if the body is weak, the spirit cannot be. The goal is to develop a conscience that is sufficiently strong to withstand temptation and avoid the inevitable guilt that comes from giving in. The conscience is there to protect the body from external assaults. The body is also problematic within the concept of addiction, but in this case the problems lie within. Mysterious, invisible, and dangerous drives, instincts, desires, appetites, and emotions rule the body. The body is always and everywhere potentially out of control. Sheer willpower and rational action are the keys to overcoming and mastering the body.

Perspectives on and discussions of food are also relevant to understanding embodiment. Again, the approaches to weight loss differ in their views of food. Discussions of food are most notably absent in the feminist perspective. To the extent that the central focus is on taking care of yourself and attending to your own needs, it is recognized that you should not use food as a reward or as a substitute for other needs. Missing is any mention of the highly gendered nature of food-related attitudes and practices in the United States. Women prepare and serve food to others, not themselves. By far the most damaging implication is that women are expected to show their love of other people by feeding them, but to demonstrate self-love by depriving themselves of food.

Ironically, food is not particularly important in the framework of addiction. Largely this is because problems with overeating and weight gain are assumed to reside within particular individual bodies, not food itself. There are parallels here with views of alcohol and alcoholism. Alcohol in and of itself is not addicting. Rather, certain individuals are genetically inclined toward addiction. Indeed, this view takes a somewhat different form in the realm of weight loss, since people cannot abstain from food in the same way that they can abstain from alcohol, cigarettes, or gambling. In the case of Overeaters Anonymous, individuals are counseled to abstain from overeating, not from food. But in the weight loss group, which is not a 12-Step program, members are cautioned to know their own weaknesses and either to eat problematic foods in moderation or to abstain entirely if need be.

The self-help and work concepts are largely similar to each other in their views of food. In both cases, food is most important as a source of fuel. In recognition of the fact that physical bodies require nourishment, the most important qualities of food are its nutritional value and its potential contribution to weight loss. High-fiber food is often touted as particularly beneficial for losing weight, as it is not only good for you but filling. Drinking water is promoted for similar reasons. From the perspective of both concepts, the overriding goal is to make rational choices when it comes to food. The successful weight-loser is the one who chooses the best foods, that is, those that are nutritionally sound and, most important, those that fill you up so that you will eat less.

Food figures most prominently in the concept of religion. It is the only framework in which taste is central. But food, especially food that tastes good, is viewed with suspicion. Good-tasting food is potentially dangerous, as it tempts you to overindulge. Theoretically, nutritionally sound food can taste good. Group leaders spend considerable time and effort trying to convince members of this fact. And yet members complain frequently that low- and nonfat alternatives often do not taste nearly as good as the regular versions. The highest compliment bestowed on low-fat food is that "it tastes just like the regular." Moderation is presumably the most reasonable solution to this dilemma. You can eat the better-tasting, high-fat version, members are told, as long as you eat it in moderation and as long as it fits into your allocation of points for the day. In reality many members find it easier to avoid tempting foods than to eat them in moderation.

The five concepts of weight loss also obviously differ from one another in significant ways, despite some similarities. Although the perspectives can and do coexist in the group as well as in the language of individual members, there is a strong tendency to translate the concepts of addiction, religion, and feminism into the concepts of self-help and work. In other words, the best way to resist temptation, overcome the weaknesses of the body, and demonstrate self-determination and self-care is to exert sheer willpower and attack the material body rationally and systematically. Several factors facilitate the translation process. First, translation is relatively easy because all five concepts share the central theme of control. Second, the weight loss organization makes a concerted effort to translate references to religion, addiction, and feminism into discussions of self-help and work. As the preferred frameworks of the organization, they provide the language most commonly used by its employees and in its written materials. But the concepts of self-help and work are not arbitrarily imposed on members. Rather, these perspectives mesh well with broader societal trends toward increased rationalization and individualism (Ritzer 1996, 1999). It is safe to say that in the contemporary United States, there is a strong and unwavering propensity to turn everything into work, including education, leisure, health, and caring for the body.

Translating the concepts of religion, addiction, and feminism into self-help and work has several consequences. First, food and eating are decidedly desensualized. At the same time that members and leaders believe that nutritional food can taste good, they downplay the sheer pleasure of eating. Leaders exhort members to "eat to live, don't live to eat." There may be some wisdom to this, but is there no middle ground? Is it possible to eat something just because it tastes good? Are there any circumstances under which it is acceptable to eat for comfort? In reducing food to its nutritional content, members and leaders also deemphasize the integral role that food often plays in social activities. Quite simply, social gatherings are turned into problems or challenges. Sometimes social activities can be avoided, but often this is not possible, or even advisable. The central concern then becomes how to manage a challenging social gathering. Holidays, family celebrations, and similar social activities become problematic events that have to be navigated. The point is to get through them. After holidays or other social events, leaders often ask members, "How did it go?" Very rarely do members describe how fun, entertaining, or satisfying the event was.

Instead, they most commonly recount the strategies they used to stick to the program, or they confess their guilt at not maintaining their weight loss efforts.

Second, weight loss is rationalized and de-emotionalized. Members experience a wide range of emotions as they try to lose weight. Members speak often of frustration, ambivalence, shame, and guilt, and celebration is filled with references to hope, pride, and camaraderie between members. But at the same time, members' complex and sometimes conflicted emotions are not confronted or dealt with in any depth. Rather, the organization tries to provide a logical plan that will result in weight loss for anyone who is committed to following it. And presumably this is what brings members to the group.

Third, both the causes of and the solutions to overweight and obesity are effectively individualized and depoliticized. In members' and leaders' minds, the most important cause of weight gain and obesity is a deficient lifestyle. Poor eating habits and not enough exercise are the primary culprits. Thoroughly ignored in these conceptualizations are the roles played by advertising, the food industry, including fast food, and the biases and deficiencies of medical research and public health campaigns that uncritically link body weight to health. Consequently, the solution for weight gain and obesity is to fix the individual. Individuals are expected to conform to societal standards for the ideal body size and shape, rather than address the political, economic, and social contributions to overweight or question the societal standards themselves. Furthermore, consumerism is the most common solution to presumably individual problems. Any problem, no matter how complex or how large, can be solved if you purchase the right product or service. Buying the right diet book, drug, herbal remedy, exercise equipment, or weight loss group membership is the key to losing weight. Spend enough money, and you, too, can buy the body you want.

So what do we make of the ways that dieting women talk about their bodies? On the one hand, there is substantial evidence that group members subscribe to traditional dualistic thinking that sees the body and self as distinct and separate entities. Members hold tenaciously to the view that "I am the same person, no matter what I weigh." In other words, members apparently believe that the material body can be manipulated and changed almost endlessly, with little effect on the self within. The body may be plastic, mutable, and infinitely transformable, but in members' views, the self is stable. Similarly, members at times appear to try to detach themselves from their bodies. This often occurs as members speak of the body as an object on which they have to work.

But it is evident at other times as well. Betty, confused by weight fluctuations apparently unrelated to her weight loss efforts, and frustrated by the elusiveness of her goal, once lamented, "My body seems to have a mind of its own." On another occasion Wendy told members, "I was at the store yesterday and I had to get dog food. I got a fifty-pound bag and I could hardly pick it up and get it in my cart. And all of a sudden I thought, wow! I've lost that much weight! It was like I had been carrying around that fifty pounds of dog food with me." At the time I found Wendy's observation interesting, but I didn't really think about it until I was in a similar situation. Having lost over sixty pounds myself, I was buying two thirty-pound bags of cat litter, and remembering Wendy's comment, I was struck by how much weight I had actually lost. But I also realized that there was something inherently problematic in thinking about weight loss in those terms. When I weighed sixty pounds more, I was not as physically fit. But nonetheless, I could walk around a store, bend over, lift, and otherwise move about without an inordinate amount of effort. I could most certainly not do the same, carrying sixty pounds of cat litter. The difference, of course, was that the sixty pounds of weight I lost were an integral part of my body; the cat litter was not.

The mind-body duality is strong. But at the same time, cracks are perceptible. Members are told to listen to their bodies. As problematic as this advice is in the context of weight loss, it does suggest that the body is not and should not be totally subordinated to the mind. Indeed, the mind can learn something by carefully attending to what the body is saying. Furthermore, in its promise of personal transformation via physical transformation, the before-and-after story can potentially destabilize the mind-body duality. Despite some members' resistance to the idea, the before-and-after narrative raises deep and puzzling questions about whether it is indeed possible to transform the body without concomitantly transforming the self supposedly housed within it.

Feminist Weight Loss?

Some women come to the weight loss group informed by feminist sensibilities, although they vary in consciousness and consistency. Theoretically these feminist sensibilities, if and when articulated, could potentially upset and destabilize assumptions and perspectives held by the organization and group members. But the potential should not be exaggerated. The feminist perspective most apparent in the group has been co-opted much in the way that advertisers have co-opted and exploited feminism to sell their products.

However, this observation begs the question of whether or not feminism and weight loss can coexist under some circumstances. Is it possible to be a feminist and simultaneously want to lose weight?

Not only do feminists raise this question; they are deeply ambivalent about it. In an article provocatively titled, " 'I'll Die for the Revolution but Don't Ask Me Not to Diet': Feminism and the Continuing Stigmatization of Obesity," Rothblum (1994) argues that feminists have failed to recognize fat as a feminist issue, in part due to deeply embedded popular associations between feminism and physical unattractiveness. At the same time, she suggests: "To recognize the social control of women's appearance does not mean that we cannot act and look in ways that make us feel beautiful. We have long been made to feel guilty and immoral because we do not meet unattainable and debilitating standards of attractiveness. It is time to take control of our bodies. As we do so, we must tolerate differences, for other women may make other choices" (Rothblum 1994:72). Similarly, Bordo (1993:30) states:

> In 1990 I lost twenty-five pounds through a national weight-loss program, a choice that some of my colleagues viewed as inconsistent and even hypocritical, given my work. But in my view, feminist cultural criticism is not a blueprint for the conduct of personal life (or political action, for that matter) and does not empower (or require) individuals to "rise above" their culture or to become martyrs to feminist ideals. It does not tell us what to *do* (although I continually get asked such questions when I speak at colleges)— whether to lose weight or not, wear makeup or not, lift weights or not. Its goal is edification and understanding, enhanced *consciousness* of the power, complexity, and *systemic* nature of culture, the interconnected webs of its functioning. It is up to the reader to decide how, when, and where (or whether) to put that understanding to further use, in the particular, complicated, and ever-changing context that is his or her life and no one else's.

With reference to the related practice of cosmetic surgery, Morgan (1991:160) takes a different tack, arguing that one feminist response to cosmetic surgery is to appropriate it, and thereby claim the female body as "the site for feminist action through transformation, appropriation, parody, and protest."

Despite their different perspectives and approaches, Rothblum and Bordo both recognize that the same action can be motivated by different factors, and interpreted in varying ways by different women. After two years in the weight loss group, I found it abundantly clear that women are motivated to lose weight for many reasons, some conscious and some not. Blind acceptance of societal standards of thinness and physical attractiveness is not the only explanation for the large numbers of women that continue to diet and try to lose weight. I do not underestimate the pervasiveness and power of cultural and institutional practices that impinge on, subordinate, and restrain women. But I am suggesting that there has been a tendency among feminist scholars to see resistance as an all-or-nothing response, and to categorize women as resisters or not, often on the sole dimension of whether or not they diet. Alternatively, we need to reconceptualize resistance. There is much value in thinking of resistance as an ongoing process that takes many different forms and is more or less conscious, systematic, and successful over the life courses of individual women.

If we concede that individual feminists, for a variety of reasons, might indeed want to lose weight, is it possible to envision what a feminist weight loss group might look like? In other words, following Morgan, is it possible for feminists to re-appropriate weight loss? I make no pretenses to be able to answer this question. But I am fairly certain that I know what a feminist weight loss group wouldn't look like. In the first place, I am convinced that dieting, based on denial, deprivation, and restriction, is inherently problematic. I am also convinced that weight loss groups that are placed within the capitalist market economy pose clear problems. The potential for exploitation is overwhelming. Furthermore, when we consider that the same corporation can own a weight loss organization and simultaneously manufacture high-fat, non-nutritious foods filled with chemicals and preservatives, we are reminded that capitalism makes for strange bedfellows.

I can go somewhat further. At times, at odd and unexpected moments, I have glimpsed the potential for feminist weight loss. A year or so ago, my seventeen-year-old daughter, Allison, took me by surprise when she said, "I want to lose weight." To my knowledge, she had never dieted, and I had gone out of my way to instill in her feelings of comfort and acceptance with regard to her body. Not entirely sure of the appropriate response, but haunted by visions of the beginning of an endless cycle of dieting, deprivation, and frustration, I sidestepped the issue of losing weight and said, "Why don't you start walking with me?" I was walking for forty-five minutes or so every day, and after some gentle prodding and encouragement, Allison agreed to join me. I began to eagerly look forward to our daily walks. During our time together, outside, undistracted by ringing phones, household responsibilities, and other disturbances, we got to know each other a little better. We both learned that while it's not impossible, it's difficult and ultimately unproductive to try to argue while keeping up a four-mile-per-hour pace. Did she lose weight? I don't know; we no longer own a bathroom scale. But I think we both benefited immensely, in numerous ways, by walking together.

I caught another glimpse not long ago while reading a magazine devoted to healthy cooking. An article described a group of women who came together, motivated by a shared interest in cooking healthy food that tasted good. Even though the women were strangers when they began meeting, they soon developed strong connections and bonds. The photographs accompanying the article showed six women of varying ages, ethnic backgrounds, and body shapes and sizes, sharing recipes, food, and companionship. It looked like a group I would like to join. I don't know that any of the women wanted to or were likely to lose weight. But they clearly enjoyed being together, and food played a central role in their gathering.

As a feminist, I also know without a doubt that any group that purports to be feminist, regardless of its focus or purpose, has to be tied to political and social action. Individual change is never sufficient. There is much that is unhealthy in our culture, political system, and economy, and the effects on women are at times devastating. When I combine this conviction with my glimpses of feminist potential, I begin to see a group of women, not motivated solely to lose weight, but simultaneously committed to finding psychologically and physically healthy ways to truly live with/in their bodies, and to restructuring society to increase the likelihood that this can happen. The failure rates of traditional approaches to losing weight are high, and they are real. But to unilaterally and uncritically interpret this observation to mean that losing weight is doomed to failure is to move toward biological reductionism. Weight loss failure rates occur within specific historical and social contexts. What would happen if cultural standards of thinness and physical attractiveness disappeared, or at least broadened significantly? Would some women, no longer motivated by trying to achieve the ideal, gain weight? Possibly. For some women, most notably those with eating disorders, this is not a bad thing. If, as a result of political action, good, nutritious food became affordable and accessible to anyone who wanted it, would some people lose weight? Possibly. But if these and other changes were to occur, most certainly women could more comfortably live with/in their bodies. And ultimately, isn't that the point?

References

Adams, A. E. 1997. "Molding Women's Bodies: The Surgeon as Sculptor." In *Bodily Discursions: Genders, Representations, Technologies,* edited by D. S. Wilson and C. M. Laennec, 59–80. New York: State University of New York Press.

Agell, G., and E. D. Rothblum. 1991. "Effects of Clients' Obesity and Gender on the Therapy Judgments of Psychologists." *Professional Psychology: Theory, Research, and Practice* 22:223–229.

Akan, G. E., and C. M. Grilo. 1995. "Sociocultural Influences on Eating Attitudes and Behaviors, Body-image, and Psychological Functioning: A Comparison of African-American, Asian-American, and Caucasian College Women." *International Journal of Eating Disorders* 18:181–187.

American Society of Plastic Surgeons. 1998. "1998 Gender Distribution: Cosmetic Procedures." *National Clearinghouse of Plastic Surgery Statistics.* Retrieved April 19, 2000, from the World Wide Web: <http://www.plastic-surgery.org/mediactr/98gendist.htm>.

Andersen, A. E., and L. DiDomenico. 1992. "Diet vs. Shape Content of Popular Male and Female Magazines: A Dose-Response Relationship to the Incidence of Eating Disorders?" *International Journal of Eating Disorders* 11:283–287.

Austin, S. B. 1999. "Commodity Knowledge in Consumer Culture: The Role of Nutritional Health Promotion in the Making of the Diet Industry." In *Weighty Issues: Fatness and Thinness as Social Problems,* edited by J. Sobal and D. Maurer, 159–181. New York: Aldine de Gruyter.

Balsamo, A. 1996. *Technologies of the Gendered Body: Reading Cyborg Women.* Durham, N.C.: Duke University Press.

Barrett-Connor, E. L. 1985. "Obesity, Atherosclerosis, and Coronary Heart Disease." *Annals of Internal Medicine* 103:1010–1019.

Bartky, S. L. 1988 [1998]. "Foucault, Femininity, and the Modernization of Patriarchal Power." Reprinted in *The Politics of Women's Bodies: Sexuality, Appearance, and Behavior,* edited by R. Weitz, 25–45. New York: Oxford University Press.

Beaman, A. L., M. Cole, M. Preston, B. Klentz, and N. M. Steblay. 1983. "Fifteen Years of the Foot-in-the-Door Research: A Meta-analysis." *Personality and Social Psychology Bulletin* 9:181–186.

Bell, R. 1985. *Holy Anorexia.* Chicago: University of Chicago Press.

Bellah, R. N., R. Madsen, W. M. Sullivan, A. Swidler, and S. M. Tipton. 1985. *Habits of the Heart: Individualism and Commitment in American Life.* Berkeley: University of California Press.

Beller, A. S. 1977. *Fat and Thin: A Natural History of Obesity.* New York: Farrar, Straus and Giroux.

Bennett, G. A. 1986. "Behavior Therapy for Obesity: A Qualitative Review of the Effects of Selected Treatment Characteristics on Outcome." *Behavior Therapy* 17:554–562.

Berg, F. M. 1995. *Health Risks of Weight Loss,* 3rd ed. Hettinger, N.D.: Healthy Weight Journal.

Blair, S. N., J. Shaten, K. Brownell, G. Collins, and L. Lissner. 1993. "Body Weight Change, All-Cause Mortality, and Cause-Specific Mortality in the Multiple Risk Factor Intervention Trial." *Annals of Internal Medicine* 119:749–757.

Blake, R. R., and J. S. Moulton. 1979. "Intergroup Problem Solving in Organization: From Theory to Practice." In *The Social Psychology of Intergroup Relations,* edited by W. G. Austin and S. Worchel, 19–32. Monterey,Calif.: Brooks/Cole.

Bolin, A. 1997. "Flex Appeal, Food, and Fat: Competitive Bodybuilding, Gender, and Diet." In *Building Bodies,* edited by P. L. Moore, 184–208. New Brunswick, N.J.: Rutgers University Press.

Bordo, S. 1993. *Unbearable Weight: Feminism, Western Culture, and the Body.* Berkeley: University of California Press.

Borkman, T. J. 1990. "Experiential, Professional, and Lay Frames of Reference." In *Working with Self-Help,* edited by T. J. Powell, 3–30. Silver Spring, Md.: NASW Press.

Boston Women's Health Book Collective. 1998. *Our Bodies, Ourselves for the New Century: A Book by and for Women.* New York: Simon and Schuster.

Bouchard, C., A. Tremblay, J. Despres, A. Nadeau, J. P. Lupien, G. Theriault, J. Dussault, S. Moorjani, S. Pinault, and G. Fournier. 1990. "The Response to Longterm Overfeeding in Identical Twins." *New England Journal of Medicine* 322:1477–1482.

Brehm, J. W. 1956. "Post-Decision Changes in Desirability of Alternatives." *Journal of Abnormal and Social Psychology* 52:384–389.

Brewer, M. B. 1979. "Ingroup Bias in the Minimal Intergroup Situation: A Cognitive-Motivational Analysis." *Psychological Bulletin* 86:307–324.

———. 1987. "Collective Decisions." *Social Science* 72:140–143.

Brewer, M. B., and R. K. Kramer. 1986. "Choice Behavior in Social Dilemmas: Effects of Social Identity, Group Size, and Decision Framing." *Journal of Personality and Social Psychology* 50:543–549.

Brown, K. M. 1985. "On Feminist Methodology." *Journal of Feminist Studies in Religion* 1:76–79.

Brown, K. M., G. B. Schreiber, R. P. McMahon, P. Crawford, and K. L. Ghee. 1995. "Maternal Influences on Body Satisfaction in Black and White Girls Aged 9 and 10: The NHLBI Growth and Health Study (NGHS)." *Annals of Behavioral Medicine* 17:213–220.

Brownell, K. D., and R. W. Jeffery. 1987. "Improving Long-Term Weight Loss: Pushing the Limits of Treatment." *Behavior Therapy* 18:353–374.

Brownell, K. D., and J. Rodin. 1994. "The Dieting Maelstrom: Is It Possible and Advisable to Lose Weight?" *American Psychologist* 49:781–791.

Brumberg, J. J. 1988. *Fasting Girls: The Emergence of Anorexia Nervosa as a Modern Disease.* Cambridge, Mass.: Harvard University Press.

Brunner, R. L., S. T. St. Jeor, B. J. Scott, G. D. Miller, T. P. Carmody, K. D. Brownell, and J. Foryet. 1994. "Dieting and Disordered Eating Correlates of Weight Fluctuation in Normal and Obese Adults." *Eating Disorders: The Journal of Treatment and Prevention* 2:341–356.

Burgard, D., and P. Lyons. 1994. "Alternatives in Obesity Treatment: Focusing on Health for Fat Women." In *Feminist Perspectives on Eating Disorders,* edited by P. Fallon, M. A. Katzman, and S. C. Wooley, 212–230. New York: Guilford Press.

Burger, J. M. 1991. "The Effects of Desire for Control in Situations with Chance-Determined Outcomes: Gambling Behavior in Lotto and Bingo Players." *Journal of Research in Personality* 25:196–204.

Bynum, C. W. 1987. *Holy Feast and Holy Fast: The Religious Significance of Food to Medieval Women.* Berkeley: University of California Press.

Cash, T. F., and P. E. Henry. 1995. "Women's Body Images: The Results of a National Survey in the U.S.A." *Sex Roles* 33:19–28.

Cash, T. F., and R. R. Roy. 1999. "Pounds of Flesh: Weight, Gender, and Body Images." In *Interpreting Weight: The Social Management of Fatness and Thinness,* edited by J. Sobal and D. Maurer, 209–228. New York: Aldine de Gruyter.

Cash, T. F., B. A. Winstead, and L. H. Janda. 1986. "The Great American Shape-Up." *Psychology Today* 19:30–37.

Caskey, S. R., and D. W. Felker. 1971. "Social Stereotyping of Female Body Image by Elementary School Age Girls." *Research Quarterly* 42:251–255.

Chapman, G. E. 1999. "From 'Dieting' to 'Healthy Eating': An Exploration of Shifting Constructions of Eating for Weight Control." In *Interpreting Weight: The Social Management of Fatness and Thinness,* edited by J. Sobal and D. Maurer, 73–87. New York: Aldine de Gruyter.

Checkoway, B., M. A. Chesler, and S. Blum. 1990. "Self-Care, Self-Help, and Community Care for Health." In *Working with Self-Help,* edited by T. J. Powell, 277–300. Silver Spring, Md.: NASW Press.

Chernin, K. 1981. *The Obsession: Reflections on the Tyranny of Slenderness.* New York: Harper and Row.

Chesler, M. A. 1990. "The 'Dangers' of Self-Help Groups: Understanding and Challenging Professionals' Views." In *Working with Self-Help,* edited by T. J. Powell, 301–324. Silver Spring, Md.: NASW Press.

Coates, T. J., R. W. Jeffery, and R. R. Wing. 1978. "The Relationship between Persons' Relative Body Weights and the Quality and Quantity of Food Stored in Their Homes." *Addictive Behaviors* 3:179–184.

Cogan, J. C. 1999. "Re-evaluating the Weight-Centered Approach toward Health: The Need for a Paradigm Shift." In *Interpreting Weight: The Social Management of Fatness and Thinness,* edited by J. Sobal and D. Maurer, 229–253. New York: Aldine de Gruyter.

Cordell, G., and C. R. Ronai. 1999. "Identity Management among Overweight Women: Narrative Resistance to Stigma." In *Interpreting Weight: The Social Management of Fatness and Thinness,* edited by J. Sobal and D. Maurer, 29–47. New York: Aldine de Gruyter.

Counihan, C. M. 1998a. "An Anthropological View of Western Women's Prodigious Fasting: A Review Essay." In *Food and Gender: Identity and Power,* edited by C. M. Counihan and S. L. Kaplan, 99–123. Amsterdam: Harwood.

———. 1998b. "Introduction—Food and Gender: Identity and Power." In *Food and Gender: Identity and Power,* edited by C. M. Counihan and S. L. Kaplan, 1–10. Amsterdam: Harwood.

Crawford, R. 1979. "Individual Responsibility and Health Politics." In *Health Care in America: Essays in Social History,* edited by S. Reverby and D. Rosner, 247–268. Philadelphia: Temple University Press.

Croteau, D., and W. Hoynes. 2000. *Media/Society: Industries, Images, and Audiences.* Thousand Oaks, Calif.: Pine Forge Press.

Dillard, J. P. 1991. "The Current Status of Research on Sequential-Request Compliance Techniques." *Personality and Social Psychology Bulletin* 17:283–288.

Douglas, S. J. 1994. *Where the Girls Are: Growing Up Female with the Mass Media.* New York: Times Books.

Durkheim, E. 1912 [1965]. *The Elementary Forms of the Religious Life.* Translated by J. W. Swain. New York: Free Press.

Ernsberger, P., and P. Haskew. 1987. "Health Implications of Obesity: An Alternative View." *Journal of Obesity and Weight Regulation* 6:58–137.

Etzioni, A. 1982. *An Immodest Agenda: Rebuilding America before the Twenty-First Century.* New York: McGraw-Hill.

Evans, S. 1979. *Personal Politics.* New York: Knopf.

Ewen, S. 1988 [1994]. "Hard Bodies." Reprinted in *Signs of Life in the USA: Readings on Popular Culture for Writers,* edited by S. Maasik and J. Solomon, 60–65. Boston: Bedford Books of St. Martin's Press.

Faludi, S. 1991. *Backlash: The Undeclared War against American Women.* New York: Crown.

Feingold, A., and R. Mazzella. 1998. "Gender Differences in Body Image Are Increasing." *Psychological Science* 9:190–195.

Festinger, L. 1954. "A Theory of Social Comparison Processes." *Human Relations* 7:117–140.

Finn, J. 1995. "Computer-Based Self-Help Groups: A New Resource to Supplement Support Groups." In *Support Groups: Current Perspectives on Theory and Practice,* edited by M. J. Galinsky and J. H. Schopler, 109–117. New York: Haworth.

Fisher, L. A. 1997. " 'Building One's Self Up': Bodybuilding and the Construction of Identity among Professional Female Bodybuilders." In *Building Bodies,* edited by P. L. Moore, 135–161. New Brunswick, N.J.: Rutgers University Press.

Fitzgerald, F. T. 1981. "The Problem of Obesity." *Annual Review of Medicine* 32:221–231.

Flannery-Schroeder, E. C., and J. C. Chrisler. 1996. "Body Esteem, Eating Attitudes, and Gender-Role Orientation in Three Age Groups of Children." *Current Psychology* 15:235–248.

Foucault, M. 1979. *Discipline and Punish: The Birth of the Prison.* New York: Vintage.

Fraser, L. 1997. *Losing It: America's Obsession with Weight and the Industry That Feeds on It.* New York: Dutton.

Freedman, R. 1986. *Beauty Bound.* Lexington, Mass.: Lexington.

Freeman, J. 1975. *The Politics of Women's Liberation.* New York: David McKay.

French, S. A., M. Story, B. Downes, M. D. Resnick, and R. W. Blum. 1995. "Frequent Dieting among Adolescents: Psychosocial and Health Behavior Correlates." *American Journal of Public Health* 85:695–710.

Freund, P.E.S., and M. B. McGuire. 1999. *Health, Illness, and the Social Body: A Critical Sociology,* 3rd ed. Upper Saddle River, N.J.: Prentice Hall.

Galinsky, M. J., and J. H. Schopler, eds. 1995. *Support Groups: Current Perspectives on Theory and Practice.* New York: Haworth.

Garner, D. M. 1997. "The 1997 Body Image Survey Results." *Psychology Today* 30:30–44, 75–84.

Garner, D. M., and S. C. Wooley. 1991. "Confronting the Failure of Behavioral and Dietary Treatments for Obesity." *Clinical Psychology Review* 11:729–780.

Geertz, C. 1973: *The Interpretation of Cultures.* New York: Basic Books.

Gerard, H. B., and J. M. Rabbie. 1961. "Fear and Social Comparison." *Journal of Abnormal and Social Psychology* 62:586–592.

Germov, J., and L. Williams. 1999. "Dieting Women: Self-Surveillance and the Body Panopticon." In *Weighty Issues: Fatness and Thinness as Social Problems,* edited by J. Sobal and D. Maurer, 117–132. New York: Aldine de Gruyter.

Gmelch, G. 1995. "Baseball Magic." In *Dress and Identity,* edited by M. E. Roach-Higgins, J. B. Eicher, and K.K.P. Johnson, 251–259. New York: Fairchild.

Goffman, E. 1963. *Stigma: Notes on the Management of Spoiled Identity.* New York: Simon and Schuster.

———. 1971. *Relations in Public.* New York: Harper and Row.

Goodman, N., S. A. Richardson, S. M. Dornbusch, and A. H. Hastorf. 1963. "Variant Reactions to Physical Disabilities." *American Sociological Review* 28:429–435.

Goodrich, G. K., and J. P. Foreyt. 1991. "Why Treatments for Obesity Don't Last." *Journal of the American Dietetic Association* 91:1243–1247.

Gordon, M., and S. Riger. 1989. *The Female Fear.* New York: Free Press.

Green, M. W., P. J. Rogers, N. A. Elliman, and S. J. Gatenby. 1994. "Impairment of Cognitive Performance Associated with Dieting and High Levels of Dietary Restraint." *Physiology and Behavior* 55:447–452.

Greenwald, A. G., C. G. Carnot, R. Beach, and B. Young. 1987. "Increasing Voting Behavior by Asking People if They Expect to Vote." *Journal of Applied Psychology* 71:315–318.

Griffiths, R., and D. Farnill. 1996. "Primary Prevention of Eating Disorders: An Update." *Journal of Family Studies* 2:179–191.

Gutierrez, L., R. M. Ortega, and Z. E. Suarez. 1990. "Self-Help and the Latino Community." In *Working with Self-Help,* edited by T. J. Powell, 218–236. Silver Spring, Md.: NASW Press.

Hamm, P., R. B. Shekelle, and J. Stamler. 1989. "Large Fluctuations in Body Weight during Young Adulthood and Twenty-five Year Risk of Coronary Death in Men." *American Journal of Epidemiology* 129:312–318.

Hanson, R. L., L. T. Jacobsson, D. R. McCance, K. M. Narayan, D. J. Pettit, P. H. Bennett, and W. C. Knowler. 1996. "Weight Fluctuation, Mortality, and Vascular Disease in Pima Indians." *International Journal of Obesity* 20:463–471.

Henslin, J. M. 1967. "Craps and Magic." *American Journal of Sociology* 73:316–330.

———. 1975. *Introducing Sociology: Toward Understanding Life in Society.* New York: Free Press.

Hesse-Biber, S. 1996. *Am I Thin Enough Yet?: The Cult of Thinness and the Commercialization of Identity.* New York: Oxford University Press.

Heywood, L. 1997. "Masculinity Vanishing: Bodybuilding and Contemporary Culture." In *Building Bodies,* edited by P. L. Moore, 165–183. New Brunswick, N.J.: Rutgers University Press.

Hochschild, A. R. 1983. *The Managed Heart.* Berkeley: University of California Press.

Holmlund, C. A. 1989. "Visible Difference and Flex Appeal: The Body, Sex, Sexuality, and Race in the Pumping Iron Films." *Cinema Journal* 28:38–51.

Honeycutt, K. 1999. "Fat World/Thin World: 'Fat Busters,' 'Equivocators,' 'Fat Boosters,' and the Social Construction of Obesity." In *Interpreting Weight: The Social Management of Fatness and Thinness,* edited by J. Sobal and D. Maurer, 165–181. New York: Aldine de Gruyter.

Institute of Medicine. 1995. *Weighing the Options: Criteria for Evaluating Weight-Management Programs.* Washington, D.C.: National Academy Press.

Iribarren, C., D. S. Sharp, C. M. Burchfiel, and H. Petrovitch. 1995. "Association of Weight Loss and Weight Fluctuation with Mortality among Japanese American Men." *New England Journal of Medicine* 333:686–692.

Jackson, L. A., L. A. Sullivan, and J. S. Hymes. 1987. "Gender, Gender Role, and Physical Appearance." *Journal of Psychology* 121:51–56.

Joanisse, L., and A. Synnott. 1999. "Fighting Back: Reactions and Resistance to the Stigma of Obesity." In *Interpreting Weight: The Social Management of Fatness and Thinness,* edited by J. Sobal and D. Maurer, 49–70. New York: Aldine de Gruyter.

Katz, A. H., and C. A. Maida. 1990. "Health and Disability Self-Help Organizations." In *Working with Self-Help,* edited by T. J. Powell, 141–155. Silver Spring, Md.: NASW Press.

Kaw, E. 1998. "Medicalization of Racial Features: Asian-American Women and Cosmetic Surgery." In *The Politics of Women's Bodies: Sexuality, Appearance, and Behavior,* edited by R. Weitz, 167–183. New York: Oxford University Press.

Keys, A. 1980. "Overweight, Obesity, Coronary Heart Disease, and Mortality." *Nutrition Reviews* 38:297–307.

Keys, A., A. Menotti, C. Aravanis, H. Blackburn, B. S. Djordevic, R. Buzina, A. S. Dontas, F. Fidanza, M. J. Karvonen, N. Kimura, I. Mohacek, S. Nedeljkovic, V. Puddu, S. Punsar, H. L. Taylor, S. Conti, D. Kromhout, and H. Toshima. 1984. "The Seven Countries Study: 2,289 Deaths in Fifteen Years." *Preventive Medicine* 13:141–154.

King, K. M. 1990. "Neutralizing Marginally Deviant Behavior: Bingo Players and Superstition." *Journal of Gambling Studies* 6:43–61.

Kirkpatrick, L. A., and P. Shaver. 1988. "Fear and Affiliation Reconsidered from a Stress and Coping Perspective: The Importance of Cognitive Clarity and Fear Reduction." *Journal of Social and Clinical Psychology* 7:214–233.

Kleinman, S. 1991. "Fieldworkers' Feelings: What We Feel, Who We Are, How We Analyze." In *Experiencing Fieldwork: An Inside View of Qualitative Research,* edited by W. B. Shaffir and R. A. Stebbins, 184–195. Newbury Park, Calif.: Sage.

Knox, R. E., and J. A. Inkster. 1968. "Post-Decision Dissonance at Post-Time." *Journal of Personality and Social Psychology* 8:319–323.

Kramer, F. M., R. W. Jeffery, J. L. Forster, and M. K. Snell. 1989. "Long-term Follow-up of Behavioral Treatment for Obesity: Patterns of Weight Regain among Men and Women." *International Journal of Obesity* 13:123–126.

Kramer, R. M., and M. B. Brewer. 1984. "Effects of Group Identity on Resource Use in a Simulated Commons Dilemma." *Journal of Personality and Social Psychology* 46:1044–1057.

Kulik, J. A., and H.I.M. Mahler. 1989. "Stress and Affiliation in a Hospital Setting: Preoperative Roommate Preferences." *Personality and Social Psychology Bulletin* 15:183–193.

Kulik, J. A., H.I.M. Mahler, and A. Earnest. 1994. "Social Comparison and

Affiliation under Threat: Going beyond the Affiliate-Choice Paradigm." *Journal of Personality and Social Psychology* 66:301–309.

Kurtz, L. F. 1990. "Twelve-Step Programs." In *Working with Self-Help,* edited by T. J. Powell, 93–119. Silver Spring, Md.: NASW Press.

———. 1994. "Self-Help Groups for Families with Mental Illness or Alcoholism." In *Understanding the Self-Help Organization: Frameworks and Findings,* edited by T. J. Powell, 212–226. Thousand Oaks, Calif.: Sage.

Laessle, R. G., P. Platte, U. Schweiger, and K. M. Pirke. 1996. "Biological and Psychological Correlates of Intermittent Dieting Behavior in Young Women: A Model for Bulimia Nervosa." *Physiology and Behavior* 60:1–5.

Lanzetta, J. T. 1955. "Group Behavior under Stress." *Human Relations* 8:29–53.

Lasch, C. 1979. *The Culture of Narcissism: American Life in an Age of Diminishing Expectations.* New York: Warner.

———. 1984. *The Minimal Self: Psychic Survival in Troubled Times.* New York: Norton.

Lerner, R. M., and E. Gellert. 1969. "Body Build Identification, Preference, and Aversion in Children." *Developmental Psychology* 1:456–462.

Lesieur, H. R. 1990. "Working with and Understanding Gamblers Anonymous." In *Working with Self-Help,* edited by T. J. Powell, 237–253. Silver Spring, Md.: NASW Press.

Lester, R. J. 1999. "Let Go and Let God: Religion and the Politics of Surrender in Overeaters Anonymous." In *Interpreting Weight: The Social Management of Fatness and Thinness,* edited by J. Sobal and D. Maurer, 139–164. New York: Aldine de Gruyter.

Lewis, R. J., T. F. Cash, L. Jacobi, and C. Bubb-Lewis. 1997. "Prejudice toward Fat People: The Development and Validation of the Antifat Attitudes Test." *Obesity Research* 5:297–307.

Lieberman, M. A., and L. R. Snowden. 1994. "Problems in Assessing Prevalence and Membership Characteristics of Self-Help Group Participants." In *Understanding the Self-Help Organization: Frameworks and Findings,* edited by T. J. Powell, 32–49. Thousand Oaks, Calif.: Sage.

Lipsitz, A., K. Kallmeyer, M. Ferguson, and A. Abas. 1989. "Counting on Blood Donors: Increasing the Impact of Reminder Calls." *Journal of Applied Social Psychology* 19:1057–1067.

Lissner, L., P. Odell, R. D'Agostino, J. Stokes, B. Kreger, A. Belanger, and K. D. Brownell. 1991. "Variability in Body Weight and Health Outcomes in the Framingham Population." *New England Journal of Medicine* 324:1839–1844.

Lupton, D. 1996. *Food, the Body, and the Self.* London: Sage.

Macdonald, M. 1995. *Representing Women: Myths of Femininity in the Popular Media.* London: Edward Arnold.

Macdonald, B., and C. Rich. 1983. *Look Me in the Eye: Old Women, Aging, and Ageism.* San Francisco: Spinsters Ink.

Maddox, G. L., and V. Liederman. 1969. "Overweight as Social Desirability with Medical Implications." *Journal of Medical Education* 44:214–220.

Maiman, L. A., V. L. Wang, M. H. Becker, J. Finlay, and M. Simonson. 1979. "Attitudes toward Obesity and the Obese among Professionals." *Journal of the American Dietetic Association* 74:331–336.

Mann, G. V. 1974. "The Influence of Obesity on Health (Part I and Part II)." *New England Journal of Medicine* 291:178–185, 245–253.

Mauss, M. 1967 [1925]. *The Gift: Forms and Functions of Exchange in Archaic Societies.* New York: Norton.

McKinley, N. M. 1999. "Ideal Weight/Ideal Women: Society Constructs the

Female." In *Weighty Issues: Fatness and Thinness as Social Problems*, edited by J. Sobal and D. Maurer, 97–115. New York: Aldine de Gruyter.

Meissen, G. J., and M. L. Warren. 1994. "The Self-Help Clearinghouse: A New Development in Action Research for Community Psychology." In *Understanding the Self-Help Organization: Frameworks and Findings*, edited by T. J. Powell, 190–211. Thousand Oaks, Calif.: Sage.

Miller, C. T. 1984. "Self-Schemas, Gender, and Social Comparison: A Clarification of the Related Attributes Hypothesis." *Journal of Personality and Social Psychology* 46:1222–1229.

Miller, W. C., D. M. Koceja, and E. J. Hamilton. 1997. "A Meta-Analysis of the Past Twenty-five Years of Weight Loss Research Using Diet, Exercise, or Diet Plus Exercise Intervention." *International Journal of Obesity* 21:941–947.

Millman, M. 1980. *Such a Pretty Face: Being Fat in America*. New York: Norton.

Mills, C. W. 1959. *The Sociological Imagination*. New York: Oxford University Press.

Modleski, T. 1982. *Loving with a Vengeance: Mass-Produced Fantasies for Women*. New York: Methuen.

Moore, P. L. 1997. "Feminist Bodybuilding, Sex, and the Interruption of Investigative Knowledge." In *Building Bodies*, edited by P. L. Moore, 74–86. New Brunswick, N.J.: Rutgers University.

Morgan, K. P. 1991 [1998]. "Women and the Knife: Cosmetic Surgery and the Colonization of Women's Bodies." Reprinted in *The Politics of Women's Bodies: Sexuality, Appearance, and Behavior*, edited by R. Weitz, 147–166. New York: Oxford University Press.

Muth, J. L., and T. F. Cash. 1997. "Body-Image Attitudes: What Difference Does Gender Make?" *Journal of Applied Social Psychology* 27:1438–1452.

Nash, K. B., and K. D. Kramer. 1990. "Self-Help for Sickle Cell Disease in African-American Communities." In *Understanding the Self-Help Organization: Frameworks and Findings*, edited by T. J. Powell, 212–226. Thousand Oaks, Calif.: Sage.

Neighbors, H. W., K. A. Elliott, and L. M. Gant. 1990. "Self-Help and Black Americans: A Strategy for Empowerment." In *Working with Self-Help*, edited by T. J. Powell, 189–217. Silver Spring, Md.: NASW Press.

Noordsy, D. L., B. Schwab, L. Fox, and R. E. Drake. 1994. "The Role of Self-Help Programs in the Rehabilitation of Persons with Severe Mental Illness and Substance Use Disorders." In *Understanding the Self-Help Organization: Frameworks and Findings*, edited by T. J. Powell, 212–226. Thousand Oaks, Calif.: Sage.

NutriSystem, Inc. 2000. "NutriSystem.com Online Weight Loss Program." Retrieved July 28, 2000, from the World Wide Web: <http://www.nutrisystem.com/tour/overview/>.

Oldman, D. 1974. "Chance and Skill: A Study of Roulette." *Sociology* 8:407–426.

Orbach, S. 1979. *Fat Is a Feminist Issue*. London: Hamlyn.

Orbell, J. M., A.J.C. van de Kragt, and R. M. Dawes. 1988. "Explaining Discussion-Induced Cooperation." *Journal of Personality and Social Psychology* 54:811–819.

Overeaters Anonymous, Inc. 1996–1998a. "About OA." Retrieved May 18, 2000, from the World Wide Web: <http://www.overeatersanonymous.org/about.htm>.

———. 1996–1998b. "Are You a Compulsive Overeater?" Retrieved May 18, 2000, from the World Wide Web: <http://www.overeatersanonymous.org/15quttxt.htm>.

———. 1996–1998c. "The Twelve Steps." Retrieved May 18, 2000, from the World Wide Web: <http://www.overeatersanonymous.org/12steps.htm>.

———. 1997. "Tools of Recovery." Retrieved May 18, 2000, from the World Wide Web: <http://www.overeatersanonymous.org/toolstxt.htm>.

Paget, M. A. 1990. "Life Mirrors Work Mirrors Text Mirrors Life." *Social Problems* 37:137–151.

Patton, G. 1992. "Eating Disorders: Antecedents, Evolution, and Course. Special Section: Eating Disorders." *Annals of Medicine* 24:281–285.

Pliner, P., S. Chaiken, and G. L. Flett. 1990. "Gender Difference in Concern with Body Weight and Physical Appearance over the Life Span." *Personality and Social Psychology Bulletin* 16:263–273.

Pliner, P., H. Hart, J. Kohl, and D. Saari. 1974. "Compliance without Pressure: Some Further Data on the Foot-in-the-Door Technique." *Journal of Experimental Social Psychology* 10:17–22.

Polivy, J., and C. P. Herman. 1992. "Undieting: A Program to Help People Stop Dieting." *International Journal of Eating Disorders* 11:261–268.

Powell, T. J. 1990a. "Self-Help, Professional Help, and Informal Help: Competing or Complementary Systems?" In *Working with Self-Help,* edited by T. J. Powell, 31–49. Silver Spring, Md.: NASW Press.

———, ed. 1990b. *Working with Self-Help.* Silver Spring, Md.: NASW Press.

———, ed. 1994. *Understanding the Self-Help Organization: Frameworks and Findings.* Thousand Oaks, Calif.: Sage.

Price, R. A., R. J. Cadoret, A. J. Stunkard, and E. Troughton. 1987. "Genetic Contributions to Human Fatness: An Adoption Study." *American Journal of Psychiatry* 144:1003–1008.

Radway, J. A. 1984. *Reading the Romance: Women, Patriarchy, and Popular Literature.* Chapel Hill, N.C.: University of North Carolina Press.

Reinharz, S. 1988. "What's Missing in Miscarriage?" *Journal of Community Psychology* 16:84–103.

———. 1992. *Feminist Methods in Social Research.* New York: Oxford University Press.

Rieff, D. 1991. "Victims All?: Recovery, Co-dependency, and the Art of Blaming Somebody Else." *Harper's* (October):49–56.

Rieff, P. 1966. *The Triumph of the Therapeutic: Uses of Faith after Freud.* New York: Harper and Row.

Riessman, C. K. 1983. "Women and Medicalization: A New Perspective." *Social Policy* 14:3–18.

Ritzer, G. 1996. *The McDonaldization of Society: An Investigation into the Changing Character of Contemporary Social Life,* rev. ed. Thousand Oaks, Calif.: Pine Forge Press.

———. 1999. *Enchanting a Disenchanted World: Revolutionizing the Means of Consumption.* Thousand Oaks, Calif.: Pine Forge Press.

Rodin, J. 1992. *Body Traps.* New York: William Morrow.

Rofe, Y. 1984. "Stress and Illness: A Utility Theory." *Psychological Review* 91:235–250.

Rosen, J., and J. Gross. 1987. "Prevalence of Weight Reducing and Weight Gaining in Adolescent Girls and Boys." *Health Psychology* 6:131–147.

Rosen, R. 1986. "Search for Yesterday." In *Watching Television: A Pantheon Guide to Popular Culture,* edited by T. Gitlin, 42–67. New York: Pantheon.

Ross, C. E. 1994. "Overweight and Depression." *Journal of Health and Social Behavior* 35:63–79.

Rothblum, E. D. 1994. " 'I'll Die for the Revolution but Don't Ask Me Not to Diet': Feminism and the Continuing Stigmatization of Obesity." In *Feminist*

Perspectives on Eating Disorders, edited by P. Fallon, M. A. Katzman, and S. C. Wooley, 53–76. New York: Guilford.

Rothman, B. K. 1986. "Reflections: On Hard Work." *Qualitative Sociology* 9:48–53.

Rucker, C. E., and T. F. Cash. 1992. "Body Images, Body-Size Perceptions, and Eating Behaviors among African-American and White College Women." *International Journal of Eating Disorders* 12:291–299.

Rush, F. 1980. *The Best Kept Secret: Sexual Abuse of Children.* Englewood Cliffs, N.J.: Prentice Hall.

Ruzek, S. 1978. *The Women's Health Movement: Feminist Alternatives to Medical Control.* New York: Praeger.

Satter, E. 1987. *How to Get Your Kid to Eat—But Not Too Much.* Palo Alto, Calif.: Bull.

Schachter, S. 1959. *The Psychology of Affiliation.* Stanford: Stanford University Press.

Schopler, J. H., and M. J. Galinsky. 1995. "Expanding Our View of Support Groups as Open Systems." In *Support Groups: Current Perspectives on Theory and Practice,* edited by M. J. Galinsky and J. H. Schopler, 3–10. New York: Haworth Press.

Schulze, L. 1997. "On the Muscle." In *Building Bodies,* edited by P. L. Moore, 9–30. New Brunswick, N.J.: Rutgers University Press.

Schwarzwald, J., A. Bizman, and M. Raz. 1983. "The Foot-in-the-Door Paradigm: Effects of Second Request Size on Donation Probability and Donor Generosity." *Personality and Social Psychology Bulletin* 9:443–450.

Seid, R. A. 1994. "Too 'Close to the Bone': The Historical Context for Women's Obsession with Slenderness." In *Feminist Perspectives on Eating Disorders,* edited by P. Fallon, M. A. Katzman, and S. C. Wooley, 3–16. New York: Guilford Press.

Shattuc, J. M. 1997. *The Talking Cure: TV Talk Shows and Women.* New York: Routledge.

Shaver, P., and M. Klinnert. 1982. "Schachter's Theories of Affiliation and Emotion: Implications of Developmental Research." In *Review of Personality and Social Psychology,* vol. 3, edited by L. Wheeler. Beverly Hills, Calif.: Sage.

Sherif, M. 1966. *In Common Predicament: Social Psychology of Intergroup Conflict and Cooperation.* Boston: Houghton Mifflin.

Simonds, W. 1992. *Women and Self-Help Culture: Reading between the Lines.* New Brunswick, N.J.: Rutgers University Press.

Snowden, L. R., and M. A. Lieberman. 1994. "African-American Participation in Self-Help Groups." In *Understanding the Self-Help Organization: Frameworks and Findings,* edited by T. J. Powell, 50–61. Thousand Oaks, Calif.: Sage.

Sobal, J. 1999. "The Size Acceptance Movement and the Social Construction of Body Weight." In *Weighty Issues: Fatness and Thinness as Social Problems,* edited by J. Sobal and D. Maurer, 231–249. New York: Aldine de Gruyter.

Spitzack, C. 1990. *Confessing Excess: Women and the Politics of Body Reduction.* Albany, N.Y.: State University of New York Press.

Starker, S. 1989. *Oracle at the Supermarket: The American Preoccupation with Self-Help Books.* New Brunswick, N.J.: Transaction.

Stinson, K. M. 1992. "Gender, Stress, and Anorexia Nervosa among College Students." Paper presented at the annual meeting of the North Central Sociological Association, Fort Wayne, Ind.

Stunkard, A. J., T. T. Foch, and Z. Hrubec. 1986. "A Twin Study of Human Obesity." *Journal of the American Medical Association* 256:51–54.

Stunkard, A. J., J. R. Harris, N. L. Pederson, and G. E. McClearn. 1990. "The Body Mass Index of Twins Who Have Been Reared Apart." *New England Journal of Medicine* 322:1483–1487.

Stunkard, A. J., T. L. Sorensen, C. Hanis, T. W. Teasdale, R. Chakraborty, W. J. Schull, and F. Schulsinger. 1986. "An Adoption Study of Human Obesity." *New England Journal of Medicine* 314:193–198.

Suls, J. M., and R. L. Miller. 1977. *Social Comparison Processes: Theoretical and Empirical Perspectives.* Washington, D.C.: Halsted-Wiley.

Taylor, V., and N. Whittier. 1993. "The New Feminist Movement." In *Feminist Frontiers III,* edited by L. Richardson and V. Taylor, 533–548. New York: McGraw-Hill.

Tiggemann, M., and E. D. Rothblum. 1988. "Gender Differences in Social Consequences of Perceived Overweight in the United States and Australia." *Sex Roles* 18:75–86.

Tisdale, S. 1994. "A Weight That Women Carry: The Compulsion to Diet in a Starved Culture." In *Minding the Body: Women Writers on Body and Soul,* edited by P. Foster, 15–31. New York: Anchor.

Tocqueville, A. de. 1848 [1969]. *Democracy in America,* translated by G. Lawrence, edited by J. P. Meyer. Garden City, N.Y.: Doubleday.

Toffler, A. 1970. *Future Shock.* New York: Bantam.

Troiano, R. P., E. A. Frongillo, Jr., J. Sobal, and D. A. Levitsky. 1996. "The Relationship between Body Weight and Mortality: A Quantitative Analysis of Combined Information from Existing Studies." *International Journal of Obesity* 20:63–75.

van Wormer, K. 1994. " 'Hi, I'm Jane; I'm a Compulsive Overeater.'" In *Feminist Perspectives on Eating Disorders,* edited by P. Fallon, M. A. Katzman, and S. C. Wooley, 287–298. New York: Guilford.

Videka-Sherman, L. 1990. "Bereavement Self-Help Organizations." In *Working with Self-Help,* edited by T. J. Powell, 156–174. Silver Spring, Md.: NASW Press.

Wadden, T. A., and A. J. Stunkard. 1985. "Social and Psychological Consequences of Obesity." *Annals of Medicine* 103:1062–1067.

Weber, M. 1904–1905 [1930]. *The Protestant Ethic and the Spirit of Capitalism,* translated by T. Parsons. New York: Scribner's.

Williams, R. M., Jr. 1965. *American Society: A Sociological Interpretation,* 2nd ed. New York: Knopf.

Williams, S. J., and G. Bendelow. 1998. *The Lived Body: Sociological Themes, Embodied Issues.* New York: Routledge.

Wing, R. R., and R. W. Jeffery. 1978. "Differential Restaurant Patronage of Obese and Nonobese People." *Addictive Behaviors* 3:135–138.

Withorn, A. 1980. "Helping Ourselves: The Limits and Potential of Self-Help." *Radical America* 1980:25–59.

Wolf, N. 1991. *The Beauty Myth: How Images of Beauty Are Used against Women.* New York: William Morrow.

Wooley, O. W. 1994. ". . . And Man Created 'Woman': Representations of Women's Bodies in Western Culture." In *Feminist Perspectives on Eating Disorders,* edited by P. Fallon, M. A. Katzman, and S. C. Wooley, 17–52. New York: Guilford Press.

Wooley, S. C., O. W. Wooley, and S. Dyernforth. 1979. "Theoretical, Practical, and Social Issues in Behavioral Treatments of Obesity." *Journal of Applied Behavior Analysis* 12:3–25.

Wuthnow, R. 1994. *Sharing the Journey: Support Groups and America's New Quest for Community.* New York: Free Press.

Yankelovich, D. 1981. *New Rules: Searching for Self-Fulfillment in a World Turned Upside Down*. New York: Random House.

Young, L. M., and B. Powell. 1985. "The Effects of Obesity on the Clinical Judgments of Mental Health Professionals." *Journal of Health and Social Behavior* 26:233–246.

Younger, J. C., L. Walker, and J. A. Arrowood. 1977. "Postdecision Dissonance at the Fair." *Personality and Social Psychology Bulletin* 3:284–287.

Index

About the Author

Kandi M. Stinson is associate professor of sociology and chair of the department of political science and sociology at Xavier University. Her teaching and research interests include women and gender roles, popular culture, religion, and qualitative research methodology.